D0346907

BANNOCKBURN
1314

THE BATTLE
700 YEARS ON

CHRIS BROWN

First published 2008 by Tempus Publishing

This new edition 2013
by Spellmount, an imprint of The History Press
The Mill, Brimscombe Port
Stroud, Gloucestershire, GL5 2QG
www.thehistorypress.co.uk

© Chris Brown, 2008, 2013

The right of Chris Brown to be identified as the Author
of this work has been asserted in accordance with the
Copyrights, Designs and Patents Act 1988.

All rights reserved. No part of this book may be reprinted
or reproduced or utilised in any form or by any electronic,
mechanical or other means, now known or hereafter invented,
including photocopying and recording, or in any information
storage or retrieval system, without the permission in writing
from the Publishers.

British Library Cataloguing in Publication Data.
A catalogue record for this book is available from the British Library.

ISBN 978 0 7509 5379 5

Typesetting and origination by The History Press
Printed in Great Britain

Contents

Introduction to the Second Edition

It is relatively rare that one has the opportunity to construct a second edition to a history book, rarer still if the volume is concerned with medieval or military history and almost unheard of for a book on medieval Scottish military history. As we approach the 700th anniversary of the battle – and, of course, the referendum on Scottish independence – it is inevitable that there should be a growth in interest in an event that has been so significant for Scots for such a long time. It is all too easy to inflate the importance of the battle as a military and political phenomenon, and forget that King Robert's war would not be concluded for more than a decade.

After 1314 the war was not generally conducted in Scotland, but in Ireland and England, and at one point there was a very real possibility that it would spill over into Wales as well. King Robert also had to face domestic opposition. In 1320 he was threatened by a widespread conspiracy of nobles whose intent was to replace him with Edward Balliol, son of the unfortunate King John.

Despite the political credibility gained through his military successes – somewhat diminished by failure in Ireland – Robert was not, strictly speaking, the legitimate king. Until the death of Edward Balliol in 1354 both he and his son David II continued to be usurpers, a fact that Edward III did his level best to exploit in his efforts to gain control over Scotland in the 1330s and 1340s.

Equally, there is no escaping the sheer artistry of King Robert's victory at Bannockburn. The defeat of the English in such a great encounter gave him political credibility at home and abroad and went some way toward confirming the innate superiority of the infantry over the cavalry. Well trained, well led and well motivated, the man on foot demonstrated that he was more than a match for the armoured knight; the lessons delivered by Robert I at Bannockburn, and then developed by men such as Henry Beaumont and Edward III at Dupplin and Crécy, would have a profound and permanent effect on the practice of war right across Europe.

Preface

Why write a book on Bannockburn at all? We can never hope to achieve a complete and undisputed understanding of any historical event, let alone a battle.

Bannockburn was only one battle in a very long war, or rather, a long series of wars, though all of them have the same issue at stake – the conquest or independence of Scotland as a political entity. The rarity of major battles of manoeuvre is such that none of the larger battles of the Wars of Independence can be considered 'typical', so Bannockburn is not really 'representative' of the general course or nature of the conflicts. Bannockburn was far from being typical in scale; in the half century between 1296 and 1346 there were only a handful of general engagements that involved more than a few thousand men – Stirling Bridge, Falkirk, Halidon Hill and Neville's Cross – and the latter is, arguably, not really a battle about the survival or otherwise of the Scottish kingdom, so much as a facet of the Hundred Years War. Even the capture of King David did not really pose a threat to the independence of his realm. Despite their defeat, the Scots seem to have had no shortage of confidence in their ability to withstand Edward III, and Edward himself seems to have taken little or no interest in restoring the short-lived administration which had held much of southern Scotland in the 1330s for the English crown.

Operationally, Bannockburn was far from being typical of the general conduct of the war. There are examples of a similar tactical policy in action at the battle of Loudon and elsewhere. Myton[1] and Culblean,[2] on the other hand, are battles in which mounted cavalry played no part at all. The majority of the actions that took place in Scotland between 1296 and 1314 – most of which are unknown outside the academic community – were encounters between rather modest bodies of heavy cavalry[3] or sieges of the towns and castles[4] which formed the focal points of local political, commercial, social and judicial activity.[5]

The battle occurred nearly 700 years ago, and so it should come as no surprise that the evidence tends to be limited, both in terms of quantity and quality. Even when studied in relation to the terrain, the material is often less informative than we might hope, indeed, study of the site may actually bring other factors into mind which might otherwise have escaped us. Relating written accounts to modern maps can be a frustrating – and not necessarily a rewarding – exercise. We may be confident that the burn we find on a map is the one referred to by this or that writer, but is it still in the same place? Has its course, width or current been affected by the construction of roads, railways or housing? Were its banks more treacherous in the past than they are today? Crucially, even if we are utterly certain that 'this' is the burn that a given force crossed on a given day, we cannot be so certain that it did so at any particular point in the water's course.

Maps or diagrams of battles often present difficulties of their own. The symbols used to denote formations on the battlefield seldom bear any in-scale resemblance to the size or shape of those formations. To some extent this is obviously a matter of ensuring that the reader can identify the formations; a product of showing the course of the battle in a map that is too small to allow the unit symbols to be depicted in the same scale as the geographical features. This is not a problem unique to battle diagrams; the symbol used to denote churches by the Ordnance Survey is not related to the physical size of the church in question. The combat elements of medieval armies were little more than specks on the landscape; they were not large and the majority of the men fought in very close order – something approaching one square metre per man for close-combat infantry, and perhaps six to eight square metres for every man-at-arms. It is quite possible that the entirety of Edward II's army at Bannockburn could have been seated in Wimbledon's Centre Court, which has a capacity of 16,000 and that all of King Robert's spearmen could – at a pinch – have stood on one full-size rugby pitch.

Further, we cannot rely on maps to show all of the features which might affect manoeuvre. A low mound or long ditch might have a dramatic influence on the course of a fight, but be too insignificant to appear on a map.[6] More importantly, few people spend enough time reading maps to really appreciate the extent to which visibility is limited by terrain. This is a matter of considerable importance. In an age when the fastest mode of transport was the horse, the advantage conferred on the army with the upper hand in reconnaissance was considerable. The commander who could obtain a position that allowed him to observe the approach of the enemy, whilst keeping his own forces hidden from view, could deploy his troops to their greatest advantage in the light of observations and deductions made from the enemy's order of march. If he could keep his own troops out of sight until the last moment, he could be reasonably confident that his enemy would not be able to redeploy his units in the most appropriate manner without considerable time and trouble.

The conduct and progress of medieval engagements once battle was joined is often, though not always, a good deal easier to follow if one has a reasonable understanding of the nature of the troops – their equipment, their approach to combat and, in many cases, some understanding of that crucial tool of medieval life, the horse. Without that knowledge it is easy to make deductions that do not stand the test of rational examination. There is, for example, a widely accepted mental picture of Sir William Wallace as a large man, clad in plaid and wielding a two-handed sword from the saddle. Putting aside the fact that two-handed swords were not the weapon of the day in the late thirteenth century, a moment's thought about the practicalities of using such a weapon on horseback, should be enough to dispel the suggestion instantly. Nonetheless, the image persists.

The purpose of this study is to relate the information contained in the contemporary sources to what we know of the military practice of the day and, so far as is possible, to the nature of the terrain. An obvious problem lies in the fact that we cannot precisely identify the sites of the different actions that took place on 23/24 June 1314, but this is not so much of an issue as one might expect. Whether an engagement occurred a thousand metres to the west or east of a specific spot is only significant if aspects of the terrain would conflict with the existing body of evidence. The action that occurred in the vicinity of St Ninians would, for example, have been radically different had it occurred at a particular distance to the east, south or north of the chapel, due to the nature of the location. All of the relevant source material puts the action on flat, hard ground, therefore it clearly was not fought two miles to the northeast of Kirkton of St Ninians – unless it was fought in the waters of the fast and powerful River Forth. Moreover, battles are not, as a general rule, static events.

Armies manoeuvre for position; they advance to contact, they retire or advance during combat. This in turn presents problems for archaeological interpretation, particularly in instances where 'finds' are few and far between.[7] The discovery of a weapon fragment – even if the fragment can be indisputably attributed to the action in question – tells us no more than the fact that at some point the weapon was lost or abandoned. It need not even have been lost at the location in which it is found, and even if it was, the fragment is not evidence that a formation of either army passed that way; it may have been lost by a man escaping from a fight that was actually taking place at some considerable distance. Even the most assiduous study of the sources, the terrain and the archaeological material cannot, therefore, give us a complete and incontrovertible account of all the different aspects of this battle, nor for most others of the period.

On the other hand, the general sequence of events and the nature of the engagements can be readily understood from the source material if we relate that information to the practices of the day. It is certainly true that the sources contradict each other to some extent; indeed, if they did not do so, we should be suspicious that they all stemmed from one common account. However the degree of inconsistency is not great and, as we shall see, the discrepancies between sources are – to a considerable extent anyway – matters of perspective in the sense that the deployment for battle and the progress of the fight may have looked very different from the points of view of the *Lanercost* chronicler's witness and that of Sir Thomas Grey – both of whose accounts of the battle are reproduced in this volume.

Contemporary accounts, however carefully written, are of limited value unless we make a real effort to understand the nature of the armies and their nature of approach to battle. Failure to do so can lead to very serious misconceptions which, in turn, can lead us to very questionable conclusions. This is, perhaps, less of an issue for the army of Edward II than for that of Robert I. There are two reasons for this. One is that English armies of the fourteenth century have been studied in far more detail than Scottish ones, which is itself a matter of source material. Not only is there a great deal more in the way of record evidence – payrolls and horse valuations records, for example – but the material has been thoroughly examined by many very talented historians for the better part of 100 years – particularly, though not exclusively, J.E. Morris, Professor G.W.S. Barrow and Doctors Michael Prestwich, Andrew Ayton and Andy King.[8]

Study of the armies and actions of a particular time and place is, of course, somewhat redundant without gaining some understanding of the political, social, economic and cultural conditions which brought about war between the nations concerned. Many fine scholars have devoted themselves to these aspects of medieval England and Scotland, and there are a number of volumes which are simply indispensable to the student who wishes to get to grips with the societies from which the political and military leaders of the day were drawn – those which provided the manpower, finance and political will to wage war. Professors Barrow and Prestwich have already been mentioned, but there are many others worthy of praise: Professors Nicholson, Keen and Duncan, and Drs Fiona Watson, Michael Brown, Norman Reid, David Ditchburn, Alexander Grant, Michael Penman and Colm McNamee, to name but a few.

There is no particular shortage of 'Bannockburn' books on the market, and one might question the value of writing another. No new source material has come to light, so perhaps it could be argued that there is nothing new to say. In a sense, this is true. There *is* nothing new to add to the existing body of evidence; however, there are a great many issues to be considered in relation to the interpretation of that evidence. To that end, I have chosen to cite and discuss all of the significant narrative sources, both in relation to one another and in the light of what we know of the military realities of the early fourteenth century as practiced in Scotland. I have endeavoured to keep endnotes to a minimum; the bulk of the significant material is contained in the chronicle accounts. I have devoted no space whatsoever to the authorship of those accounts; in this context it is the writing that is significant, not the writer. The one exception is Sir Thomas Grey, whose personal experience as a career soldier cannot be ignored.

No medieval battle can be perfectly understood; there is no-one alive today who has experienced the terror of an arrow-storm or the ferocity of a full-blooded charge by armoured cavalry, but I hope that the material contained in this book will give the reader a reasonable practical understanding of this remarkable battle which, despite modern claims to the contrary, was very much more than a clash between medieval gangsters. For Scottish people at least, it was an expression of the political preference of the majority of the community for independence.

Without the active support of a very wide segment of Scottish society, from labourers to lords, King Robert would never have been able to restore the sovereignty of his nation. The war was not, however, a simple matter of allegiance to a king, but a subtle and complex combination of issues of national and regional identities, traditions of support for, or opposition to, local leaders, perceptions of the political realities of the day, resentment of domination by a foreign power, personal ambition and ties of familial and social relationships. All of these factors, and probably many others which defy identification at a distance of seven hundred years, were instrumental in persuading many thousands of men to risk their lives at Stirling in the summer of 1314.

The Story So Far:
The War of Independence,
1296–1313

An extensive body of books, articles and essays on the wars of King John, Robert I, Edward I and Edward II has been published over the last hundred years or so, but the extent to which many of these works has contributed to our understanding of the 1314 campaign is questionable. Even the most cursory survey of the secondary material currently most accessible to the public – entries in encyclopaedias, general histories, Internet sites and dictionaries of battles – shows the enormous influence of the works of S.R. Gardiner[1] and C.W.C. Oman.[2] Both of these men still enjoy very positive reputations for their efforts in different fields; Oman's account of the Peninsular campaigns against Napoleon is still an invaluable piece of work after a century.[3] For Oman and Gardiner the battle took the form of an opposed crossing, one of the most hazardous approaches to battle. The challenge of forcing a passage over the deep muddy-banked stream that divided the armies was further complicated by the fact that the Scots had dug innumerable pits along the bank of the Bannock Burn. These inflicted many casualties on the English cavalry, who exhausted themselves in repeated attacks on the serried ranks of the Scots before eventually giving up the contest and abandoning the field to the enemy. None of this bears very much resemblance to any of the contemporary or near-contemporary accounts, but the fame of the writers has ensured that their interpretations and maps have gained a very real currency – so much so that they still have an influence on academic understanding of the events of June 1314 today.

Undermining the Gardiner/Oman interpretation is not a modernist 'debunking' exercise. In 1913 Rev. MacKenzie published his study of the battle – still one of the better works on the topic. MacKenzie's volume was not simply a counterblast to Oman and Gardiner; it was an attempt to consider all of the sources in relation to one another and in relation to examinations of the terrain. One might make a number of criticisms of MacKenzie's conclusions and of his preference for some medieval writers over others, but he certainly examined all of the significant material from the relevant contemporary accounts – Barbour's *Bruce*, Thomas Grey's *Scalacronica*, Fordoun's *Chronicle*, the *Lanercost Chronicle*, Bower's *Scotichronicon*, and *Vita Edwardus Secundus*.[4]

MacKenzie was not the only Scottish historian of his time to examine Bannockburn in some detail. Evan MacLeod Barron's work, *The Scottish War of Independence*,[5] still exerts an influence on Scottish medieval history nearly a century after its first publication. There are numerous weaknesses to Barron's understanding of Bannockburn that have been explored in detail by Professor Barrow.[6] Barron's contribution to the topic largely revolved around his conviction that the contribution of Highland communities to the cause of independence had been obscured by a concentration on Lowland magnate politics, and that the viability of the patriotic cause had been continually undermined by the capacity of lowland nobles and gentry to defect to the English. Barron could certainly provide many examples of serial defections among the Scottish magnates – Robert Bruce, for example, changed sides in 1297, 1301–02 and again in 1306. In the view of Barron, the southern nobility were less committed than their northern counterparts, a reflection of differing values between what he saw as two distinct Scottish cultural, social and political entities, the 'Teutonic' (southern/lowland) and the Celtic (Gaelic/northern). This aspect of Barron's interpretation has been thoroughly discredited by Professor Barrow, but continues to exert a considerable influence on the popular perception of the Battle of Bannockburn and of the war in general. Barron's intention was to redress what he saw as a tendency on the part of historians to focus on the activities of the southern magnates. His view was not without validity, but he exaggerated some pieces of evidence and marginalised others to make his case. He was not the first writer to draw attention to this perceived north–south imbalance. In 1909, John Shearer, in his *Fact and Fiction in the Story of Bannockburn*,[7] wrote:

> … there is nothing in Barbour that even gives a hint that the chiefs, with their men, from the hills and glens of Loch Lomond, Loch Katrine, Loch Tay, Loch Ness and Loch Shin, were fighting at the Battle Bannockburn. This is surely a great omission on the part of Barbour, and a terrible injustice to the Celts of Scotland.

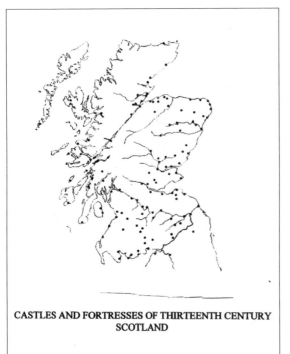

**CASTLES AND FORTRESSES OF THIRTEENTH CENTURY
SCOTLAND**

Map of the more important castles and strongpoints of medieval Scotland. Most of these lie in the south and east of the country. There were of course a great many castles and fortresses in the far north, west and isles, however medieval conflict in Scotland was dominated by the Wars of Independence. The occupation of governments of Edward I, II and III failed to make much headway in the north and west. Even in the brief period of unchallenged English occupation in 1304–1306, Edward I was largely reliant on the power of indigenous lordship outwith the southern and eastern portions of the country.

Cities and significant towns of Scotland c. 1300. The loss or retention of administrative and economic centres was a crucial indicator of success or failure in war throughout the medieval and early modern periods.

Popular perception is one of the barriers to understanding the battle at all. Scottish romantic tradition tends to see the action as a struggle between impoverished Scottish peasants – unarmoured and ill-equipped – against endless hordes of armoured English knights, a triumph of the peasants over the nobility – a myth greatly enhanced by the popularity of the film *Braveheart*. There is also the question of the extent to which the Wars of Independence can be seen as a 'civil war' between Scottish factions rather than a war of aggression and conquest inaugurated by Edward I.[8] There was certainly an element of domestic political strife before 1291 which revolved around the question of whether Robert Bruce or John Balliol should have inherited the crown – an issue that led to the presence of the Bruces and others in the English camp. The objective of the Bruces was to acquire Scottish kingship, not to subject themselves to the authority of Edward I.

The 'civil war' theory, however, does have some validity in the sense that many Scots, for a variety of reasons and at different times, did align themselves with the Plantagenet cause, but that in itself is a long way short of proving that the War of Independence was a 'civil' war as such. There was no sense in the entirety of a series of conflicts – which lasted intermittently from 1296 to 1328 (and resumed in 1332) – when the war was exclusively, or even primarily, a conflict between Scottish political factions. Even Edward Balliol's invasion depended on the resources of English lords with Scottish ambitions. The presence of English garrisons[9] and field armies was always the most significant aspect of the military dimension of the struggle and, with the exception of the period between the death of Wallace and the inauguration of Robert I, there was always a part of Scottish society, from the labourers to the great lords, which was prepared to unite across barriers of class and culture in defence of the independence of their country. As the chronicler Guisborough wrote of the Scottish aristocracy, their bodies might be with the King of England, but 'their hearts were always with their own people'.

Despite assertions such as –

> the misery and bloodshed in the wars between England and Scotland lies at the door of those rebellious Scots who adhered neither to their King, nor to their oaths of fealty to their supreme overlord, Edward[10]

– the basic cause of the Wars of Independence was the ambition of Edward I. It is of course true that without Edward's involvement in the period after the death of the young Queen Margaret on her voyage from Norway,[11] there would almost certainly have been a genuine civil war in Scotland between the Bruce and Balliol parties. It is worth bearing in mind, however, that both Robert Bruce and John Comyn were prepared to join forces against Edward in a joint Guardianship despite their very real political differences.[12]

Although the two men were far from being happy allies, it was not the prospect of military defeat at the hands of the English that made Robert Bruce defect to Edward I, but the increasingly strong possibility that King John might be restored to his throne, thus compromising any possibility that Robert might eventually become king himself. Again, this was a matter of domestic Scottish politics, but the key issue which had united Bruce and Comyn in the first place was that of political independence.

It is also true that Robert had to wage campaigns against powerful Scottish interests in the early part of his reign, primarily against the Comyn and MacDougal families, but it is misleading to see these campaigns simply as aspects of 'civil' war. After 1304 each of these groups had been drawn into an English administration of Scotland;[13] they were not assets of an alternative Scottish government acting in opposition to the Bruce party.

This, however, does not mean that either the MacDougals or the Comyns would necessarily have remained in English allegiance regardless of political developments. King Philip of France had been forced to abandon the Scots in the wake of the Battle of Courtrai,[14] but circumstances do change. If Philip had felt that it was in his interests (and within his capabilities) to deploy a significant force to Scotland in an attempt to restore King John after the collapse of the Balliol party in 1304, it is quite possible, even probable, that the Comyns would have reverted to their traditional role of supporters to the Scottish crown, a role from which they – and the crown – had profited greatly over a period of more than 100 years. In practice, of course, this was not an option that the French could pursue; they had problems enough already. Diplomatically it suited Edward I and Edward II to depict their Scottish campaigns as a purely domestic matter; lawful kings exercising their right to discipline recalcitrant subjects in rebellion against their liege-lord. That they enjoyed some success is apparent from the tendency for English – and sometimes Scottish – historians to describe men like Comyn and Bruce as 'rebels'.

Naturally, the commitment of the Comyns to the Plantagenet cause was enhanced by their opposition to the Bruce party – hardly surprising given Robert's murder of John Comyn of Badenoch in February 1306.[15] But it was also encouraged by their defeat at Robert's hands in his Buchan campaign of 1308.[16] Once they had been driven out of the northeast, their only hope of recovering their property and, with it, their position of political power, was the hope that Edward II might defeat and destroy the Bruce party. By the close of 1313, this must have seemed increasingly unlikely, unless Bruce could be brought to battle on a grand scale. In terms of territorial control, King Robert was close to winning his war. He had gained control of all Scotland north of the Forth and Clyde, his armies were able to pass through those areas which were still in Plantagenet hands in order to mount operations in England, and the remaining assets of Edward II's administration were increasingly isolated and vulnerable – even Berwick had nearly fallen in 1312.[17] The commitment of a field army does not seem to have brought much progress. The campaign of 1310–11 had achieved little in the way of recovered ground for the expenditure of a very considerable sum – essentially a failure for the English and therefore a major propaganda coup for King Robert. The position of the Comyn family, and others who had remained in Plantagenet allegiance, became precarious throughout the military successes of a Scottish rival – Robert Bruce – however the Comyns were fighting not for an alternative Scottish kingship, but for the King of England. This is also true of Robert's western enemies, the MacDougalls and McCans. Their rivalry with the MacDonalds gave Robert an ally, but the MacDougalls – like the Comyns – were fighting to preserve Plantagenet kingship, not to bring back King John. Their conflict with the Bruce party had a 'civil' element, but was still the operational expression of a war between English and Scottish kings.

As a conflict between nations, it is hardly a surprise that nationalism – in all its guises – is a factor in itself. As we shall see, both Scottish and English people were perfectly aware of their nationality, but nationalism is also an issue within some of the source material. We need only compare the *Lanercost* chronicler's generally hostile views of the Scots with those of Sir Thomas Grey, who spent the greater part of his professional life in Scotland. Nationalism and concepts of national destiny were already an important part of English historiography by the time of the Wars of Independence. To a great degree, this was bound up with a view that the King of England was the rightful and acknowledged superior of the whole of the British Isles. One need look no further than Geoffrey of Monmouth's assertion that Scotland was a dependency of England, which Professor Mason calls the 'Brut tradition'.[18] The 'evidence' on which Monmouth's case depended was that Brutus the Trojan, having escaped from the fall of Troy, had travelled to Britain and divided the British Isles between his sons, with the eldest, Locrinus, enjoying the kingship of England and superiority over his brother-kings, Albanactus of Scotland and Kamber of Wales.

The Trojan legend was supported in more recent times (by medieval standards) by the 'fact' that Arthur had been king of all Britain and, more cogently perhaps, the fact that at different times a number of Scottish kings had accepted the superiority of their English counterparts, the most recent being William the Lion in December 1174. In practice, William's acceptance of Henry II's feudal superiority was given under duress and was, in any case, soon traded away by Richard I of England for ready money under the terms of the Quitclaim of Canterbury in 1189.[19] It has been suggested that the terms of the Quitclaim were sufficiently vague to mean anything to anyone, however the key cause is very straightforward:

> ...We (Richard of England) have freed him (William of Scotland) from all compacts which our good father, Henry, king of the English, extorted from him by new charters and by his capture.

More generally, the popular view of the society and economy of the northern kingdom has been shaped by what Dr Fergusson[20] called:

> the peculiarly English Victorian Gothic version of early medieval Scotland in which Gaels and Norse and Anglians and even Britons live in different parts of the country, separated by geography, culture, language and pretty much tribal kingdoms in themselves ... not to mention Northumbrians and Galwegians.

There has also been something of a tendency for English historians to view any action contrary to English interests as being a threat to good practice and desirable outcomes. May McKisack[21] saw the development of a strong political alliance between Scotland and France in 1294–97 as being 'among the most sinister developments of the war of independence', rather than being the only practical response to the ambitions of an aggressive and predatory neighbour. Few reputable English medievalists of recent times would choose to see Edward's behaviour in Scotland as the reasonable and lawful actions of a well-intentioned and benign neighbour, however the prevalence of that attitude in the past still exerts an influence on 'popular' history. One need look no further than John Harvey's book *The Plantagenets*, which clearly makes the Scots the villains of the piece. According to Harvey, the judicial murder of Sir William Wallace was a fate he brought upon himself:

Had his offences been merely political he would have found the same mercy that Edward's other opponents never sought in vain; but Wallace was not the hero of romantic legend, but a leader of well-organised criminals in an assault upon society. For three hundred years the Borders suffered cruelly for this one man's misdeeds.[22]

In reality, Wallace was executed because his death suited Edward's own political purposes on a number of levels. The high-profile public execution and dismemberment of Wallace did more than provide a spectacle for Londoners, it gave a superficial veneer of 'closure' in the wake of the Strathord armistice. The execution was popular at home and, to some extent anyway, politically practical in Scotland. Edward could not afford to execute any of the men who had until recently been the leaders of the Balliol party since he needed their influence and military power if he was to make his conquest effective. If Wallace had been a great and powerful magnate, Edward would probably not have had him killed, but, since his defeat at Falkirk and his resignation from the Guardianship in 1298, Wallace had ceased to be a figure of any real importance in the Scottish political community. He was, however, very famous, so his capture and execution could be presented – in England at least – as a triumph.

In fact, Wallace's murder was probably a serious mistake on the part of Edward and for the future of his Scottish administration, since it 'raised the political temperature in Scotland'.[23] Wallace may not have been a great favourite of the senior aristocracy in Scotland, but he was still a popular figure in wider society. Wallace is a heroic figure to Scots – and others – and hero-worship can get in the way of a realistic appraisal of his career; the same applies to King Robert and Edward I as a hero to the English. To cite Harvey again:

> ... it is impossible not to regret that the peace-lover, the arbitrator, the fountain-head of his country's prosperity and justice, should have exhausted himself in constant war.[24]

But in reality Edward's wars in Scotland and in Wales were problems that he brought upon himself, and the various financial and political crises faced by the English crown at the end of the thirteenth century were in fact products of Edward's military ventures. Edward's reputation as an outstanding soldier is something of a barrier in itself; had he lost the battle of Falkirk it is hard to see how that reputation could ever have flourished. Edward cannot have assumed that his 1296 campaign had really finished the Balliol cause, but presumably he did expect that the manpower and money he committed to the project would be adequate to the task of quickly overcoming any residual resistance and erecting an occupation administration. His strategic and tactical expertise failed him on both counts.

Traditionally Scottish historians have shied clear of describing Edward's rule as an 'occupation', partly perhaps for fear of giving offence, but chiefly because of the number of Scots who were involved in Edward's government, particularly in the period after the Strathord armistice of 1304. This is something of an over-simplification. There were certainly a great many Scottish men and women who accepted Edward as their king, some through conviction, some through duress. No doubt there were quite a few who were not really terribly concerned about who was king, so long as they could maintain their own position in society and either felt that Edward was too strong to resist or that he offered the best chance of stability.[25] There would probably have been some who felt that the country had been failed by the Bailliol monarchy and who were prepared to accept Edward – at least temporarily – for want of any other source of political leadership. To assume that Plantagenet kingship was the preferred option for all of these people is to do them a considerable injustice, comparable to assuming that men and women who retained their posts under the Germans or the Japanese during World War Two had embraced Nazi or Japanese imperial ideologies. Accepting authority for the sake of keeping one's job or one's business is not tantamount to being a collaborator.

On one level there was the question of avoiding forfeiture, imprisonment or even death for failing to accept Plantagenet rule, but there were also many internal Scottish political issues. Just because someone did not accept the Bruce party does not mean that they wholeheartedly endorsed the Plantagenets. Aryeh Nusbacher,[26] referring to the example of the Earl of Angus who responded to the summons to fight for Edward II in 1314, points out that, with him:

> … were a number of Scottish knights who had decided that their allegiance to their English sovereign was more important than their allegiance to the claimant of the Scottish throne.

Though typical of the conventional English view of the wars of independence articulated by Oman and others, there is an implication here that cannot go unchallenged. Scottish 'knights' might choose to support Edward II because they believed that his cause was legally sound or because they believed that the Plantagenet administration offered the best prospect of peace. They might, alternatively, choose Edward II's lordship for no better reason than that they rejected the Bruce party. Robert's conduct over the previous two decades had not been consistent in the sense of supporting the 'patriotic cause'; he had murdered his chief political rival and he was most certainly a usurper so long as there was a legitimate heir of the Balliol family. Further, many of the Scots who served as men-at-arms in the English army of 1314 were the tenants, relatives and associates of men who had firmly rejected the Bruce party and had lost their estates as King Robert extended his rule.

Some, no doubt, served Edward II (as they had served Edward I) for fear of losing their estates in England, though in reality these are likely to have been few in number since only a handful of Scots held estates of any great significance outside Scotland. The converse is true as well; some of the gentry and nobility who joined the Bruce cause, particularly after the defeat of the Comyns in 1308, surely did so because their properties, or at least their most significant estates, lay in areas dominated by the Bruces. As the Bruce party gained ground the chances of retaining those properties without accepting Robert's kingship must have seemed increasingly remote. This applied equally to great lords and minor gentry. The Earl of Ross, a Balliol supporter in 1291–92,[27] was firmly in the Plantagenet camp in 1306 when he captured King Robert's queen, Elizabeth de Burgh[28] and dispatched her to Edward I as a prisoner, but by 1308 his earldom had become very isolated and he was obliged to accept a truce with the Bruce party until June and then entered King Robert's peace on 31 October. Without the armed support of Edward II's forces to help him resist the Bruce party, the Earl was doomed to defeat and forfeiture unless he accepted Robert's kingship and authority. William of Ross's circumstances were, perhaps, particularly difficult. His earldom was vulnerable, not only to Robert's land-based forces, but also to raids mounted from the Hebrides by Robert's allies. The Earl of Angus, on the other hand, presumably felt that he was more likely to retain his earldom through giving his allegiance to Edward II. As it turned out he was mistaken and by the time of Bannockburn had already been an émigré for some time.

Individual Scots aligned themselves with the Bruce party for a wide variety of reasons, some political, some personal. Many people believed – rightly – that the legitimate King of Scotland was John Balliol or, after John's death in 1313, his son, Edward. The collapse of the Balliol cause in 1304 did not mean that all of the Balliol supporters defected to the Plantagenet cause, merely that the leaders of the Balliol party had come to the conclusion that, abandoned by the French[29] and by John himself,[30] their cause was no longer militarily viable.

It does not, of itself, imply a preference either for the Plantagenets over the Bruces or a general preference for the occupation government. Clausewitz's observation that a nation might see defeat – even overwhelming defeat – as a 'temporary misfortune' that might, in due course, be reversed through a resumption of hostilities, is most appropriate here.[31]

Acceptance of the rule of the government of the day did not imply political sympathy so much as a matter of keeping one's job and one's head; accepting that this or that party offered the best hope of stability and security and that it could provide 'good lordship'.[32] Similarly, people might be dissuaded from giving overt support to their favoured party because they doubted the ability of that party to impose its will on the country as a whole. As Barrow has shown, King Robert enjoyed support from nobles across the country from his inauguration as king.[33] Some of Robert's early supporters fell away through Plantagenet pressure in 1306–07, but many more joined as he began to look more credible, particularly after his campaigns of 1308.

Naturally, some Scottish landholders would have been deterred from joining the Bruce cause by the military power of the occupation government. Other than those periods in which Edward I and Edward II lead or despatched major field armies to Scotland the power of their administration depended on the resources of Scottish lords in English allegiance and the garrisons. A good many Scots served in these garrisons; some through the attractions of wages and the potential for career advancement, others for political reasons. Recruiting Scottish men-at-arms and archers was an attractive proposition for the Plantagenet government; partly because it was often difficult to recruit adequate numbers from elsewhere, but also – particularly after 1308 – because there were increasing numbers of men whose properties lay in territory dominated by the Bruce party. Having been disadvantaged for their loyalty, these men could hardly be abandoned; they needed to be supported financially until such time as their heritage could be recovered. This was all well and good as long as the prospect of an English recovery in Scotland seemed a viable proposition. By mid-1314 this must have seemed an increasingly unlikely prospect unless the decay of Plantagenet government could be reversed by a major military initiative, however there were, by this point, relatively few Scots in English allegiance other than associates of the Comyn and MacDougal families. Although there were still several garrisons at the close of 1313, they had largely lost the capacity to impose lordship in their localities. Increasingly, the surviving garrisons were becoming – if they had not already become – assets of an 'outpost' policy rather than a genuine attempt to provide secure government.

This had come about through the increasing ability of the Bruce party to deploy greater numbers of men-at-arms at critical locations at given moments. In order to contain the garrisons the Scots did not necessarily have to find a general superiority in heavy cavalry, just local superiority of an order that would prevent the garrisons from venturing too far from their stations. This is a matter of some importance, since the purpose of the garrisons was not, at least until 1313, to guard the castles themselves, but to impose the will of Edward II, ensure the collection of rents and other issues, to be a visible political presence in the community and, of course, to prevent the Scots from extending their area of influence.

That the ability of Robert to attract the support of the people without necessarily having the support – overt or otherwise – of the aristocracy added to the problems of the administration, is clear from this letter from the commander of the Plantagenet garrison at Forfar Castle to an English courtier at Carlisle. It is dated May 1307 and relates recent events and current situations:

I hear that Bruce never had the good will of his own followers or of the people generally so much with him as now. It appears that God is with him, for he has destroyed King Edward's power both among the English and Scots. The people believe that Bruce will carry all before him, exhorted by 'false preachers' from Bruce's army, men who have previously been charged before the justices for advocating war and have been released on bail, but are now behaving worse than ever. I fully believe, as I have heard from Duncan of Frendraught and Gilbert of Glencairnie, who keep the peace beyond the Mounth and on this side, that if Bruce can get away in this direction or towards the parts of Ross he will find the people all ready at his will more entirely than ever, unless King Edward can send more troops; for there are many people living loyally in his peace so long as the English are in power.

May it please God to prolong King Edward's life, for men say openly that when he is gone the victory will go to Bruce. For these preachers have told the people that they have found a prophecy of Merlin, that after the death of 'le roy coveytous' the people of Scotland and the Welsh shall band together and have full lordship and live in peace together to the end of the world.

This is Professor Barrow's translation, published in 'Robert the Bruce and the Community of the Realm of Scotland', p.245. The letter is listed and described in CDS ii, No. 1926.

This letter, probably from Sir Alexander Abernethy, a staunch officer and sup-porter of the Plantagenet government, is worth examining in some detail. It is clear that the writer was convinced that Robert enjoyed a good deal of popu-lar support in both the northeast and the northwest – neither of them regions with a strong tradition of Bruce lordship. Moreover there were strong, well-established local political leaders who were adamantly opposed to the Bruce party; Duncan of Frendraught and Gilbert of Glencairnie were men of some prominence, and the Earl of Ross, the most significant mainland magnate in the northwest, was definitely still a member of the Plantagenet camp. Clearly the author of the letter hoped to encourage the deployment of more English troops (Bain's presentation of this letter refers to men-at-arms in particular), which is in itself an indication that the leaders of the local administration were feeling the strain of confronting Bruce sentiment. The most significant assertion, however, is that Bruce would find the people 'ready at his will more entirely than ever'. The letter dates from May 1307, while Edward was still alive and at a time when Bruce's kingship, though more than a year old, had largely been passed in exile or in hiding. Robert had had little opportunity to show himself in the far north, so it is surprising that he should have had the support of any significant propor-tion of the common people. This is quite at odds with traditional views of local political leadership in the later Middle Ages, which tends to be heavily focused on the behaviour of the nobility and gentry to the exclusion of the balance of the community. Kings were certainly only too well aware of the power of the magnate classes, and of their capacity to defy the crown if pushed, but they could also demonstrate an awareness of the importance of popular political opinion. Edward I issued at least one document in which he attempted to enlist the sup-port of the wider community for his kingship by accepting that his government had been too harsh. He hoped to secure their support, but also to deny that sup-port to the enemy. It would seem that Robert was convinced of the importance of popular support, since he clearly went to some effort to ensure that the peo-ple were informed of his actions. The prophecies of Merlin, among other aspects of Arthurian legend, were widely held to be significant, and were evidently sufficiently well known to provide a propaganda vehicle for the Bruce cause. Identifying Edward I as the *Roy Coveytous* (greedy king) would have been a reasonably easy prospect to 'sell' to the people given Edward's general behaviour in Scotland. The prospect that the Scots and the Welsh would enjoy 'full lordship' (political independence) after Edward's death would also make an attractive and credible ambition, given that Edward was now an old man (by the standards of the fourteenth century) and was not in the best of health.

Had there been an accommodation between the Comyns, traditional leaders in the northeast, and the Bruce party, we might expect that Comyn political alignment would find an expression among the people at large, but of course the opposite was the case; the Comyns were utterly opposed to Robert's kingship – the murder of John Comyn had made sure of that. It is possible, though there is no evidence to support such a possibility, that the Comyns had lost the support of the wider community of the northeast through their support of the Plantagenet cause, or through their abandonment of King John in 1304. This would still be a demonstration of popular political sentiment. If the men and women of Buchan, Aberdeenshire and Kincardineshire rejected the leadership of the Comyns because the Comyns no longer represented the interests of Scottish kingship, then the people were making a political choice between independence and integration into the domain of English kingship. It is difficult to see any motivation other than national sentiment for the assertion that the people would be willing, even eager, to adopt the Bruce cause in 1307, particularly when we bear in mind that Robert could not yet impose his authority effectively in areas of strongly established Bruce lordship.

Accepting Bruce kingship did not necessarily mean that an individual was utterly convinced of the merits of Robert's claim to the throne. In 1306–07 Robert's campaign cannot have looked very promising, so one might assume that early commitment to the Bruce cause was a product of a conscious political decision. This was no longer the case by the close of 1308. By that time, Robert had brought a considerable swathe of territory under his sway so, in much the same way as Plantagenet lordship continued to be acceptable in the far south, acceptance of Bruce lordship in the far north was probably – to some extent at least – a matter of accepting the *de facto* government of the day regardless of personal preference. Once again, there may be an element of national consciousness underlying the growth of the Bruce party in the north of Scotland after 1307–08. Alignment with Bruce may, for some, have been no more than the product of rejecting Plantagenet rule. Men and women who had given their support to King John between 1292 and 1296 may have accepted the settlement negotiated by the magnates in 1304, but they were not obliged to like it. They may not have needed any great sympathy with the ambitions of King Robert, but still accepted him on the basis that any 'home grown' king was preferable to any foreigner.

The existence of the garrisons may have been a factor in encouraging support for the Bruces in the northeast. Between 1297 and 1304 the north had been little affected by the activities of English field armies and most of the garrisons installed by Edward I after the campaign of 1296 had fallen to the Balliol party within a matter of a year or so. There is no reason to suppose that the garrisons installed after 1304 were particularly harsh or even obtrusive, but they were still a visible demonstration of the will of a foreign power. Even if the men in the garrisons were largely Scots, a garrison as an institution was an instrument of an alien king, and therefore may well have been an irritant to the communities of the region. The same is true of the rest of Scotland inasmuch as there were garrisons scattered throughout the realm. About forty castles were held by Plantagenet garrisons in the later years of Edward I's reign, but there were also several baronial castles held by men in Edward's employ or sympathetic to his cause. By 1306, many of these, particularly in the south and east, had been in place for a decade. The local communities may not have liked the garrisons, but they must surely have become accustomed to them over the preceding ten years.

National sentiment is one of the factors that continue to make Bannockburn so prominent in Scottish opinions of the War of Independence to the present day; another is class sentiment. There is a rather romantic view that the Scots at Bannockburn represent the people in arms whereas the English army represents the power of kingship. Neither of these propositions bears examination. King Robert was well aware of the importance of attracting and retaining the support of the noble class as a political tool and as the source of military power. The men who served in his army of 1314 were far from being the 'common husbandmen and tribesmen' beloved of Scottish romance – and, unfortunately, of several historians. The popular mental picture of plaid-clad peasants armed with sharpened logs – and possibly blue face paint – prepared to risk their lives in a perilous, desperate throw of the dice against the rich and finely mounted English, cannot be taken seriously. The rank and file of Robert's army consisted primarily of the more prosperous farm tenants (as opposed to farm labourers), burgesses and other townspeople[34] and he had access to men from the West Highlands and Western Isles for whom soldiering was a normal part of life. The rest – possibly as much as ten to fifteen per cent of the total – were men-at-arms who, almost without exception, were drawn from the nobility. In terms of class representation, there would have been little social difference between the English and Scottish armies other than the contingents from the Western Isles and the northwest Highlands.

Another reason for the prominence of Bannockburn is of course the scale of the victory. In Scottish romance Bannockburn tends to figure as one of only two Scottish victories, the other being Stirling Bridge in 1297. This tradition steadfastly ignores several very important engagements – Roslin, Myton and Culblean, to name but a few. Similarly, this view tends to inflate the importance of various English victories, primarily Falkirk and Halidon Hill. In practice, Edward I derived very little benefit from his victory at Falkirk and in the long term his grandson gained nothing from his 1333 victory at Halidon, since his administration in Scotland had dwindled to a handful of increasingly isolated fortresses by 1338. To a certain extent, the same applies to Bannockburn. Victory allowed Robert to confirm his hold on the southeast and gave him a very enviable martial reputation but, contrary to popular perception, Bannockburn did not give him the political victory he sought. Edward II may have been roundly defeated, but he was not prepared to have peace on the basis of accepting Robert as King of Scotland. He did not even accept that he had actually lost his war irrevocably, but mounted fresh invasions. He did not do so simply in the hope that he would destroy Bruce, though that would have been highly appreciated; he did so to recover what he saw as part of his heritage from his father. Edward II was not the brightest man ever to wear the English crown, but he was not an imbecile. If he was prepared to make the financial and political effort to raise an army for service in Scotland he clearly believed that conquest was not beyond his means. His army had been destroyed in 1314, but his will – and that of many English magnates – to bring Scotland under his rule was still strong and would remain so until his death. It was not Edward II who eventually acknowledged Robert's kingship in 1328, but the government of Edward III.

In the century and more that has passed since Gardiner, Oman, MacKenzie and several others have made their contributions to the study of Bannockburn, most historians have followed the template provided by one or the other. The actual process of any battle is not really that important in relation to the general march of events. Whether the outcome of the battle was decided by this or that incident, by this or that practice, by this or that feature in the terrain is, arguably, a trivial question in comparison to the effects of that outcome. Had Edward II been victorious at Bannockburn, the political consequences might have been far more interesting to historians than the means by which he achieved that victory, unless he had done so through a dramatically innovative approach to battle.

It would be rash to assume that victory at Bannockburn would have brought the War of Independence to a conclusion. Had Robert I and his brother Edward both been killed in action, the Bruce party would probably have come to an end since there was no legitimate male heir to pursue the

Bruce claim to kingship, but that does not mean that the cause of independence would not have been taken up by another candidate, specifically Edward Balliol, son of King John, who had been deposed in 1296, and who would mount a serious challenge to the Bruce party a generation after Bannockburn.

The Nature and Extent of the Evidence

The body of contemporary and near-contemporary documentary evidence relating to the battle of Bannockburn is not extensive, and none of what there is can really be considered as a full account of the action.

More positively, none of them really contradicts any of the others in any material sense, though Barbour pretty certainly 'invented' an extra Scottish formation for the main battle in order to provide a role for Sir James Douglas and for Walter the Stewart, the father of Barbour's patron, Robert II. This can serve as an example of the sort of thing that could influence medieval writers to include material that causes confusion for generations. Barbour wrote his epic poem half a century or more after the events that he described. This was close enough to prevent wholesale invention if the narrative was to have credibility. The account was written to entertain members of the noble class, men who saw themselves as the inheritors of a great military tradition. On a practical level, they were well aware of the nature of battle and well aware of the physical and emotional stresses of active service, but they were also aware of the tales of their fathers and grandfathers – men who had served in the Wars of Independence and who had known Douglas, Randolph and King Robert himself. If Barbour strayed too far from the realities of fighting, his audience would be unimpressed; on the other hand, he had every incentive to raise the profiles of his heroes and, indirectly, the prestige of Robert II.

Further, from Barbour's perspective in the 1360s/70s it would have been unthinkable that so great a figure as Douglas had had no prominent role in the greatest battle of the age. In 1314, Douglas had yet to attain great political stature. He was, no doubt, already the possessor of a serious reputation as a man-at-arms, but was still only a baron, and a fairly minor one at that. This does not imply that barons were not men of some substance, but they were not a homogeneous group in terms of influence and wealth. John Comyn, Lord of Badenoch, was a baron of the very highest order, a man of enormous power – so much so that he was acceptable to the political community as a national leader, serving as Guardian of the Realm from the aftermath of

Falkirk to the appointment of Sir John de Soulis as sole lieutenant of King John. However the barons were not, as a rule, the class of society that provided the most senior political level of leadership. The sheriffdom of Lothian, for example, had at least thirty baronies within its bounds in the early fourteenth century. Obviously none of these Lothian barons enjoyed the status of John Comyn, whose wealth and power were sufficient to make him a major player on the national political stage, but their leadership and influence at a more local level was a vital part of the administrative, judicial and military structures that enabled kings to pursue their objectives.

In the years after Bannockburn Douglas became one of Robert I's principal lieutenants, and acquired vast estates across Scotland, while Walter the Stewart married the King's daughter, Marjorie. This is the Douglas that Barbour knew of – a great lord and military leader so, although every other source clearly describes the Scottish army as having three divisions, Barbour provides a fourth one for Douglas. His audience would be unconcerned about such an invention so long as there were plenty of passages about the fighting itself. Barbour's instinct told him that Douglas should have a narrative of his own within the wider description of the battle. To an extent, he was applying a rationale from his own experience, judgement and the literary needs of the narrative to produce a condition that was what he *wanted* to have been the case. This can also affect historians. In the same way that Barbour's addition of a fourth Scottish formation has conditioned the generally accepted picture of the battle, historians have shaped our perception through the presentation of the process of the action in such a way as to 'fit' their view of the nature of medieval combat. The account of Bannockburn presented by S.R. Gardiner and developed by Sir Charles Oman a century ago still dominates the popular view of the battle. Even a very cursory examination of the modern accounts available in popular histories or on the Internet will show that many of them are no more than paraphrases of Oman's work. Like Barbour, Oman was lead by his experience and instinct. He reasoned that since English arms enjoyed such great success throughout the medieval period – Falkirk, Crécy, Neville's Cross, Poitiers – there must have been curious factors in play for the Scots to defeat the English. How, after all, could the Scots win against the mighty longbow?

Since the conclusion of the fight was inescapable – the English lost and the Scots won – Oman sought to develop a scenario and sequence of events that could explain defeat without compromising the view of English martial ability that he had already adopted. In doing so he rejected the conclusions of the contemporary evidence, all of which clearly indicates a Scottish attack, in favour of his own interpretation in which the English attacked and exhausted themselves by repeated charges against unflinching Scottish spearmen. Not content with that, he placed the Scots and the English on opposing sides of the Bannock Burn itself, thus turning the action into an opposed river crossing, unquestionably a very difficult and challenging manoeuvre to effect, but not one that came to the notice of any of the contemporary writers.

One can make the same observation about issues that seem rather minor. Oman may have been the first historian to declare that Scottish archers carried a short bow, unlike their English and Welsh counterparts, who wielded the famous longbow. This is a distinction that eluded medieval writers, though it is exactly the sort of observation that a professional soldier like Sir Thomas Grey (author of *Scalacronica*) would be likely to make. Grey and his contemporaries were clearly unaware of any great difference between Scottish and English archers as individuals, indeed many of the archers recorded as serving in English garrisons during the occupations of Edward I, Edward II (between 1296 and 1314) and Edward III (in the 1330s), were in fact Scotsmen.[35] The same applies, perhaps to a greater degree, to men-at-arms. There is a romantic view that the armies raised by William Wallace, Andrew Murray, John Comyn and Robert Bruce consisted almost entirely of spearmen with very modest contingents of archers and heavy cavalry. It would be easy to form the impression that knights and men-at-arms were almost an anomaly among Scottish troops of the Middle Ages. This is an impression that is sustained, superficially, when we consider the nature of the great battles of the age – Stirling Bridge, Falkirk, Bannockburn, Dupplin Muir, Halidon Hill and Neville's Cross. At each of these actions, the majority of the Scottish troops were spearmen, however we might reasonably consider that the battles themselves were anomalies since general engagements were so few and far between, and in any case, many of the spearmen at Bannockburn, Dupplin, Halidon and Neville's Cross (at least) were actually dismounted men-at-arms.

The usual practice of war between the English and the Scots throughout the fourteenth century was not a matter of bringing about general engagements, but of achieving local supremacy in order to maintain or extend political control over the community; to impose the lordship of one side at the expense of the other. The overwhelming majority of military action between the Scots and the English throughout the Wars of Independence consisted of clashes between rather small bodies of men-at-arms and the sieges of castles and towns. The bulk of the men who served King John or Robert I or David II at sieges were unquestionably infantrymen discharging their military obligations to lord, community and king. Even in that context there is some doubt about the amount of combat that these men might expect to experience. Most sieges conducted for the Balliol and Bruce parties seem to have been sieges of containment aimed at starving the garrison into surrender, though despondency seems likely to have been as significant a factor as starvation. Several castles and towns fell to coup-de-main operations, though some of these instances occurred during the process of a close siege and should be seen as part and parcel of the wider operation.

It would be unnatural if the primary combatants in such an attack were anything other than men-at-arms. They were, obviously, the best equipped and – as a general rule at least – the most comprehensively trained element of the army, but they also had greater personal motivations. A great feat of arms, even if committed in the context of a siege rather than the better-regarded arena of the open battlefield, could have profound career implications for an ambitious fourteenth-century noble; acquiring a good martial reputation almost invariably enhanced an individual's social and political standing. When we read of the Earl of Moray's successful attack on Edinburgh Castle during the siege of 1314, we should be in no doubt that the picked men who clambered up the Castle Rock in the middle of the night were – for the most part anyway – members of the gentry and aristocracy giving service as men-at-arms for properties held in exchange for a mixture of cash, administrative, social and military obligations. They were emphatically *not* the common peasantry in arms.

2

What did the Combatants Fight for?

Although Edward II carries the weight of blame for the defeats in Scotland generally and at Bannockburn in particular, he is something of a scapegoat. The martial reputation of his father and the defeat of the Scots at Falkirk have rather obscured the fact that the Scottish war which undermined Edward II's authority was, in every sense, the fault of Edward I. His ambition to annex Scotland by force of arms led to 300 years of cross-border antipathy, so it is worth giving a little thought to his reasons for doing so. In part Edward simply wanted to achieve primacy throughout the British Isles, but he surely did not want to do so at the cost of landing himself and his successors with a long-term drain on the resources of the English state. It would seem likely that Edward did not fully understand the scale of the project. This is not to imply that he had no knowledge of Scotland, but rather that he was misled by the nature of his experience. He was aware that Scotland was worth having for economic reasons. He spent time there in 1291–92,[1] but his visits were limited to southern and eastern parts of the country – the areas that were most prosperous and most vulnerable to the sort of military pressure that his resources could most easily provide. Having manipulated the Scottish political class to temporarily cede him a very considerable degree of administrative authority for the duration of the 'great cause',[2] Edward was well aware of the income and liabilities of the Scottish crown.[3] He could see that there was potential for raising his own income and, perhaps, furnishing himself with an additional source of manpower. When he chose to push King John into armed resistance he was familiar with many of the leading figures of the Scottish political establishment, some of whom, notably the Bruce family, hoped to advance their own careers by supporting Edward or, at the very least, by failing to support King John. Even if John had been able to depend on having the military resources of all of the political community for the campaign of 1296, he would have toiled to raise a force capable of resisting Edward's army. Without that level of support, he was facing almost inevitable defeat.

The rout of the Scottish nobility at Dunbar and the rapid and unopposed progress as far north as Elgin led Edward to believe that he had conquered Scotland to such an extent that he could resume his projects on the continent, leaving his lieutenants to finish the job of installing an occupation government. The success of the 1296 campaign was remarkable, but deceptive. Edward failed to grasp two important factors. He did not appreciate the importance of national sentiment and he would seem to have failed to grasp that his progress to Elgin[4] had not really given him, or his lieutenants, a valid understanding of the resources of his enemy. The greater part of the northern and western parts of Scotland remained virtually untouched by English forces by the end of 1296. Additionally, he may have assumed that since so many Scottish nobles had fallen prisoner at Dunbar or had been obliged to give him their allegiance by appending their seals to the Ragman Roll,[5] that there was no realistic prospect of a Scottish recovery. Confident that he had dealt with Scotland, and with several other military commitments, Edward failed to ensure that his Scottish government had the necessary resources to impose his rule in the face of opposition. Although he installed garrisons in castles and towns throughout the country, the numbers involved were very small and his lieutenants were not provided with a standing force of any stature that could be quickly brought into action against a 'revolt' among the Scots. In part, the size of the garrisons may have been a political, rather than military, decision. Edward would have liked the Scots to accept his kingship with equanimity, and may have felt that installing garrisons on a similar scale to the forces which had been available to Scottish sheriffs in the reigns of Alexander III and his predecessors would be sufficient to maintain law and order without giving offence to the populace. Essentially, Edward seems to have preferred to adopt a 'business as usual' ethos in both local and national government functions.

Clearly he was very much mistaken, as Hugh Cressingham, Edward's treasurer for Scotland, had discovered before the end of July 1297,[6] when he wrote to inform Edward that only two Scottish counties – Roxburghshire and Berwickshire – were fully under English control and properly provided with Plantagenet officials. Edward's government had possession of the castles, but had failed to gain power over the rest of the country. Furthermore, the Plantagenet cause was not prospering; in fact, the Balliol party was gaining ground steadily, appointing baillies and other officials to gather issues and recruit troops. They worked to make it clear that even though John was a prisoner, government in his name was not yet dead. Clearly a good many Scots were still willing to fight, but what did they hope to achieve, and what did they risk by resistance?

It is almost axiomatic that Scottish nobles were lukewarm in their support for independence in order to protect their estates in England. A number of Scottish nobles – some of them very obscure men and women – did hold land in England, either from more substantial persons than themselves or from the king himself. Very few of them were landholders of any great significance. The Bruce family held a variety of valuable properties in the south of England, but were not sufficiently important to be figures of any real significance in the local political community, let alone on the national stage. In Scotland, on the other hand, they held a major lordship (Annandale) and an earldom (Carrick), a heritage that ensured a place at the very highest level of Scottish society. Like most cross-border landholders, their Scottish property was the focus of their life and the source of their wealth and influence. Their English properties were well worth having, but not at the risk of losing their position in Scotland. Bruce's defection to the Scots in the wake of the battle of Falkirk risked the forfeiture of his heritage in England, but failure to support the Balliol party might have eventually excluded him from the entire political process in Scotland, possibly leading to the loss of Carrick and Annandale.

The challenges of cross-border landholding were not limited to the upper ranks of the nobility. A very minor landholder in Midlothian, Hugh de Penicuik, was forfeited of two small properties in Northumberland for his adherence to the Balliol party in 1298.[7] Hugh was precisely the sort of man who might be expected to give his allegiance to the Plantagenet party. He had appended his seal to the Ragman Roll in 1296 and he lived in an area which was – at least nominally – securely held by Edward I's administration. He stood to lose valuable property rights by opposing that administration, but he nonetheless chose to do so.

No doubt his decision to resist was influenced by the same factors that affected the rest of the community, and it is worth giving a little thought to what those factors might have been. Resistance to Edward I grew from several issues: a fear that taxation might rise; that new laws and procedures would be imposed; that men might be conscripted to serve in Edward's armies in France and Flanders and, in all probability, a degree of resentment at the presence of English garrisons in Scottish towns and castles. There is no reason to believe that any of the material burdens would have been heavier in Scotland than in England, but they would have been heavier than those to which the community were already accustomed.

In part this was a product of the lighter demands of Scottish kingship. The medieval belief that a king 'should live of his own' – that is, from the proceeds of the crown estates – was not a realistic proposition given the responsibilities of the crown, but the financial demands on Scottish kings were certainly much lighter than those on their English counterparts. Consequently, Scottish kings had not had any great need to impose regular taxation on their subjects and were, as a general rule, able to live from the rents of their properties and the export duty on wool.

Scots might also have to face a considerable extension of military obligation as subjects of Edward I. A good deal of Edward's career had been taken up with warfare, indeed he had issued demands for military service to several Scottish magnates and King John himself for a campaign against France.[8] If Edward could secure Scotland he would undoubtedly make full use of the military obligations of the political class, and probably of the wider community as well.

The appointment of English sheriffs, constables and other officials to posts in Scotland, not to mention the installation of garrisons, surely provoked some degree of resentment as the visible evidence of defeat and conquest, but it had another aspect in terms of local political life. Posts that were filled by Englishmen could not be filled by Scots. The installation of English candidates disrupted the existing patterns of custom. The patronage of English kings might therefore lead to a diminution in the status of the existing political community. Perhaps more significantly the erection of English kingship in Scotland would unquestionably move the focus of political life. Like their counterparts in England or France, the kings of Scotland lived a fairly mobile life, passing through the kingdom from one royal castle to the next. The economic value of sojourns at different locations was considerable. Moving the court to another location was frequently more cost-effective than bringing the produce of crown estates to wherever the king happened to be at a particular moment, however there were also significant political benefits to be gained from travelling through the country.

Moving between communities gave the king the opportunity to monitor his officers and to be seen by his subjects, but it also provided members of the political community with an opportunity to seek favour or justice from the monarch. If the king of England became king of Scotland he would inevitably spend most of his time in other domains; not just England, but a substantial portion of France as well. Access to a king based in Edinburgh, Perth and Aberdeen might be difficult for Scottish lords from Dumfries or Skye, but still very much easier than gaining access to a king based in London. For the magnates of Scotland, there was also the question of personal political status. The earls and great lords of Scotland were very big fish in a rather small pond. Few of them could command the sort of wealth that would accord them similar status in the much larger 'pond' in which the magnates and baronage of Edward I operated.

Loss of political independence at a national level had, potentially, implications for the more senior members of the Scottish political community. Scottish earls enjoyed a considerable degree of political, judicial and military authority within the boundaries of their lordships. Although neither Edward I nor Edward II made any concerted effort to reduce the powers of the earls and barons of Scotland, the men and women who held these positions could not be sure that integration into the dominions of the Plantagenets would not in due course lead to a reduction in their authority. Any candidate for the Scottish throne would have to acquire the support of the senior nobility, support that was hardly likely to be forthcoming if the nobility had any doubt that their privileges might be compromised under Bruce or Balliol rule.

There has been a tendency to assume that Edward I entertained an ambition to annex Scotland from an early date, perhaps even from the time of the death of Alexander III. In the widest sense this is not impossible. Edward and Alexander had certainly planned to bring about a wedding between Alexander's granddaughter, Margaret, and Edward's eldest son, Edward of Carnarvon.[9] This attempt to secure a dynastic union of the two countries might well have been successful had it not been for Margaret's premature death in 1290. Edward was willing to commit himself to the preservation of Scottish laws and procedures and the Scottish aristocracy do not seem to have felt unduly threatened by the prospect of a joint monarchy, however this was in the context of the later thirteenth century. England and Scotland had developed strong cultural, economic and political bonds over a lengthy period of peace. The events of the tail end of the thirteenth century and of the fourteenth century would render such a proposition utterly unacceptable for the next 300 years. Margaret's death did more than change Edward's hopes for a union through marriage; Margaret had no clear heir. The issue of the Scottish succession became a thorny and dangerous problem for the Scots, but it was also an event that Edward could not afford to ignore. Any problem that might bring about instability in Scotland might have difficult repercussions for English kings in the future. Edward may not have taken very much interest in the northern sheriffdoms of his country, but he would not be prepared to ignore their plight in the event of a Scottish civil war that could spill over the border or dislocate the local economy. Additionally, the death of Margaret gave Edward an opportunity to become directly involved in Scottish affairs, possibly with a view to resurrecting the claims of English kings to be the feudal superiors of Scottish monarchs. This was not a new gambit on Edward's part. In 1278 he had attempted to extract homage for Scotland from Alexander III, only to be informed that Alexander owed homage 'to God alone' for his kingdom.[10]

Edward had not abandoned all hope of procuring feudal superiority; his actions in relation to the 'competition' of 1291–92 make it perfectly clear that he was willing to conduct the court which would eventually decide the issue, but only if all of the candidates were willing to accept his superiority.

On the death of Alexander, a regency council had been entrusted with the government of the country on behalf of the young queen,[11] but they could not rule forever. Even if there had been no ambitious nobles with a desire for kingship, the credibility of a regency rests on the premise that – in due course – the monarch will come of age and take the reins of power into his own hands. There were, however, several men who did harbour ambitions for the throne, primarily John Balliol and Robert Bruce of Annandale (grandfather of Robert I). Neither of these men had any interest in standing aside in favour of the other, and both had sufficiently strong cases that neither could be dismissed out of hand. Furthermore, both men had considerable military resources of their own or powerful allies to support their ambitions.

The possibility of a civil war was very real and clearly some action would have to be taken to avert it. The council of Guardians (regents) faced a problem that they did not have the resources to resolve. Robert Bruce of Annandale was, seemingly, prepared to go to war to make good his claim to the throne – a claim which, according to himself anyway, had been endorsed by Alexander II as long ago as 1238. If his resources had been limited to the lordship of Annandale and the various lesser properties in his hands, the guardians might have been able to suppress any attempt to bring about a Bruce kingship through force of arms. However, Robert's son – also Robert – had married the great Celtic heiress, Marjorie, Countess of Carrick,[12] whose earldom greatly extended the power and influence of the Bruce family. He too enjoyed the support of a number of Scottish magnates who, collectively, might be able to secure military victory.

His chief competitor, John Balliol, could not deploy the same degree of military strength from his own resources as the Bruce family, but he did enjoy the support of Scotland's foremost noble family, the Comyns. The Comyns had come to prominence through a long tradition of support for the crown[13] and held several great lordships and important offices of state, as well as the support of numerous noble families across the length and breadth of the country. With the prospect of a major national war and no internal means of preventing it, the guardians had little choice but to seek the intervention of an outside party. To all practical intents and purposes, the only candidate worthy of consideration was Edward I. The guardians had been the target of a great deal of criticism, not to say vilification, for their actions in this regard, but in reality they had very little choice. Only Edward could apply the level of military force sufficient to cow the Bruce and Balliol parties, and even if the matter came to blows, Edward would obviously only have to fight one of the two candidates. As the king of Scotland's only neighbour, Edward could hardly be ignored.

Over a period of more than a year (1291–92)[14] Edward served as the administrator of a court which gave consideration to the claims of all the declared claimants, though in practice only Robert Bruce and John Balliol were considered viable choices. Out of 104 'auditors' appointed to hear the case, forty were chosen from the Bruce party and forty from the Balliol party.[15] The eventual outcome of the hearing gave the throne to John Balliol, though the decision of the court was not accepted by Robert Bruce, who transferred his claim to his eldest son. It has often been claimed that Edward chose to favour the Balliol party because he believed that John would be a more malleable figure than Robert, and because John was willing to accept Edward as his feudal superior, however there is no evidence to support that contention. In practice, all of the candidates had been obliged to accept Edward's lordship as a condition for consideration, and there is no reason to believe that Edward feared Robert Bruce any more than he feared John Balliol.

Claims of feudal superiority of English kings over their northern counterparts had been accepted under duress by several Scottish kings in the past, but they had never been an important aspect of the general pattern of Anglo–Scottish relations. Unlike his predecessors, Edward was determined to put such claims into practice. Again, it has been suggested that Edward chose John because he believed that it would be easier to impose his will as the superior of John than of Robert. Obviously it is impossible to put such an assertion to the test, but it is difficult to believe that Edward would have treated a Bruce monarch any differently to a Balliol monarch. Even if Edward had been more accommodating to Robert – perhaps for personal reasons, since they had known one another for decades – it is worth bearing in mind that Robert was now more than eighty years old and could not be expected to live for very much longer. Robert's son does not seem to have been either a very ambitious or a particularly strong-willed person; undoubtedly Edward would have undermined him in the same way as he undermined John Balliol.

As it turned out, King John's rule was compromised by Edward in several ways. Within a matter of months, Edward was hearing appeals from John's courts, claiming much the same rights over the Scottish king that he enjoyed over English barons. The sequence of events of 1292–95 have been examined at length by several scholars[16] and do not bear repeating here, but the final issue that drove John – or possibly a council of nobles acting on his behalf – was military service. In 1295 Edward issued writs to several Scottish earls and barons and to John himself, demanding troops for his war with France.[17] This was too much to be borne, and the Scots turned to the only quarter from which they could reasonably hope for succour – Philip, King of France.

The decision to enter into a formal alliance against England gave Edward an excuse to take up arms against the Scots, but since he was already on campaign himself, he could not react to this development immediately, and so was obliged to wait until the spring of 1296 before he could take direct action. In theory, the Scots precipitated events inasmuch as they were the first to mount operations by raiding into England, including an abortive attack on Carlisle.

In short, the Scots simply had no real plan for victory and were therefore almost bound to experience defeat. It had been so long since the Scots had been involved in a major war that there was no reservoir of experience in conducting operations. Edward, on the other hand, may not have been an especially accomplished soldier, but he was certainly an experienced one. Moreover he was the undisputed ruler of a much larger realm. The Scots were far from united as well as being inexperienced. The Bruce and Dunbar families may have been the most prominent of the Scottish nobles who elected to either fight for Edward or to not fight at all, but they were not alone. In practice, the absence of the Bruces and the Earl of Dunbar probably had no effect whatsoever on the campaign. On 30 March 1296 Edward's troops stormed the town of Berwick and slaughtered the inhabitants in their thousands.

Criticism of his behaviour is justified in moral terms, but it was an effective strategic gambit. The horrors of the sack of Berwick would have lost nothing in the telling, and any intention to fight entertained by other Scottish towns must have evaporated very swiftly indeed. Four weeks after this the Scots suffered another signal reverse at the battle of Dunbar. Despite the claims of one contemporary writer that the Scottish casualties at Dunbar amounted to more than 11,000,[18] it seems likely that the action was not in fact a particularly large one. There is no evidence to suggest that a great battle of manoeuvre took place at all, rather that the Scottish cavalry – or a portion of it – met a division of Edward's cavalry in the vicinity of Dunbar Castle and were roundly beaten in short order. At least 100 Scottish nobles were taken prisoner and dispatched to various castles in England, but only one fatal casualty – Patrick Graham – is mentioned and there is no evidence to indicate that the Scottish infantry were engaged at all.

Over the next five months Edward was able to make his way through Scotland as far as Elgin, accepting the surrender of Scottish towns, castles and eventually of King John himself. The complete collapse of the Scottish military and political establishment in the summer of 1296 is rather misleading – it may have misled Edward himself. Quite simply, given the defeat of the nobles and the apparent disintegration of the balance of the army, there was no incentive for garrisons to resist the English army. Edward clearly had a considerable train of siege equipment – his troops bombarded Edinburgh Castle for five days before it surrendered – but there would have been no point in forcing the English to mount a lengthy siege since there was no Scottish army to provide a relief force, nor was there any member of the senior nobility available to raise and lead such a force since virtually all of the magnates were either in the peace of Edward I or were prisoners of war in England – a factor which must have encouraged Edward to believe that he had achieved the conquest of Scotland.

The assumption was, however, very seriously flawed in several ways. First and foremost, a shortage of Scottish political and military leadership between the summer of 1296 and the spring of 1297 did not mean that there was no will to resist, merely that there was no stable structure to guide that resistance. The absence of a Scottish force under arms did not mean that there was an absence of men willing to continue the fight given the opportunity to do so. Little more than a year after Edward's return to England, the Scots had found new leaders in the shape of William Wallace and Andrew Murray, who restored Scottish government through most of the country and won a significant battle at Stirling Bridge.[19] Over the following seven years, Edward invested vast sums in his Scottish project, but despite a resounding victory at Falkirk, which propelled Wallace from the post of Guardian, the capture of towns and castles, and the construction of several peels at Linlithgow, Selkirk and Livingstone, Edward was unable to impose his rule through force of arms alone. In February 1304 he came to terms with the Scots. A number of individuals, including William Wallace and the garrison of Stirling Castle – captured by the Scots in 1299 – were specifically excluded from the agreement. Wallace and his small band of men-at-arms continued to mount operations until his capture in August 1305 but, superficially at least, Edward had achieved his objective.

Even at this point, the extent to which he actually believed that the business of conquering Scotland was really concluded is open to question. The relatively easy terms allowed to the Scots are probably a reflection of Edward's urgent need to bring the war to a close for reasons of cost and personal prestige. He was an old man, not in the best of health, and eager to leave a clear legacy of success. By bringing the Balliol party into his peace he achieved his objective of unifying the British Isles under one central authority – that of English kingship – but his achievement was more apparent than real. The Strathord agreement was short-lived and by the spring of 1306, a new threat to Plantagenet rule in Scotland emerged as Robert Bruce declared himself King of Scotland. For the next year and more his prospects were not exactly promising, but by 1308 he had established himself as a serious threat to the occupation.

Continued success brought Robert new supporters and undermined the authority of the Plantagenet administration in Scotland. Edward hardly needed a war to add to his difficulties, but he could hardly have abandoned his father's Scottish project even if he had wanted to. Withdrawing his troops and admin-istrators from Scotland would have undermined his prestige and authority, not just in England and Wales, but in the great lordships that he held from the king of France. Furthermore, there was a degree of pressure from those members of the political community of England who had received grants of land in Scotland from Edward I, and from those Scots who continued to support the provisions of the Strathord agreement of 1304.

As the Bruce party gained ground over the years after 1307, the plight of English nobles with claims to Scottish titles and from those Scottish nobles who had been displaced by Robert's campaigns increased the pressure on Edward to restore Plantagenet administration in Scotland. Edward mounted several campaigns against the Bruce party, none of which helped to improve his prospects, but they all cost him money and political credibility and may have helped to push some Scots into the Bruce camp. Finally, there was the issue of the credibility of England as a military power and the practicalities of national security. Defeat at the hands of the Scots would undermine the reputation of the English as a nation in arms, but it would also compromise one of the attractions in conquering Scotland in the first place. So long as Scotland was under English control, Edward had a secure northern border. Without that control there was always the prospect that the Scots would ally themselves with the French, which was of course one of the issues that had brought about the campaign of 1296. Edward was caught between a rock and the proverbial hard place. He could not afford to abandon the war in Scotland for political reasons, nor could he achieve the military success necessary to put the Bruce party out of business.

By late 1313 the problem of Scotland had reached crisis proportions. When Edward came to the throne in July 1307 the English administration had covered most of the country, but by the close of 1313 it had been reduced to a mere rump in the southern counties. Even in the counties of the southeast, where a strong chain of castles and fortresses had been developed to prevent the Bruce party from seizing complete control, the ability of the Plantagenet administration to impose Edward's rule had become very isolated. The garrisons may have been able to preserve a veneer of power, but were unable to mount effective operations against the Scots. On the other hand the Scots were increasingly inclined to carry the war to the enemy by mounting operations into England demanding ransoms in cash and produce, which damaged the morale of the communities concerned and undermined Edward's credibility. Just as importantly, the funds raised were a godsend to King Robert. The operations allowed him to develop a considerable resource in the way of men with some experience of war and enabled him to pay his men well enough to prevent them raiding and pillaging at will. This was vital to the success of his policy. If the people of northern England were to pay Robert's blackmail they needed to have confidence that they would not suffer from indiscriminate robbery, rape and murder.

It must have been obvious in the winter of 1313–14 that failure to take positive action against Robert would eventually result in the loss of all that remained of the English administration in Scotland, but there was an even greater threat. One of the most important factors in medieval government was the ability – or otherwise – to provide 'good lordship'. Clearly Edward was failing to provide this for his adherents in Scotland, but he was also failing to provide it for his subjects in Northumberland, Westmorland and Cumbria. Regardless of whether or not Robert ever harboured ambitions to extend his borders southwards, there was always the possibility that the political communities of northern England might eventually seek his lordship – as indeed was the case in the years after Bannockburn. If Edward was to restore his credibility at home and in Scotland, he desperately needed to defeat Bruce.

The political pressures on Edward to seek battle with the Scots are fairly self-evident, however we should not assume that there were no political considerations for Robert. His military initiatives in the period between 1307 and 1314 are generally characterised as 'guerrilla' campaigns. In fact, Robert's general war policy was quite conventional by the standards of the time. Throughout the medieval period the practice of destroying an enemy's willingness and ability to continue the fight through what we might think of as economic warfare was a perfectly normal approach to campaigning. There was certainly plenty of warfare across Europe throughout the thirteenth and fourteenth centuries, on the other hand many campaigns, even those involving large forces, failed to result in a general engagement, and even fewer brought about more than one major battle. In Scotland there had been more or less continual warfare from 1296–1304, but the number of actual battles was very small and only two of these involved more than a couple of thousand combatants in total – Stirling Bridge and Falkirk. This does not mean that battle was necessarily regarded as undesirable or unimportant, merely that a large engagement was not something to be undertaken lightly. It must surely have been apparent to King Robert – and to King Edward for that matter – that the removal of English garrisons from Scottish towns and castles and repeated raids into England, however profitable, would not be sufficient to bring about a political settlement of the issue of Scottish independence. Robert needed more than military success if his dynasty was to sit securely on the throne. He also needed more than domestic acceptance of his rule; he needed to achieve the recognition of his right to the throne both at home and abroad. Military success would not be enough to provide him with long-term political credibility and security. If his kingship rested on military means alone then it could also be disrupted, even destroyed, by military means.

Above all, he needed to achieve recognition of his kingship from England. It is not impossible that he might have brought this about through continued success in war, though it is difficult to see quite how that could have come about. Arguably, it might have been achieved through the annexation of large tracts of northern England which could have been returned to England in exchange for a permanent peace agreement, but there are two major flaws to such a possibility. Firstly, it assumes that Edward II would have been prepared to surrender his claims to Robert in exchange for counties of very limited economic value to the crown of England, and secondly, the long-term military occupation of Northumberland, Westmorland and Cumbria would unquestionably have been an insupportable drain on his resources. Even if such an occupation could have been achieved, it would have done nothing more than give Robert the same problems that Edward faced in Scotland – the challenge of maintaining a military occupation in the face of a hostile population. More importantly perhaps, Scottish occupation of English counties might well have inspired the wider political community of England to redouble their efforts in support of Edward's Scottish ambitions, serving to unite the magnates of England behind a king who was somewhat less than popular.

Assuming that Robert's English campaigns were intended to bring Edward to the negotiating table, it was a policy that had clearly failed by the spring of 1314. Edward had been willing to allow his representatives to enter into truces with the Bruce party,[20] but only on the understanding that they were acting – at least in theory – on their own initiative, not on the orders of, or even with the acquiescence of, the English crown. Clearly Robert needed to develop another dimension to his strategy. It would be rash to assume that he had come to the conclusion that victory in battle was the only means of achieving his aims, but equally it would be unrealistic to assume that he did not have it in mind as an option. Another option would have been to continue with his existing policy in the hope that Edward's domestic political difficulties would eventually cause revolution and civil war in England. This was certainly possible given Edward's relationship with some of his nobles. In the recent past, Edward had been obliged to accept the banishment of his closest friend, Piers Gaveston, and the constraints of a set of conditions imposed by a coalition of magnates known as the 'Ordainers'.[21]

Edward may not have been either popular or particularly secure at the end of 1313, but the worst of the crisis was past and so was any immediate chance that political instability in England might provide an opportunity for Robert to gain recognition as King of Scotland.

Another avenue for a non-military political settlement was diplomacy. Robert may have entertained hopes that recognition by the King of France and the Pope might be a precursor to inclusion in a wider political settlement of outstanding issues between Edward and Philip relating to French lordships held by the king of England. However, there were significant barriers to anything of that nature, not least the fact that Robert was an excommunicate on account of the murder of John Comyn at the Greyfriars church in Dumfries. More to the point, Edward would have had little to gain and a great deal to lose by reaching an accommodation with Robert. Any attempt to discard what was seen as the 'right' of his father – and himself of course – to lordship over Scotland would have been seen as a betrayal of the nation and the vast sums that he had expended on his Scottish campaigns and garrisons would have been thrown away for the sake of bringing an end to a war that most English magnates had yet to see as a lost cause.

Given the very limited prospects for a political settlement that would bring recognition of his kingship abroad, it would be unreasonable to assume that Robert did not give serious consideration to the possibilities that might arise from a major victory on the battlefield. It is certainly true that a repeat of his strategy of avoiding combat might yet bear fruit. If Edward were to lead another great army into Scotland but fail to force battle on the Scots, the damage to his political prestige might be enough to reopen the question of his political authority in England. The expense of a major expedition which did not bring the restoration of Plantagenet rule in Scotland would have been a blow to Edward's prestige and might have led to widespread resentment at the increased burden of taxation that would have been necessary to pay for the troops and munitions committed to the operation. On the other hand, both Edward and his father had been through this process before and neither had felt obliged to give up on the conquest of Scotland. Indeed, even a relatively successful invasion that did result in a major victory for English arms might not produce any tangible benefits. In 1298 Edward I had destroyed the army of Sir William Wallace at Falkirk, but all that had been achieved was the removal of Wallace from the office of Guardian. That victory had not brought about the collapse of the Balliol party, but had provided the opportunity for the traditional political leadership of Scottish society to assert itself.

An English victory in 1314 therefore, might or might not have a positive effect on Edward's prospects, but a defeat would certainly have had very real benefits for Robert. If the Scots scored a victory, even a marginal one, Edward's credibility would have been seriously impaired at home and also in Scotland. Failure to defeat Robert in the field would unquestionably jeopardise the remaining garrisons, but it would also undermine the loyalty of those Scots who still adhered to the Plantagenet cause. This was an issue of some importance to King Robert in the winter of 1313 – English garrisons and administrators still retained a measure of control in some southern counties.

As it turned out, by the summer of 1314 the crucial strongholds of Edinburgh and Roxburgh had already been recovered and the English administration in Lothian, Roxburghshire and Berwickshire had virtually ceased to exist. Mr Nusbacher is quite wrong in his assertion that:

> The Lothian fortresses were firmly in English hands, making it difficult indeed for King Robert to muster his army in Lauderdale.[22]

Edinburgh fell in March 1314[23] and there is no English record material to indicate that any of the other Lothian castles still contained English garrisons or any material to indicate that Robert ever had any intention of mustering his army in Lauderdale.

There were still some Scots in the southern and eastern counties who were prepared to turn out to support the Plantagenet cause and probably rather more who, though no longer active for King Edward, were not yet prepared to turn out for King Robert, but the few remaining garrisons, such as Bothwell and Berwick, were no longer able to impose Edward's lordship in the surrounding communities. The failing strength of the English garrisons did not, in itself, mean that Robert's kingship had been fully established in Lothian, Lanarkshire, Roxburghshire, Berwickshire and Dumfriesshire, so even in the spring of 1314 the southern counties must still have represented something of a challenge to the Bruce cause. If an English invasion could be defeated without battle then these communities would, in all probability, have fallen into King Robert's hands, but the process would surely be hastened if he could inflict a defeat on his rival.

There was also the wider question of Robert's credibility throughout the country as a whole. Bluntly, most of the political community must have been aware that, even with the best will in the world, Robert was not the legitimate king. Victory on the battlefield would not in itself give him political legitimacy, but it would certainly enhance his prestige and damage the prospects of any movement to restore the Balliol monarchy. This was not such a far-fetched prospect bearing in mind that despite his victories – military and political – King Robert was threatened by a coup in 1320.[24] Although it is known to history as the De Soulis Conspiracy, the real objective of the conspirators was to replace Robert with Edward Balliol. If there was still a strong sympathy for the Balliol party in 1320 it would be unreasonable to assume that there was none at all in 1314 or that Robert was unaware that there were people in his allegiance who would be willing to transfer their loyalty to the man who was, after all, the legitimate heir to the throne.

If victory on the battlefield held potential benefits in the military, diplomatic and political spheres there was also, arguably, a religious dimension; victory could be construed as an endorsement by God. It is quite possible that some people would have seen defeat of the English as an indication that

God favoured the Bruce cause, or that defeat of the Scots would have been an indication that he favoured the Plantagenets; however there is very little evidence to support such a view. Neither the Scots nor the English could claim to have enjoyed continual success in their campaigns at different times, which would rather undermine the idea that divine intervention was a major factor in warfare. Naturally, both sides claimed to have God on their side; the bishop of Moray[25] going so far as to claim that taking up arms against the English was as worthy as going on crusade. No doubt there was a limited degree of propaganda value among the more credulous, but given the severity of the defeat at Falkirk in 1298, it is hard to imagine that many people were deeply affected by the theological considerations or by whether or not the conflict could be categorised as a 'just war' for either the Scots or the English. In practice, most people probably saw the conflict for what it was – a political struggle between kings and nations, and not a demonstration of God's will.

3

Lions and Leopards: The Careers of Robert I and Edward II

The Leopard: Edward II

In many respects Edward II was a very similar man to his father. He was strong, handsome and personally courageous; he was fond of the outdoor life and strenuous exercise including swimming and wrestling. He was a literate man, partial to romances and drama. His hobbies and passions have led to him being seen as a man who was not in sympathy with the members of his court. To a great extent he was not, but not because of the pleasure he took in literature – there was nothing 'unmanly' or 'anti-aristocratic' or even unusual about a man of his class owning books or enjoying plays. He also had some of his father's faults. He was partial to gambling and prone to promoting men because he liked them, not because of their abilities. Both father and son were ambitious men, though not perhaps in quite the same sense. Edward I was eager to conquer Scotland; Edward II was eager to retain her, but not perhaps so much as a demonstration of his will and ability, as a sheer reluctance to give up any part of what he viewed as his 'heritage'.

He was not a very successful soldier, but he was not devoid of military experience either. In 1301[1] he was in command of a substantial force at Carlisle that had been tasked with operations against the Scots in the south west in the hope, according to his father, that he would acquire 'the chief honour of taming the pride of the Scots'. The campaign that ensued was not a great success, but it was not a complete failure either. By September, the Bruce stronghold of Turnberry had fallen to the Prince Edward's troops.[2]

Shortly after he came to the throne, Edward married Isabella, daughter of King Philip of France. It was not a very happy union, though it did produce four children and Edward had at least one other child out of wedlock.[3]

By the time of his marriage, Edward had already formed a close relationship with Piers Gaveston and before the end of 1308 there was already a rumour that Edward was rather more partial to the company of his friend than of his queen. She was described as a 'most elegant lady and beautiful woman',[4] but it is worth noting that she was also just twelve years old. She would have to have been a most precocious teenager to be capable of offering better company than the witty, elegant and entertaining Gaveston, even if he and Edward were not lovers, and if they *were* lovers – as seems most likely – she would have had no chance at all of ousting Gaveston from the king's favour.

Edward did not spend much time with his queen, and seems to have made no great effort to involve her in either his political or social life. At the time of Bannockburn, Isabella would only have been about eighteen years old and therefore still unlikely to be a stimulating companion for any grown man, let alone one who was homosexual. On the other hand he did not neglect her entirely. He showed considerable interest in her physical comfort and well-being and he seems to have been very fond of his children. Even after she elected to remain in France, Edward seems to have been genuinely upset and not a little confused at her reluctance to return to England.

The blame for the failure of Edward and Isabella's marriage has often been laid at the feet of Piers Gaveston or, more reasonably, attributed to Edward's preference for, and generosity to, his close friend. Gaveston himself is generally seen as a 'nobody' plucked from obscurity by the king's friendship. Gaveston certainly benefited from Edward's largesse; he did not stem from an especially humble background, but from a prominent Gascon noble family. He was widely resented among the English magnates, not least for his practice of giving uncomplimentary nicknames to prominent members of Edward's court. Gloucester was 'whoreson', Pembroke was 'Joseph the Jew' and Warwick – who would eventually kill Gaveston – was 'The Black Dog of Arden.' As well as his fierce wit, Gaveston was resented for his remarkable rise in status and wealth, particularly after Edward made him Earl of Cornwall. A more circumspect and tactful person might have found a way of smoothing ruffled magnatial feathers and integrating themselves into the community of earls and great lords, but Gaveston seems to have had a real talent for offending the mighty.

Gaveston served Edward in Scotland during the abortive campaign of 1310–11, and appears to have discharged his duties in a reasonably effective manner, however the army raised was not adequate to the task of carrying the war to the Scots. Indeed, the main purpose of mounting the campaign at all seems to have had much more to do with Edward's desire to avoid his domestic political problems and protecting his favourite than it did with pursuing the recovery of the Plantagenet government. If Edward thought that a Scottish campaign would defuse opposition he was sadly mistaken; few English magnates heeded his call to arms, and by the summer of 1312 matters had come to a head, with several English magnates taking up arms against the king's government. It was at this point that the Ordainers, who had forced Edward to accept the existence of a committee of twenty-one magnates charged with producing a blueprint for government reforms, over-reached themselves. Gaveston, besieged in Scarborough Castle, surrendered to Aymer de Valence, Earl of Pembroke, but was snatched from De Valence's custody by Warwick, who promptly had him executed. This was a gross insult to De Valence and to John de Warenne, Earl of Surrey, who had given their word to Gaveston that he would not be harmed in their hands. Warwick's actions pushed Pembroke and Surrey into the king's party, and Gaveston's death eased Edward's domestic situation to some degree. His queen, Isabella, had resented Gaveston's prominence, which, she felt, diminished her own position. This in turn helped Edward's relationship with his father-in-law, the King of France, despite the fact that Philip had, effectively, though not formally, recognised Robert's kingship. While Edward tried to deal with his domestic and political problems, the Scots continued to apply military pressure, but not just in Scotland. As early as 1309, the community of Northumberland was incapable of contributing to a crown subsidy due to the impact of raids by Robert's troops.[5]

The opposition of the English magnates prevented Edward from waging war in Scotland and a truce was arranged early in 1309 which would run to the summer of 1310, at which point Edward was able to renew the conflict.[6] However, the increasingly strong position of Robert and the slender force that Edward could commit to the campaign meant that little was achieved. He returned to England and entered into negotiations with his opposition – the Lords Ordainers – to bring matters relating to taxation and the royal prerogative to a mutually acceptable conclusion. It seems to have been a tortuous business, but an agreement was reached at Edward's Parliament of October 1313.

The range of events that transpired at this time – King Robert's declared intention to forfeit Scottish lords who failed to come to his peace over the next twelve months,[7] a petition of Sir Adam Gordon and the Earl of Dunbar seeking protection against both the Bruce party and the troops of the Plantagenet garrisons[8] and the increasing isolation of his remaining Scottish assets – suggest, perhaps, that Edward was prepared to make more concessions to the Ordainers than he would have liked. But he was obliged to go some way toward meeting their demands in the interests of raising troops for a campaign in 1314, a matter eased by a grant of taxation from his 1313 Parliament.

It would be unfair to suggest that Edward's need to mount an offensive in 1314 was simply the product of his failure to address the situation earlier in his reign. It is true that he abandoned the campaign that his father had mounted in 1307, but he did have pressing problems, not least the enormous debt which Edward I had incurred over the previous twenty years and more. This amounted to something in the region of £200,000 – a massive sum, even for government debt, and well beyond Edward's immediate resources. That he managed to discharge his obligations and even put away a substantial sum by the time of his deposition and death was a remarkable achievement, but it could not have been done in the short-term, and the pursuit of a 1307 campaign against Robert would only have made matters worse. In addition to his immediate financial difficulties, Edward faced a good deal of political opposition from the very first days of his reign. Some of these – particularly his determination to shower lands, wealth and power on Gaveston – were of his own making, but others were inherited from his father's reign. Edward I had also had to deal with a lot of opposition from his magnates, but he had always been able to face them down before anger turned into defiance. Edward II was not so astute a politician as his father, and certainly did not have such a weight of experience. It would not be surprising if some part of the opposition to Edward II had its roots in the resentment of men who had been out-manoeuvred by his father.

Edward II's reign was hardly an example of English kingship at its best; his reputation as an incompetent and ill-advised monarch is, by and large, justified. On the other hand, he was not the only English king to experience serial misfortunes, nor the only one to bring many of his problems on himself. Henry II faced opposition from his sons, let alone his barons; Richard I managed to become a prisoner; Henry III had to deal with an extensive civil war and Edward I's ambitions had brought on a financial crisis – but none of them carries the weight of censure and opprobrium heaped onto Edward II. Defeat in Scotland was not Edward's only problem by a long way, but it is the issue with which he is most closely associated. National leaders – until modern times at least – have often had to bear the responsibility for national disasters, and Edward has had to carry the blame for Bannockburn. To an extent, this is neither surprising nor unrealistic, but it is not altogether fair. War with Scotland was not Edward's project, it was a situation that had been engendered by his father. He was not responsible for the dire financial situation of 1307, nor was he entirely responsible for the difficult relationship between the crown and the senior nobility, but he is widely held to be entirely responsible for the defeat at Bannockburn and the depredations of the Scots in northern England.

The latter was a product of the inability of the English crown to impose a settlement on the Scots through force of arms, and is a rather wider issue than victory or defeat in one battle. The former was certainly Edward's problem, but the extent to which he was personally responsible for losing the battle can be exaggerated. Edward was not alone at Bannockburn; he was surrounded by several very experienced and competent soldiers – Aymer de Valence, Sir Robert Clifford and Henry Beaumont to name but a few. None of these men seem to have been dismayed at the prospect of bringing the Scots to battle and none seem to have been responsible for the location chosen for the English camp on the night of 23/24 June 1314 – probably the single most significant factor in the Scots' victory.

Edward's most crucial failure in relation to Scotland was his decision to carry on the fight at all. Edward I had failed to impose Plantagenet rule despite a decade of massive political, military and financial effort. However, even if he had wanted to do so, Edward could not have abandoned his father's project. Accepting Robert as King of Scotland and disbanding the garrisons in 1307 would have been seen as an admission of defeat and weakness. Furthermore, the military situation at the time of Edward I's death did not indicate massive support for the Bruce cause, so withdrawal would have had an adverse impact on Edward's prestige. Additionally, in the period since 1296, a number of prominent English lords had developed interests in Scottish properties. Some of these were men of great status who had provided the English crown with troops in 1296 with a view to receiving grants of land at the expense of Scottish lords who resisted Edward's invasion. Some were men who had made their careers in Scotland, men like Pier de Lubaud[9] and the Hastangs family,[10] whose service as soldiers and administrators in the occupation had been rewarded with substantial landholdings. Both of these groups had a vested interest in maintaining English rule, since they stood to lose their acquisitions if the Bruce party (or the Balliol party between 1296 and 1304) were to restore Scottish kingship. These were not the only factors that put pressure on Edward to continue the war. By the close of 1308 several Scots who had aligned themselves with the Plantagenet cause had been driven off their estates and had become pensioners of the English crown pending the recovery of English fortunes in Scotland. Defections to the Bruce party from this group would have a deleterious effect on Edward's credibility; if he were to retain their loyalty, he would have to take steps to restore them to their former prominence.

The repeated incursions of the Bruce party into the northern counties of England must have diminished Edward's standing at home.[11] The economic burden of these raids was marginal in terms of the damage to Edward's income, though highly significant to King Robert. Failure to protect his subjects in the far north may not have had a great impact on the magnates of the far south, but Edward could not afford to ignore Scottish operations indefinitely; if Robert's campaigns were not stopped, the political communities of Northumberland and Cumbria might eventually turn to Robert for 'good lordship'. There were no signs of this in 1314, despite the huge sums levied by Robert's lieutenants and the ability of the Scots to demand free passage through the most northern English counties in order to pursue campaigns further south, but the risk of disaffection and defection among the landholders and burghal communities of northern England must surely have been apparent to Edward and his counsellors.

Finally, there was the question of Edward's personal prestige. As the king of a major European power, he could not afford to be defeated by a relatively minor nation like Scotland. Moreover, if he could bring the Scots to battle and defeat them, his political stock would rise at home since he would have been following in the footsteps of his father, a man more popular in death than he had been in life. A successful campaign would do more than damage the Bruce party – it would provide an opportunity to bring the political community of England together in defence of the 'right' of their king at a time when Edward was in sore need of a unifying influence among his nobles.

Whether the conquest of Scotland was really a viable project given the resources of late medieval English kings is another matter. Edward's father's achievements in Scotland had probably already become inflated in the perception of the English, and any reduction in Edward's power in Scotland may have been seen as a betrayal of the late king. With hindsight it is easy to see that Edward I's Scottish ventures had not brought a real victory, just transitory gains in periods when he could maintain a large force north of the border. At best he had procured a peace of sorts in February 1304, but was not able to put an end to Balliol resistance until the summer of 1305 when Wallace was captured. Edward I may have wished to believe that he had finally achieved his goal with Wallace's death, but it was hardly a 'final' peace. Little more than six months after Wallace's death, Robert Bruce renewed the struggle for Scottish independence.

The rise of the Bruce party and the diminution of the occupation through 1308–1313 had not been marked by any large-scale battles; there had been no large-scale general engagements since Falkirk in 1298. The experience of the English during that period was that it was exceptionally difficult to force battle on the Scots, but if a battle could be brought about, the superior numbers of the English army in general and of the heavy cavalry element in particular, would be more than sufficient to ensure victory. The experience of Falkirk had demonstrated the effectiveness of a 'combined arms' approach to battle. The cavalry had proved incapable of crushing the Scottish schiltroms without archer support, but the Scots had no effective answer to massed archery.

We should not assume that the English command was utterly complacent about combat. On the contrary, we should be safer to assume that Edward and his lieutenants – some of whom, like Clifford, Beaumont and De Valence, had served in 1298 – had analysed what they knew about Falkirk and had developed policies and plans to make the best use of English assets when attacking an army in a strong defensive position. We should not doubt that Edward intended to take the initiative and force the Scots to fight and that he – or his subordinates – had adopted a plan for victory based on their knowledge and experience. They may of course have hoped, even expected, to score a victory without actually coming to blows at all. The Scots had avoided combat during the 1303–04 and 1310–11 campaigns and might well attempt to do so again. Failure to bring the Scots to battle would not reflect well on Edward's abilities, but both he and his lieutenants seem to have been perfectly confident that the Scots could be defeated if they could be forced to fight. Without a battle, Edward could only hope that Robert's credibility might be fatally undermined if, having raised a large army, he did not take the field, but instead returned to his usual policy of evasion.

Edward was eager to fight, and the composition of his army illustrates that. Aware of the likely nature of a campaign in Scotland, Edward had called for a large number of infantry, but he had also ensured that a very powerful cavalry army was mustered. Essentially he hoped to have an overwhelming superiority in foot should the Scots give battle and an equally impressive superiority in men-at-arms to pursue them if they did not. None of this proves that Edward really expected to have to fight. The sheer size of his army might be enough to persuade the Scots to decline battle and retire to less accessible terrain, but if the Scots were to accept battle, Edward had an army suitable for the purpose. Further, Edward and his lieutenants had a healthy knowledge and understanding of Robert's military resources. They knew that Scottish men-at-arms, spearmen and archers were no different to English ones, but that the numbers available to Robert were very much inferior. In the campaigns of small actions and sieges that had characterised the preceding years, this superiority had not been too significant; English troops could not be everywhere at once, so the Scots only needed to achieve local superiority.

It would be a different matter if they could be manoeuvred into a major action; the Scots might even be so demoralised by the scale of the English army that 'shock and awe' might drive them into total flight.

The Lion: Robert I

When King John's army assembled at Caddonlea to resist Edward I in March 1296 there were a number of notable absences in its ranks. Three of Scotland's most prominent magnates – Gilbert D'Umfraville, Earl of Angus (an Englishman with extensive properties south of the border), Patrick, Earl of Dunbar and Robert Bruce, Earl of Carrick – had chosen to give their allegiance and their military resources to Edward I. It is more likely that none of them actually saw any combat during the 1296 campaign, but they were certainly in the peace of the King of England and were therefore in a state of rebellion against the King of Scotland. Each had his own reasons for failing to support their monarch. For Dunbar, there was the risk to his property. Virtually all of his landholdings lay in the counties of Roxburghshire, Berwickshire and Lothian and were therefore extremely vulnerable to an English invasion. Dunbar evidently did not feel confident that the Scots would be able to offer the kind of resistance to Edward that would protect his property, but was in the curious position of not having possession of his chief residence, Dunbar Castle, which was being held for the Balliol cause by his own wife.[12]

Like Dunbar, the Bruce family was no longer in possession of its heritage. Failure to endorse the recent treaty made with France and to respond to the summons for military service had resulted in the family estates of the Lordship of Annandale and the Earldom of Carrick being seized and put into the hands of John Comyn, but Bruce ambitions were probably more significant than the loss of property. Robert's grandfather had never accepted his rejection for the throne, and had passed his claim to his heirs. His eldest son, also Robert, does not seem to have entertained any regal ambitions and remained steadfast in Plantagenet allegiance until his death in 1304. His grandson – another Robert – was rather more ambitious. By supporting Edward I against King John he hoped to do more than achieve the restoration of his lands and titles, he apparently still harboured hope of a resurrection of the Bruce family's claim to the throne. If so he was to be sorely disappointed. Edward swept Robert's ambitions aside and then set about forming a new administration that would govern Scotland in his name.

By the summer of 1297 the Balliol cause had made a remarkable recovery under the leadership of the heir of a senior northeast baron, Andrew Murray and the younger son of a minor gentry family, William Wallace. The uprising of Wallace and Andrew Murray is the most well-known act of resistance to Edward, but the fame of these young men and the battle they won at Stirling Bridge has rather obscured another significant attack on Edward's rule. The bishop of Glasgow, James the Stewart of Scotland and Sir William Douglas (father of King Robert's lieutenant, Sir James) gathered troops and conducted some minor operations against the occupation in the southwest while William Wallace and Andrew Murray did the same in central and northeast Scotland respectively. It is by no means certain that all three of these insurrections were planned as a concerted effort, though it is difficult to imagine that the bishop and the Stewart thought they would be capable of defying Edward's government on their own. They were both men of considerable wealth and influence, but their resources were very limited in comparison to those of the English crown.

They did, however, have the backing of one other great lord, Robert Bruce. As Professor Barrow has pointed out,[13] Bruce had '... everything to gain by loyalty to Edward, everything to lose by supporting the hopeless and reckless enterprise of Wishart and the Stewart,' but join them he did. What is most remarkable about Bruce's defection is that he was supporting King John, the very cause that he had refused to espouse in 1295–96. His motivation for doing so is not at all clear. There were rumours that he had the crown in his sights, but no real evidence to support this. By the end of June, the forces of this 'noble revolt' were at Irvine, where they were approached by a major English force under Sir Robert Clifford and Sir Henry Percy. The troops assembled by the Scottish lords were no match for the army, and no sooner had Percy and Clifford arrived at Irvine than the Scots were seeking terms for surrender. Percy and Clifford do not seem to have been anxious to force battle and negotiations continued for a month and more before a settlement was reached.[14] In the meantime, Wallace and Murray were able to gather more men, conduct more operations and, most importantly, start to erect a Balliol administration in competition with Edward's government. Robert himself managed to avoid surrendering and was still at liberty and probably active in the Balliol cause until at least November 1297, but the noble revolt had fizzled out by September, when Wallace and Murray led their troops to victory at Stirling Bridge.

By November Murray was dead, possibly from wounds incurred at Stirling and Wallace, now a knight, had become the sole leader of the Balliol party. For the next ten months Wallace carried on the process of restoring government in the name of King John,[15] but was utterly defeated by Edward at the Battle of Falkirk in July 1298. Wallace's political power had been a product of his military success rather than the more traditional basis for political influence, landed wealth. Before the end of the year he had either resigned or been removed from the post of Guardian of the Realm[16] and returned to the role that had brought him to prominence in the first place – leader of a company of men-at-arms.

Before the end of the year he had been replaced by two magnates, men whose leadership of major family and geographical affiliations gave them a degree of political weight that Wallace could not aspire to – John Comyn of Badenoch and Robert Bruce of Carrick and Annandale. Comyn's participation is hardly surprising; his family had been strong supporters of the Scottish crown for generations. But the continuing presence of Robert Bruce in the Balliol party makes less sense. Why should Bruce, a candidate for Scottish kingship himself (at least in his own opinion), act in support of a king that he had opposed in arms as recently as the spring of 1296, and a cause that had recently suffered a major defeat at the hands of King Edward? Politically, if Robert was ever to acquire the crown, it was vital that he be seen in a favourable light in regard to the struggle for independence. He could hardly claim to be active in the patriotic cause if he was in the service of Edward I. His alignment with the Balliol party does not necessarily imply that he was confident of King John's reinstatement, merely that he saw the Balliol cause as the best avenue for political independence in current circumstances. Militarily, the situation of the Balliol party was not so precarious as we might at first expect. Edward had scored a victory at Falkirk, but had made little real progress in bringing the country under his control. Wallace and Murray's efforts had led to the recovery of Balliol administration throughout most of Scotland north of the River Forth, and the Plantagenet garrisons, though powerful, were failing to extend Edward's rule. Further, though Bruce and Comyn must have been all too well aware of the relative weakness of the Scottish military establishment compared to that in England, they will also have been aware that Edward already had other military objectives to pursue and that he was facing increasing antipathy from his own lords.

The Bruce–Comyn alliance was not an easy one; there was political rivalry and a personal animosity that resulted in violence on at least one occasion, but they did manage to keep the war going and even to extend the scope of Balliol rule. Hugh and Margaret de Penicuik were active in the Balliol interest in Lothian,[17] Stirling Castle fell to a force under Sir Herbert Morham before the end of 1299[18] and the Balliol party were able to hold two Parliaments in 1300,[19] but it had already become necessary to redefine the Guardianship. In August, a fight broke out at a meeting of the Scottish leadership at Peebles, in the course of which Comyn had taken Bruce by the throat.[20] Clearly there needed to be a calming influence in the upper echelons of the Balliol party, and William Lamberton, the Bishop of St Andrews, was elected as the chief guardian with Bruce and Comyn as his lieutenants. This arrangement was short-lived. At some point before the spring of 1302 Bruce defected to Edward I. He may have done so because of the actions of King Edward, who led a large army into southwest Scotland in that summer. Apart from lifting the Scottish siege at Lochmaben, laying siege to Caerlaverock and scattering a force of Scottish in a modest action on the River Cree,[21] the English army – the first really significant force to be committed to Scotland since the Falkirk campaign – achieved very little. Edward, obliged to attend to his other pressing concerns, agreed a truce with the Scots which was to last from the end of October to 21 May 1301. Although Edward continued to pursue his campaign, the Scots were able to hold their own and on 26 January 1302 he was obliged to make another truce with them, this time for a duration of nine months.

Since Edward was making little, if any, progress against the Balliol party it should seem curious that Robert should defect to the English before the middle of February 1302, but there had been a considerable change in the Scottish political arena. In place of the joint guardianships, Sir John Soulis had been appointed as sole Guardian, probably with direct authority from King John.[22] The issue that prompted Robert's defection was probably the news that John, who had been entrusted to Papal custody, had now been given into the custody of the King of France. The prospect of a Balliol restoration was now a very real threat to Robert's position, for although he had been active in the Balliol cause between 1297 and late 1301 or early 1302, he had been one of the most significant absentees from John's army in 1296 and was of course a potential threat to John's kingship.

Naturally, if he was to defect, Robert needed to reach an accommodation with King Edward. The terms of the agreement have been discussed by historians at great length and there are two particular items which have been the occasion of comment. The first refers to Edward's promise that he would do his utmost to ensure that Robert would not be disinherited of his heritage lands, whether in England or Scotland; the second is his acceptance that Robert should be free to 'pursue his right' in the event of King John returning to Scotland.[23] The precise nature of 'his right' is not stated, but it has been suggested that the only 'right' Robert might wish to pursue in 1302 would have been his claim to the throne. This raises the possibility that Edward was prepared to consider acceptance of Robert as the Scottish king, presumably on the basis of the feudal superiority that he had demanded of John in 1292. This might have led to a schism among the Scots which would, obviously, be in Edward's interests, but it is difficult to imagine that Edward would have been prepared to promote the interests of a man who had but recently been a sore thorn in his flesh.

Bruce's defection was only one of a number of blows that the Balliol party suffered over the next two years. The defeat of the French at Courtrai weakened King Philip's negotiating position with Edward, and the Scots were excluded from the terms of a peace agreement between England and France. The Balliol cause was not yet dead, but it had been fatally wounded. Edward led another army into Scotland, and this time stayed there for the whole winter, driving the Scots to surrender on terms at Strathord in February 1304. There were still minor elements of resistance – Fraser and Wallace were still in the field and the garrison of Stirling continued to defy Edward until July, but the Balliol cause had ceased to be a viable one.

The siege of Stirling was a major event. Edward even built a special viewing platform so that his queen and her courtiers could observe its progress.[24] A number of Scottish magnates were present, but the most significant among them were Robert Bruce and Bishop Lamberton. The two men made a pact that bound them not to undertake any hazardous ventures without the consent of the other.[25] The document does not state explicitly the nature of what such ventures might be, but the only logical possibility is that they were referring to Robert's claim to the throne; a major change in the position of Lamberton who had, until this point, been a faithful and constant prop to John's kingship. For the next year or so, Robert seems to have largely devoted himself to the business of lordship, but at Edward's Parliament of 1305 he, along with Bishop Wishart of Glasgow and Sir John Moubray – a prominent baron – was called upon to advise Edward on the future of Scotland.[26] In due course this led to the appointment of a lieutenant for Scotland who, with the aid of a chancellor and chamberlain and the advice of a number of Scottish and English nobles, would appoint a council to help draw up an ordinance for the future government of Scotland – a council that would include arch-rivals Robert Bruce and John Comyn.

E.M. Barron has suggested that Bruce had already fallen from favour by the time the Ordinance was finalised in September 1305, in part because of one of the entries, which reads:

Also, it is agreed that the Earl of Carrick shall be commanded to put Kildrummy
Castle in the keeping of such a man as he himself will be willing to answer for.[27]

The wording conveys – as Professor Barrow has pointed out – a 'tone of
mistrust', however exactly the same phrase appears in another document,
requiring the same commitment from Aymer de Valence,[28] who can hardly
have been considered suspect. He was, after all, a senior and trusted aide, advi-
sor and friend of King Edward.

Robert's attempt to restore independent Scottish kingship was probably
premature, but his hand was forced by his own actions. In February 1306
he met with his chief rival on the Scottish political scene, John Comyn. In
Barbour's narrative, Robert offered Comyn a deal which would allow the
Comyn and Bruce parties to co-operate against Edward's administration. In
a meeting at the Greyfriars Church in Dumfries, Bruce offered to cede his
lordships to Comyn if Comyn would give him unequivocal support as king,
or, alternatively, Comyn would transfer his lordships to Bruce and take the
throne himself. However Professor Duncan suggests that it was 'unlikely' the
meeting was arranged to discuss Scottish kingship, accepting the Guisborough
interpretation that the Earl of Carrick was accusing John of undermining his
position with Edward I.[29]

The chief problem with Barbour's story is that neither Bruce nor Comyn
really had a legitimate claim to the throne as long as King John or his heir,
Edward Balliol, was still alive. Moreover, if the Bruce claim were invalid, any
Comyn claim would be even less credible. It is difficult to see how either
Bruce or Comyn could commit themselves to the pact described by Barbour.
Whichever stood aside to allow the other the throne would be in a very vulnerable position. Had Robert passed his lordships to John Comyn he would
have been giving up his family's heritage lands in exchange for the properties
of the crown, but only if he could make his kingship a reality; the Comyn family on the other hand would have gained an enormous addition to what was
already a vast range of properties. In addition to being the most significant magnates in the northeast, they would become the most powerful political force
in the southwest and therefore potentially too strong a force to be contained
should they decide to desert the Bruce cause. On the other hand, who could
they look to for aid if they were persecuted by King Robert and were unable to
defeat him from their own resources? By helping Robert to become king they
would have forsaken any chance of appealing for aid from the King of England.
The reverse would also hold true if the Comyn heritage passed to the Bruces.

Any chance of future co-operation between the Bruce and Comyn parties was, in any case, made impossible by Robert's actions since the Greyfriars meeting was concluded by Robert – or possibly one of his adherents – stabbing John Comyn to death at the altar of the church. Comyn's murder pushed Robert into premature action. He could either attempt to defend himself against criminal charges in court, take to the hills and hope to negotiate a pardon from King Edward, or attempt to put himself on the Scottish throne. The first of these possible courses of action would have had to depend on principles of law – possibly a claim that he had acted in self-defence. The second would have depended on acquiring the favour of King Edward. Neither of these courses seems to have held out much hope for Robert, and he immediately set about gathering support for his kingship. On Lady Day, 25 March, 1306 he had himself installed as King of Scotland in a ceremony conducted by three of the twelve Scottish bishops – Glasgow, St Andrews and Moray – and the Abbot of Scone. This was followed by a second ceremony on Palm Sunday, 27 March.[30] By tradition the Earls of Fife played a major part in the inauguration of Scottish kings. The current Earl, Duncan, was still under age, and was, in any case, effectively in the custody of Edward I. It would seem that his role was taken by his sister, Isabel.

Her participation is interesting on two accounts. It is generally accepted that women had no position in the political life of the Middle Ages, yet here is an example of a woman performing a significant political act and nobody at the time seems to have regarded this as an unnatural or even very innovative event. Additionally, Isabel was more than the sister of the Earl of Fife, she was the wife of John Comyn, Earl of Buchan, a sworn enemy of Robert Bruce.

Robert threw himself into the business of enlisting political and military support, but his future did not look bright, even his great ally Bishop Lamberton was sufficiently dubious about the outcome that he opened negotiations to rejoin Edward's peace sometime before 9 June.[31] Before the end of that month Aymer de Valence had assembled a strong force and captured Perth, an action which attracted the attention of the newly inaugurated king, who moved to recover the town. Robert may have been misinformed about the scale of De Valence's force or simply over-confident about the capacities of his own army. Far from containing the enemy in the town and laying siege to it, Robert's army was attacked and scattered by De Valence.[32] Robert led the remainder of his force westward, only to be defeated again, this time by John MacDougall.[33]

His primary objective for the next six months and more was survival, and he spent the winter of 1306–07 in hiding – possibly in the West Highlands, possibly on the island of Rathlin off the northeast coast of Ireland, or possibly in Norway, at the home of his sister, queen of the late King Eric. He had not given up the fight, and around the beginning of February mounted two operations against the English, one in Galloway led by his brothers Thomas and Alexander, and the other under his own leadership, to Carrick.[34] Neither of these operations was successful. Thomas and Alexander were captured and executed and, although Robert's force inflicted a minor defeat on men of the Turnberry castle garrison, the weakness of his following and the strength of the occupation forced him to take to the hills of Carrick and Galloway. By May, however, he had gathered enough men to meet and defeat an English party at Glen Trool[35] and, on 10 May, to confront a more significant force under De Valence at Loudon[36] and another led by the Earl of Gloucester just three days later.[37]

The Bruce cause seems to have started to gain real political momentum after these actions, but Robert's war was still little more than a localised problem for the occupation, and a major invasion was in hand for the summer of 1307. The operation was delayed by the long-expected death of Edward I in July, but it was not abandoned. The new king led his troops northwards, but only as far as Cumnock, Ayrshire, before returning to England. This, rather than the death of Edward I, was a turning point for Bruce's fortunes. Edward II has borne a great deal of criticism for not pursuing the objective of destroying the Bruce cause, but he did have several pressing concerns to deal with. Bruce had scored a few minor victories, but Edward had no reason to presume that the forces of the occupation government were not adequate to the task of defeating Bruce, or at least containing him until such time as Edward could raise another army. In the meantime, Edward had to attend to the issues that confronted any new king: asserting his authority; entering negotiations about giving homage for his lordships in France; and seeking a bride who would provide him with an heir.

Bruce's actions over the next few years have been examined and analysed in great detail by several scholars – most notably Professor Barrow and Dr McNamee. They do not need to be rehearsed here, suffice to say that by the spring of 1314, Robert had brought virtually the whole country under his control, restoring the forms of administration that had existed under Alexander III, King John and the Guardians. Although he was a very successful soldier in the years after 1307, he was not committed to war as the only means of achieving recognition of his kingship. He was prepared to negotiate truces with Edward's officers and with specific communities, but would only consider a final peace on the basis of acceptance of kingship free from any suggestion of English superiority – a condition that was utterly unacceptable to Edward II. Robert may not have been committed to offering battle in the summer of 1314, but his only tool of any consequence was war.

4

Sources and Interpretation

The shortcomings of medieval chroniclers are all too familiar to historians – chronicle accounts of battles are particularly prone to exaggeration of numbers and to political and national prejudices. Even so, they provide narrative accounts of events that can be very revealing when they are analysed in relation to the record material and, in the case of campaigns and actions, to the terrain and to aid our understanding of military practice. The compilers of medieval chronicles did not, as a rule, set out to wilfully mislead their readership, but they did endeavour to portray their favoured figures in a very sympathetic light. Prejudices, exaggeration and the considerations of literature, patronage and patriotism should not, however, lead us to dismiss chroniclers as ignorant. It is true that almost all of the chronicles of England and Scotland were written by churchmen, but their occupation should not be construed as a barrier to any understanding of military affairs. Most of the chroniclers – and Barbour is a very clear example – were men with an extensive classical education, much of which was focused on the martial qualities and activities of heroes from antiquity. Additionally, almost all of them were the children of noble families and as such training with arms and horses would have been part of their cultural and social background.

One of the common observations about Bannockburn is that there is very little 'of what an historian calls primary source material'.[1] It is certainly true that the contemporary record and narrative source material is very limited; the only account by an indisputable eye-witness is that of Friar Baston, who was captured at the battle. Sadly, Baston's poem gives very little information of any value for the purposes of strategic or tactical analysis. Of the other contemporary or near contemporary material, two accounts demand to be taken seriously: Thomas Grey's *Scalacronica* and *The Lanercost Chronicle*. Neither of these were written by an eye-witness, however the *Lanercost Chronicle* is, in general, quite well informed about Scottish issues and the chronicler specifically tells us that his information was provided by a 'reliable' person who was present.

Grey's *Scalacronica* was compiled some forty years after the battle from a variety of Scottish verse and narrative chronicles while the author was a prisoner of war in Stirling and Edinburgh castles. Grey's father, taken prisoner during the first day's fighting at St Ninians can reasonably be assumed to have had a rather better understanding of the sequence of events than most. There is no reason to assume that Grey's captors would have prevented him from watching the main engagement, but even if they did, he must have discussed the action with some of the men who had the misfortune to join him in captivity at the end of the battle. As a professional soldier of considerable practical experience his understanding of the sequence and significance of the events of 23/24 June 1314 must command some respect.

Chronicle accounts are not, however, the only source of information. Surviving Scottish crown records of the early fourteenth century are somewhat thin on the ground, though not, perhaps, quite as sparse as one might expect. But there is a great quantity of English record material that applies to Scotland, so much in fact that three extensive collections of English documents with Scottish subject matter were published in the second half of the nineteenth century – McPherson's *Rotuli Scotiae*,[2] Stevenson's *Documents Illustrative of Scottish History*[3] and Bain's *Calendar of Documents Relating to Scotland*.[4] Of these, Bain's work contains by far the largest body of material relevant to the nature and practice of the English occupation government of Scotland between 1296 and 1314. Naturally only a very tiny proportion of the many thousands of documents calendared by Bain relate specifically to the battle at Stirling in June 1314, but a great many of them pertain to the business of raising troops, money and provisions to the English garrisons and armies that operated in Scotland under Edward I and Edward II. The documents cover a vast range of subjects including petitions for financial aid, demands for supplies, valuations of horses, pardons granted in exchange for military service, the forfeiture of Scots defecting to the Bruce party, the restoration of other Scots defecting to the Plantagenet party and notes of indentures. Indentures were contracts by which an individual contracted to supply the crown of England with a given number of troops, usually men-at-arms, for a given period and for an agreed fee. Indentures became an important means of raising troops, particularly – in Scotland at least – for garrison service in the widest sense, that is to say, the provision of men-at-arms to mount active operations against the Scots rather than for the defence of a castle, town or pele.

Some of the documents in Bain and McPherson's compilations do refer specifically to Bannockburn or 'the battle at Stirling'. Many of these relate to the heirs of men killed at the battle, rather than to the fighting; some are appeals for help with ransoms or 'protections' for men travelling abroad in search of financial aid from other quarters. Collectively, the English record material gives us some insight into the military practices of the day relating to garrison work and, occasionally, to operations against the Scots. They do not provide us with a detailed guide to the tactical practices of field armies, but they do give us some idea of the policies, actions and intentions of the occupation government.

The amount of English government record specifically relating to the army of 1314 is rather more limited than we might usually expect for a major army of this period. To a considerable degree this is a product of defeat. The records of the 1314 army would have included a great deal of information that historians would dearly love to have, in particular those records that deal with enlistment. It is all well and good that we have records of the number of infantrymen demanded from English counties, but without pay records we have no way of estimating the number of men who actually served. It does not help that the various summonses issued by Edward II are either contradictory or ambiguous or both. Equally, though we can identify a very large number of men seeking and obtaining 'protections' for the duration of their service, we have no way of knowing what proportion of the total complement of men-at-arms sought such protections.[5] The complete absence of pay records and 'restauro' (horse valuation) rolls prevents us from making any detailed assessment of the army of 1314 compared to the armies of 1296 and 1298. There is of course a simple explanation for the paucity of army records for 1314. The destruction of Edward's army as a viable force was accompanied by the loss of the army's administrative documents. In the main, information relating specifically to the actions at Bannockburn is to be found in chronicle accounts rather than from record sources, and they are worth examining in some detail.

English Narrative Sources

The Scalacronica of Sir Thomas Grey

Of the various accounts of Bannockburn, that of Sir Thomas Grey, though brief, is in some senses the most valuable. Grey was not an eye-witness himself, but his father was, having been made prisoner during the first day of the action. It would be reasonable to assume that Grey was aware of his father's view of the battle, but he also had access – so he tells us – to verse and narrative chronicles, possibly including a 'life' of Robert I and perhaps a 'life' of Sir James Douglas, while he was himself a prisoner of war a generation later. These accounts no longer exist, but there is no reason to suppose that Grey invented them. Barbour, writing half a century later, seems to have had access to accounts of both King Robert and Sir James that have since disappeared and it is by no means impossible that he worked from at least some of the same sources that were available to Sir Thomas. Additionally, Grey was himself a professional soldier who spent most of his career serving against the Scots and was therefore a better judge of what Colonel Burne called 'inherent military probability' than many of his contemporaries (his fellow-chroniclers, were, without exception, clerics) or for that matter, modern historians. As a member of the nobility he was chiefly concerned with the deeds of other nobles, but this should not be taken as an indication that he was not aware of the wider picture:

> The said King Edward planned an expedition to these parts, where, in attempting the relief of the castle of Stirling, he was defeated, and a great number of his people were slain [including] the Earl of Gloucester and other right noble persons; and the Earl of Hereford was taken at Bothwell, whither he had beaten retreat, where he was betrayed by the governor [of the castle]. He was released [in exchange for] the wife of Robert de Brus and the Bishop of St Andrews.
>
> As to the manner in which this discomfiture befell, the chronicles explain that after the Earl of Atholl had captured the town of St John [Perth] for the use of Robert de Brus from William Oliphant, captain [of the town] for the King of England, being at that time an adherent of his, although shortly after he deserted him, the said Robert marched in force before the castle of Stirling, where Philip de Moubray, knight, having command of the said castle for the King of England, made terms with the said Robert de Bruce to surrender the said castle, which he had besieged, unless he should be relieved; that is, unless the English army came within

three leagues of the said castle within eight days of St John's day in the summer next to come, he would surrender the said castle. The said King of England came thither for that reason, where the said constable Philip mat him at three leagues from the castle, on Sunday, the vigil of St John, and told him there was no occasion for him to approach any nearer, for he considered himself as relieved. Then he told him how the enemy had blocked the narrow roads in the forest.

The traditional view that the Earl of Carrick agreed a pact for the surrender of Stirling, and that his brother, King Robert, was dismayed and angered, is seriously undermined by Grey's account. In Grey's view, the pact was made between Moubray and the king; Edward Bruce is not mentioned at all. In the absence of powerful evidence to the contrary it would be unreasonable to assume that the king was not involved in this operation. The other major operations of Spring 1314 consisted of the capture of Edinburgh Castle by a force under the Earl of Moray and the capture of Roxburgh by a force under James Douglas. The king must have been somewhere, and where better than at the very centre of his country, conducting operations against a strategically vital installation. Compacts of this nature were not in any sense extraordinary; it seems likely that Dundee[6] had fallen to the Scots under a similar arrangement. By agreeing to the compact the Scottish leadership was able to remove a large force from the tedious business of conducting a siege and either redeploy them elsewhere or send them home on leave.

Philip Moubray was technically correct to point out that his garrison had been relieved within the terms of the agreement, but politically and militarily Edward was still obliged to force battle on the Scots if it were at all possible. The political, administrative and financial effort to raise a large army for foreign service was considerably more than could be justified by the bloodless relief of one castle, however significant. Once the army was brought to Stirling, failure to bring the Scots to battle – and defeat them – would do little or nothing to restore Edward's government in Scotland. This was, of course, the real object of the exercise. The loss of Perth and Dundee had reduced the area of English administration in eastern Scotland to Lothian, Roxburghshire and Berwickshire; the loss of Roxburgh and Edinburgh castles had reduced it to a little more than a toe-hold in the southern corner of Berwickshire. If Edward could defeat King Robert – preferably resulting in Robert's death or capture – he would be in a good position to recover the towns and castles that had fallen to the Scots since 1307 and to reimpose his administration.

If, however, he failed to do so, he could not maintain a large field army in Scotland for very long, and would, sooner rather than later, have to withdraw his army. This in itself would represent a major victory for the Bruce party and further diminish any prestige and authority that Edward's rule might retain north of the border.

Edward was not alone in his determination to bring about a general engagement, as Grey reports:

The young troops would by no means stop, but held their way. The advanced guard, whereof the Earl of Gloucester had command, entered the road within the Park, where they were immediately received roughly by the Scots who had occupied the passage. Here Peris de Mountforth, [Grey is referring to Henry de Bohun] knight, was slain with an axe by the hand of Robert de Brus, as was reported.

While the said advanced guard were following this road, Lord Robert de Clifford and Henry de Beaumont, with three hundred men-at-arms, made a circuit upon the other side of the wood towards the castle, keeping to the open ground. Thomas Randolph, Earl of Moray, Robert de Brus's nephew, who was leader of the Scottish advanced guard, hearing that his uncle had repulsed the advanced guard of the English on the other side of the wood, thought that he must have his share, and issuing from the wood with his division marched across the open ground towards the two afore-named lords.

Sir Henry Beaumont called to his men 'Let us wait a little; let them come on; give them room!'

'Sir', said Sir Thomas Grey [father of the author], 'I doubt that whatever you give them now they will have all too soon.'

'Very well!' exclaimed the said Henry, 'If you are afraid be off!'

'Sir,' answered the said Thomas, 'it is not from fear that I shall fly this day.' So saying he spurred in between him [Beaumont] and Sir William Deyncourt, and charged into the thick of the enemy. William was killed, Thomas was taken prisoner, his horse being killed on the pikes, and he himself being carried of with them on foot when they marched off, having utterly routed the squadron of the two said lords, some of whom fled to the castle, others to the king's army. Which having already left the road through the wood had debouched on a plain near the water of Forth beyond Bannockburn, an evil, deep, wet marsh, where the said English army unharnessed and remained all night, having sadly lost confidence and being too much disaffected by the events of the day.

Although it is generally accepted that medieval spearmen could not stand against men-at-arms without the support of archers and/or the benefit of terrain that would present a challenge to mounted troops, Sir Thomas (junior) does not seem to be surprised by the ability of Moray's force to defeat the English cavalry, indeed, his father seems to have expected no other result. Clearly it was perfectly possible for well-drilled spearmen to dominate the field as long as they were not subjected to the attention of archers. This had in fact been amply demonstrated at the Battle of Falkirk in 1298. Although Wallace's army was roundly defeated in that action, his schiltroms proved impenetrable to Edward I's cavalry until their formations had been disrupted by the shooting of the English and Welsh archers. Having described the state of affairs in the English camp, Grey goes on to relate the deliberations at King Robert's headquarters:

> The Scots in the wood thought they had done well enough for the day, and were on the point of decamping and marching through the night into the Lennox, a stronger country, when Sir Alexander de Seton, who was in the service of England, and had come thither with the King, secretly left the English army, went to Robert de Brus in the wood. And said to him 'Sir, this is the time if you ever intend to undertake the reconquest of Scotland. The English have lost heart and are discouraged, and expect nothing but a sudden, open attack.
>
> Then he described their condition, and pledged his head, on pain of being hanged and drawn, that if he would attack them on the morrow he would defeat them easily without loss. At whose [Seton's] instigation they resolved to fight, and at sunrise on the morrow marched out of the woods in three divisions of infantry. They directed their course boldly on the English, which had been under arms all night with their horses bitted.

According to Grey, then, the English army had not rested properly through the night. This is less remarkable than it seems if, as Seton allegedly told King Robert, they expected to be attacked. Alternatively, if the English expected the Scots to withdraw during the night, there might be an opportunity to attack them as they marched away from the field, but only if the English army, and the cavalry in particular, were ready to give chase at first light. There can be little doubt that the English command were eager to bring the Scots to battle and equally little doubt that they considered it unlikely that the Scots would choose to stand and fight, let alone attempt to force battle on the English. The experience of both Edward I and Edward II and of their senior lieutenants – Aymer de Valence, Robert Clifford and others – was that campaigning in

Scotland tended to be a matter of pursuing an elusive enemy who would avoid a major engagement if at all possible. Edward I had failed to bring the Scots to battle between 1298 and 1304 and Edward II had experienced the same problem in his campaign of 1310. Edward senior had managed to bring his Scottish war to a conclusion of sorts in 1304, but the 1310 campaign had not only failed in its objective of forcing battle on the Scots, it undermined Edward's credibility in England and among his supporters in Scotland, while simultaneously enhancing the prestige of King Robert:

They [the English] mounted in great alarm, for they were not accustomed to fight on foot; whereas the Scots had taken a lesson from the Flemings, who before that, had, at Courtrai, defeated on foot the power of France. The aforesaid Scots came in line of 'scholtroms' and attacked the English columns, which were jammed together and could not operate against them, so direfully were their horses impaled upon the pikes. The troops in the English rear fell back upon the ditch of Bannockburn, tumbling one over the other.

The English squadrons, being thrown into confusion by the thrust of the pikes upon the horses, began to fly. Those who were appointed to the King's rein, perceiving the disaster, led the King by the rein off the field towards the castle, and off he went, though much against the grain. As the Scottish knights, who were on foot, laid hold of the King's charger in order to stop him, he struck out so vigorously behind him with a mace there was none whom he touched that he did not fell to the ground.

As those who had the King's rein were thus drawing him always forward, one of them, Giles de Argentine, a famous knight who had lately come over the sea from the wars of the Emperor Henry of Luxembourg, said to the King; 'Sire, your rein was committed to me, you are now in safety; there is your castle where your person may be safe. I am not accustomed to fly, nor am I going to begin now. I commend you to God.' Then, setting spurs to his horse, he returned to the melee, where he was slain.

The King's charger, having been piked, could go no further, so he mounted on a courser and was taken around the Torwood, and so came to the plains of Lothian. Those who were with him were saved; all the rest came to grief. The King escaped with great difficulty, travelling thence to Dunbar, where Patrick, Earl of March, received him honourably, and put his castle at his disposal. And even evacuated the place, removing all his people, that there might be neither doubt nor suspicion that he would do nothing short of his devoir [duty] to his Lord, for at that time he [Patrick] was his liegeman. Thence the King went by sea to Berwick and afterwards to the south.

As far as Sir Thomas Grey was concerned, neither the course of the main action, nor its outcome, was in any sense mysterious. The Scots were simply the better army on the day of the battle. Unlike Barbour he does not seem to have thought that the fighting was a drawn-out affair, but rather that the English army, caught against the 'ditch of Bannockburn' were unable to deploy properly for the fight or derive any benefit from their numerical superiority. Interestingly, in common with the *Lanercost* chronicler and the author of *Vita Edwardus Secundus*, Grey makes no mention of Scottish cavalry, asserting that the entirety of the Scottish army, including the nobles, fought on foot. Nor does he mention any attempt by the English commanders to bring the archers into the action. This is remarkable insofar as the importance of archery had been amply demonstrated at Falkirk in 1298, which was the last major tactical success for English arms in Scotland. Edward I had been able to force the Scots to an accommodation in 1304, but he had done so through strategic and political pressure, not by success on the battlefield. The archers were not the only arm of service to fail to get a mention in Grey's account. The majority of the English army were undoubtedly spearmen, as we might expect of any major western European army of the day, but Grey makes no reference to them at all. To a certain extent this might be explained by Grey's social background and the literary demands upon a narrative aimed at an aristocratic readership, however both the chronicler and his father were professional soldiers, and were surely well aware of the power of close combat infantry; indeed Grey specifically refers to the defeat inflicted on French men-at-arms by the Flemings at Courtrai more than a decade before Bannockburn.

Vita Edwardus Secundus

Vita Edwardus Secundus (The Life of Edward II) was written some years after the events he describes. Although somewhat dramatic in style, the *Vita* is one of the best narrative sources for Edward's reign. The following extract follows the course of the campaign from the spring of 1314 to the flight of King Edward and his immediate entourage to Berwick:

> About the beginning of Lent messengers came to the King with news of the destruction of Scottish cities, the capture of castles and the breaching of the surrounding walls. The constable of Stirling came too, and pointed out to the King how he had been compelled by necessity to enter upon the truce. He persuaded the King to lead an army into Scotland, to defend his castle and the country.

When the King heard the news, he was very much grieved, and for the capture of his castles could scarcely restrain his tears. He therefore summoned the earls and barons to come to his aid and overcome the traitor who called himself King. The earls replied that it would be better for all to meet in Parliament and unanimously decide what ought to be done in this matter rather than to proceed so inadvisedly; this moreover would be in accord with the ordinances. But the King said that the present business was very urgent and he could not therefore wait for the Parliament. The earls said that they would not fight without Parliament, lest it should happen that they infringed the Ordinances. Some counsellors and household officials therefore advised the King to demand their due service from all, and set out boldly for Scotland. It was certain that neither Robert Bruce nor the Scots would resist. What of the Earl of Gloucester, the Earl of Hereford, Robert de Clifford, Hugh Despenser and the King's household and the other barons in England? All these would come with their knights; there was no need to worry about the other earls. The King therefore demanded due service from all, and ordered the necessary stores to be provided. The Earl of Pembroke he sent ahead with a force of knights, to seek out the ambushes of the Scots and prepare the King's route into Scotland.

As far as the writer of the *Vita* was concerned, the stimulus for the invasion of 1314 was the threat to Stirling Castle, which the constable, Sir Philip Moubray, had promised to surrender to King Robert unless his garrison was relieved by Midsummer, though in fact Edward had been under pressure from his Scottish supporters since November 1313 if not before. The growing success of the Bruce party and the depredations of the English garrisons, particularly that of Berwick, had seriously undermined the prestige of Plantagenet lordship. Edward's kingship was not entirely secure at home either. The Ordinances that the writer refers to were a series of conditions imposed on Edward by the magnates of England in the hope of procuring a better standard of government. Edward, naturally enough, resented both the implication of poor governance and the restrictions placed on royal authority. Equally, the earls and barons who had forced him to accept the Ordinances in the first place were determined to keep their king within the bounds of the agreement, hence their request that the project of invading Scotland should be considered in Parliament. Most of the magnates of England could be depended upon to follow the king to war at the head of their retinues. The Earl of Pembroke had been instrumental in imposing the Ordinances on Edward II, but had parted company with the other chief instigators over the execution of Piers Gaveston.

Gaveston had surrendered to Pembroke on assurance of his personal safety, but had been executed by the Earl of Lancaster (see above) thus tarnishing Pembroke's word of honour – a serious breach of aristocratic protocol. The writer puts a brave face on the absence of several leading English magnates from the army, but there can be little doubt that Edward was weakened both militarily and politically by the failure of such important men as Thomas, Earl of Lancaster, to take part in the campaign:

> When all of the necessaries had been collected, the king and the other mag-
> nates of the land with a great multitude of carts and baggage-wagons set out for
> Scotland. When the lord king had reached Berwick, he made a short halt there
> to await the arrival of the rest of the army. But the Earl of Lancaster, the Earl
> Warenne, the Earl of Arundel and the Earl of Warwick did not come, but sent
> knights equipped to do their service for them in the army. On the sixth and
> seventh days of the feast of St John the Baptist, our king with all his army left
> Berwick and took his way toward Scotland. The cavalry numbered more than
> two thousand, without counting a numerous crowd of infantry. There were, in
> that company, quite sufficient to penetrate the whole of Scotland, and some
> thought that if the whole of Scotland had been gathered together, they would
> not have strayed to face the king's army. Indeed, all who were present agreed that
> never in our time has such an army gone forth from England. The multitude
> of wagons, if they had been placed end to end, would have taken up a space of
> twenty leagues.
>
> The king therefore took confidence and courage from so great and so dis-
> tinguished a multitude and hastened to the appointed place, not as if he were
> leading an army to battle, but as if he were going to St James's. Brief were halts
> for sleep, briefer still for food; hence horses, horsemen and infantry were worn
> out with toil and hunger, and if they did not bear themselves well it was hardly
> their fault.

The *Vita* writer was eager to convince his readers of the strength and mag-
nificence of Edward's army in general, and the cavalry force in particular.
A body of 2,000 men-at-arms was indeed a powerful force, but not really an
exceptional one by the standards of other major English armies of the period.
The army that Edward I led to victory at Falkirk in 1298 had included at least
that number of men-at-arms and the invasion force of 1296 had probably been
even stronger. The writer may have relied on the estimates of men who had
taken part in the 1314 campaign, or may have simply plucked a figure from the

air. Alternatively he may have been aware that more than 2,000 men-at-arms had had their horses valued for *restauro* or that the number had been in receipt of crown wages. This would not, however, have given him an accurate reckoning of the armoured cavalry force, since not all of the men serving in the cavalry would have been entitled to pay. Great lords might refuse wages for both themselves and their retinues as a matter of personal prestige and men who served in exchange for pardons – a common practice in thirteenth- and fourteenth-century England – served at their own expense and risk. If they lost a horse in action they would not be recompensed by the crown, nor could they expect any help with ransoms if they were taken prisoner. Although the writer stressed the power of the army, he also prepared his readers for the actual outcome of the fight by mentioning the speed with which the army moved north, highlighting the 'brief' breaks in the march for eating and sleeping which resulted in the army arriving at Stirling in a tired and hungry condition through no fault of their own.

Interestingly, he writes only of a 'numerous crowd' of infantry, aware, no doubt, that the men and women who might read his work would be of the noble class, and would be chiefly interested in the deeds and fortunes of the men-at-arms. However Edward was well aware of the significance of the infantry and had been careful to demand large quotas of men from English communities since the army would probably have to fight the Scots in terrain that would be difficult for cavalry operations:

The Earl of Gloucester and the Earl of Hereford commanded the first line. On Sunday, which was the vigil of St John's day, as they passed by a certain wood and were approaching Stirling Castle, the Scots were seen straggling under the trees as if in flight, and a certain knight, Henry de Boun [Bohun] pursued them with the Welsh to the entrance of the wood. For he had in mind that if he found Robert Bruce there he would either kill him or carry him off captive. But when he had come thither, Robert himself came suddenly out of his hiding place in the wood and the said Henry, seeing that he could not resist the multitude of Scots, turned his horse with the intention of returning to his companions; but Robert opposed him and struck him on the head with an axe that he carried in his hand. His squire, trying to protect his lord, was overwhelmed by the Scots.

The fight between Bruce and de Bohun is one of the great tales of King Robert's martial prowess, and is sufficiently well recorded that there is no doubt that the incident took place. The *Vita* account differs somewhat from that of Grey and Barbour in that de Bohun is depicted as leading a body of Welsh troops – presumably infantry – and that he was attacked by the King, rather than vice versa. This is the only account of the battle that involves any action on the part of Edward's infantry on the first day of the battle, however it would be rash to dismiss the writer's assertion out of hand. While it is clear that the approach to the Entry was made by a force of men-at-arms, it would have been an example of 'good practice' if they had been accompanied by an infantry force which could take to the woods in pursuit of the Scots should they be broken by the cavalry. The writer does, perhaps, undermine his inference that de Bohun was the leader of the Welsh infantry by telling us that de Bohun was trying to make his way back to his 'companions' – surely his fellow men-at-arms – when he was set upon by King Robert. Moreover, it seems very likely, both from other accounts and from the *Vita* writer's own words, that de Bohun was actively seeking a confrontation with the King. Evidently the writer saw the demise of de Bohun and the repulse of the English at the Entry as a pointer to the course of the rest of the action:

> This was the beginning of their troubles! On the same day a sharp action was fought, in which the Earl of Gloucester was unhorsed and Robert de Clifford disgracefully routed and, though our men pursued the Scots, many were killed on either side.

Here the writer describes the action between a body of Scots under the Earl of Moray and a party of English men-at-arms under the Earl of Gloucester. His statement that 'our men pursued the Scots, many were killed on either side' rather contradicts the balance of the source material. Grey and Barbour have no doubt that the Scots enjoyed the upper hand in this engagement, Barbour even claiming that the Scots suffered very few casualties at all. That would seem unlikely, since there was obviously a hard fight, but it is clear that the English force was completely routed. This does not necessarily mean that many deaths, or even injuries, were inflicted on Gloucester's force, merely that they were driven from the field. None of the contemporary writers name many men killed in this part of the battle, though at least one relatively prominent English soldier, Sir Thomas Grey (father of the chronicler) was taken prisoner. Whether or not casualties were significant, the outcome of this action must have had a damaging effect on English morale. Not only had the cavalry failed to overcome a rather modest force of spearmen, they had been roundly defeated and had failed to accomplish either of the two most likely objectives of their mission. The intention of the operation was probably either to effect a technical relief of Stirling Castle or to perform a major reconnaissance in force to locate the main body of the Scottish army or both. By this point the day was too far gone for any other initiatives, and the English army made camp:

> The day being spent, the whole army met at the place where it was to bivouac that night. But there was no rest; for they spent it sleepless, expecting the Scots rather to attack by night than to await battle by day. When day came it was abundantly clear that the Scots were prepared for the conflict with a great force of armed men. Wherefore our men, the veterans that is, and the more experienced, advised that we should not fight, but rather await the morrow, both on account of the importance of the feast and the toil that they had already undergone. This practical advice was rejected by the younger men as idle and cowardly.

The *Vita* author clearly believed that Edward's army concentrated in the bivouac area through the later part of the day on 23 June, and that the army 'stood to' throughout the few hours of darkness. The fear of a night attack was not unreasonable. It would be entirely realistic for the English command to assume that the Scots were numerically weaker in general and very much weaker in terms of men-at-arms and archers. Equally, it would have been reasonable to expect the Scots to withdraw through the night. King Robert had, after all, achieved two rather dramatic successes on the previous day, and could therefore withdraw with his military prestige intact. He would have failed to force the surrender of Stirling Castle, but Edward's failure to force battle on the Scots and achieve a major victory would have been damaging to English morale and to Edward's political credibility. He would have spent a vast sum of money and good deal of political capital in gathering a large and powerful army but have gained nothing tangible in the process. Stirling Castle, one of only two first-class royal fortresses still in English hands (the other being Berwick; Bothwell was a baronial castle, held by the Earl of Hereford from Edward II and commanded by Sir Walter FitzGilbert), would have been saved, but only so long as Edward's army remained in Scotland. The financial strain of maintaining a force of such magnitude for an extended period would have been beyond his resources, but even if it had been possible his army would inevitably have melted away through desertion and illness, potentially putting him in a very high-risk situation. He might have chosen to pursue the Scots into the more arduous terrain to the north and west of Stirling, but there would have been little prospect of forcing battle on them, save under conditions that put the English at a great disadvantage. Robert would most certainly have been aware that a major victory on the battlefield would enhance his prestige, but he would have been equally aware that he was not obliged to offer or accept battle in order to achieve a success in the campaign; he merely needed to avoid defeat.

The prospect of having a day of rest before moving against the Scots seems, superficially at least, to have been a reasonable and pragmatic suggestion, which, according to the writer, was proposed by the 'veterans and the more experienced'. The problems with such a policy were, however, quite valid. If the English made no effort to force battle on the Scots, Robert would be able to withdraw his troops to more advantageous terrain unimpeded, which would in itself add to his credibility as a wise and effective leader in war while Edward would be made to look indecisive. The enormous expense of mounting the operations of 1314 would have been a complete waste and might well have compromised Edward's ability to mount another invasion in the future. Whatever the rationale behind the decision to accept or force battle, Edward was not open to persuasion:

> The Earl of Gloucester counselled the King not to go forth to battle that day, but to rest on account of the feast, and let his army recuperate as much as possible. But the king spurned the earl's advice, and, growing very heated with him, charged him with treachery and deceit. 'Today' said the Earl 'it will be clear that I am neither a traitor nor a liar,' and at once prepared himself for the battle.
>
> Meanwhile Robert Bruce marshalled and equipped his allies, gave them bread and wine and cheered them as best he could. When he learned that the English line had occupied the field he led his whole army out of the wood, About forty thousand men he brought with him and split them into three divisions; and not one of them was on horseback, but each was furnished with light armour, not easily penetrable by a sword. They had axes at their sides and carried lances in their hands. They advanced like a thick-set hedge, and such a phalanx could not easily be broken. When the situation was such that the two sides must meet, James Douglas, who commanded the first phalanx of the Scots, vigorously attacked the Earl of Gloucester's line. The Earl withstood him manfully, once and again penetrated their wedge, and would have been victorious if he had had faithful companions. But look! At a sudden rush of the Scots, the earl's horse is killed and the earl rolls to the ground. Lacking defenders, and borne down by the weight of his body armour he could not easily arise, and of the five hundred

cavalry whom he had led to the battle at his own expense, he almost alone was killed. For they saw their lord unhorsed, they stood astonished and brought him no aid. Accursed be the chivalry whose courage fails in the hour of greatest need! Alas! Twenty armed knights could have saved the earl, but among some five hundred men, there was not one found.

Interestingly, the author of the *Vita* agrees with Barbour in according a major command position to James Douglas. Unlike Barbour, but in agreement with all of the other sources, he has the Scots deploy in three divisions rather than four. This has certain implications for the author's view of the Scottish command structure. If we are to assume that King Robert commanded the central division of his army, how was command of the others allocated without disparaging at least one of his senior officers? With Douglas leading one division and the king another, there would have only been one major command position left to be allocated either to the king's brother, Edward, Earl of Carrick, or to Sir Thomas Randolph, Earl of Moray. The author may have been misled by his knowledge of the campaigns of the latter years of Edward's reign. By the time of the Battle of Myton or Byland, Edward Bruce was dead and Douglas had become one of King Robert's chief lieutenants. He had also achieved a spectacular military reputation, both as a commander and as an individual paladin.

Regardless of who was in command of the first division of the Scots, the author is in no doubt that the Scots mounted forward to attack the English and not vice versa. In this he is in complete agreement with all of the contemporary sources, though not, it must be said, with a considerable number of historians. It would have been unthinkable for the English cavalry to stand fast in the face of advance by enemy infantry, so a counter charge was inevitable, but there may have been a delay in deploying properly for such a manoeuvre due to a disagreement about command responsibilities.

The reported argument between Gloucester and Hereford was not simply a matter of aristocratic precedence and posturing, significant as that may have been. Medieval armies were not simply mobs of armed men; the importance of cohesion on the battlefield was thoroughly understood. There are many examples from record evidence of men being disciplined for failure to follow orders, particularly the serious offence of moving in front of the chief banner of the formation. Again, this was not an issue of precedence and manners, but one of vital operational importance. To derive the greatest benefit from a charge – whether mounted or on foot – it was crucial that the front ranks of the formation arrived 'on target' at the same moment, thus it was important that men should not scatter in search of personal glory, but adhere to the most effective formation. In the opinion of the writer of the *Vita* failure to co-ordinate the attack properly led to Gloucester's force advancing in disorder, resulting in a piecemeal descent on the Scots rather than a concerted blow. Additionally, the lack of cohesion meant that Gloucester was not adequately supported by his own formation and so, when unhorsed, was vulnerable to the Scots. The failure of Gloucester's charge drew other men into that part of the conflict:

> Giles de Argentine, a fighting soldier and very expert in the art of war, while in command of the king's rein, watched the fate of the earl, hurried up in eager anxiety to help him, but could not. Yet he did what he could, and fell together with the earl, thinking it more honourable to perish with so great a man than to escape death by flight; for those who fall in battle for their country are known to live in everlasting glory. On the same day Robert de Clifford, Payn Tibetot, William Marshal, famous, powerful and active knights were overcome by the Scots and died in the field.
>
> When those who were with our king saw that the earl's line had been broken and his men ready to run, they said that it would be dangerous to tarry longer and safer for the king to retreat. At these remarks the king quitted the field and hastened to the castle. Moreover when the royal standard was seen to depart, the whole army quickly dispersed. Two hundred knights and more, who had not drawn their swords nor even struck a blow, were reduced to flight.

The *Vita* author seems to have reduced the scope and duration of the action compared to the other sources. It seems improbable that Edward would be prepared to abandon the fight because one formation of one branch of service had been defeated. He makes no reference at all to the other Scottish formations closing on the English lines and no reference to the rest of the English army other than to relate their flight and subsequent entrapment.

> Thus while our people fled, following the king's footsteps, lo! A certain ditch entrapped many of them and a great part of our army perished in it. The king, coming to the castle and thinking to find refuge there, was repulsed as if he were the enemy; the drawbridge was raised and the gate closed. Wherefore the castellan was thought by many to be not innocent of treason, and yet that very day he was seen in armour arrayed for battle as if to fight for the king. I neither absolve the castellan nor accuse him of treachery, but I think that it was God's doing

that the king of England did not enter the castle, for if he had been admitted he would never have escaped capture.

When the king saw that he was thus repulsed and that no other refuge now remained to him, he turned his steps toward Dunbar, and coming there, took ship. He landed with his following at the port of Berwick. Others having no ship came by land. The knights shed their armour and fled without it; the Scots continually harassed their rear; the pursuit lasted fifty miles. Many of our men perished and many, too, were taken prisoner. For the inhabitants of the countryside, who had previously feigned peace, now slaughtered our men indiscriminately, wherefore it was proclaimed by Sir Robert Bruce that they should take prisoners and hold them to ransom. So the Scots busied themselves with taking prisoner the magnates in order to extort large sums from them. There were captured the Earl of Hereford, John Giffard, John de Wylyntone, John de Segrave, Maurice de Berkely, undoubtedly barons of great power, and many others whom it is not necessary to specify, of whom many agreed their ransoms and paying the money were set free. Cognizances were no advantage there, because ransom was then more difficult. Five hundred and more were thought to be dead who had been taken captive and were later ransomed. Indeed, amidst all their misfortunes, this at least turned to the advantage of our army, that, while our people sought safety in flight, a great part of the Scottish army was occupied in plunder, because, if all the Scots alike had been attending to the pursuit of our men, few would have escaped. So while Robert Bruce with his men attacked our baggage train, the greater part of the English came back safe to Berwick.

This account suggests that the battle was a short-lived affair, and that the English army was so disrupted and demoralised by the first clash of arms that it descended into disorder and rout extremely quickly.

For the writer of the *Vita*, the blow to the English at Bannockburn was one very much of their own making, and an exceptional event. He goes on to suggest that:

> ... someone will ask why the Lord smote us on this day, why we succumbed to the Scots, when for the last twenty years we have always had the better of them.

This was some way from being a valid description of the ebb and flow of the preceding two decades. The English had certainly enjoyed major battlefield success at Falkirk and, on a smaller scale, Methven. Equally, they had suffered significant reverses at Stirling Bridge, Roslin and Loudon Hill. More importantly, they had been steadily losing their war with the Scots for several years. With the exceptions of Stirling and Berwick the castles and towns which formed the backbone of Plantagenet administration had all fallen to the Scots by the spring of 1314. This capture was much more than a matter of military success and failure. Without the support of a well-found network of garrisons the officers of Edward II's Scottish administration could not maintain their position in the face of competition from the Bruce party.

The Lanercost Chronicle

The Lanercost Chronicle is one of the most useful sources for Anglo–Scottish affairs in the fourteenth century. The compiler of the chronicle was, by and large, well informed about events north of the border. This does not mean that the chronicle is always accurate, or that the information is necessarily presented in a non-partisan manner. The Abbey did, after all, suffer from time to time from Scottish invasions of the north of England. King Robert availed himself of the Abbey's hospitality on at least one occasion, using it as the headquarters for his raiding operations. To the *Lanercost* chronicler, Edward's campaign of 1314 was an attempt to restore the situation of 1304 in the face of treacherous and recalcitrant Scots led by the turncoat and sacrilegious murderer Robert Bruce. To some extent he had a point. The settlement of 1304 had been accepted by the Scottish political community and in England that was seen as a reasonable conclusion to the matter of Scottish political independence as a nation. Edward's intention of recovering Scotland for the English crown was, therefore, a matter of administering royal discipline to vassals acting in defiance of their rightful lord and not a question of war between kingdoms:

> Thus before the feast of the Nativity of St John the Baptist, the King having massed his army, advanced with the aforesaid pomp towards Stirling Castle, to relieve it from siege and to engage the Scots, who were assembled there in all their strength. On the vigil of the aforesaid Nativity, the King's army arrived after dinner near Torwood; and upon information that there were Scots in the wood, the King's advanced guard, commanded by Robert de Clifford, began to make a circuit of the wood to prevent the Scots escaping by flight. The Scots did not interfere until they [the English] were far ahead of the main body, when they showed themselves, and, cutting off the King's advanced guard from the middle and rear columns, they charged and killed some of them and put the rest to flight. From that moment began a panic among the English and the Scots grew bolder.

The chronicler's description of the activity on the first day of the battle is clearly at odds with the material from the *Vita* and *Scalacronica*. There is no mention of the action at the Entry, nor of the duel between King Robert and de Bohun. Instead of two reconnaissance operations that go awry, the chronicler's informant – 'a trustworthy person who was an eye-witness' – believed the Scots deliberately positioned themselves to separate one division of the English from the rest of the army, and defeated it in isolation. The informant, evidently serving in Edward's army, was also of the opinion that the English army comprised three divisions in total. If that was the case, it would be most likely that each of these divisions had contingents of all of the branches of service – archers, spearmen and men-at-arms – which could be construed as supporting evidence for the *Vita*'s description of the action at the Entry. In the *Vita* account the unfortunate de Bohun was a leader of Welsh infantry.

Barbour does not mention a close-combat infantry fight at the Entry, but that should not be construed as evidence against the *Lanercost* interpretation. If the English army really was arrayed in three divisions it would be realistic to see each of these formations as a body of troops fighting as an independent formation, operationally identical in concept to the use of the term 'Division' in military terminology since the Napoleonic wars if not before. This still does not contradict Barbour. Merely because a 'Division' is in contact with the enemy does not mean that all of the elements of the division are engaged. It is therefore possible that the 'Division' as a whole had approached the Scots, but that only the cavalry element of that 'Division' actually made contact with the enemy. This does not contradict the assertion that de Bohun was a leader (or even the leader of a contingent of infantry), since he was also a man-at-arms. It is not impossible that he chose to leave his command at some distance from the fighting in order to pursue personal glory or, more charitably perhaps, to reconnoitre the area.

Obviously, the *Lanercost* chronicler's 'eye-witness' account only describes one of the actions of the first day's operations, however it is important to remember that the account reflects the experience of one individual. Since he refers to Robert Clifford as the commander of the division in question and does not mention the de Bohun incident it is reasonable to conclude that he is referring to the action between Moray's force below St Ninians chapel, rather than the fight at the Entry:

> On the morrow – an evil, miserable and calamitous day for the English – when both sides had made themselves ready for battle, the English archers were thrown

forward before the line, and the Scottish archers engaged them, a few being killed and wounded on either side; but the King of England's archers quickly put the others to flight.

This segment of the *Lanercost* account does seem very credible; a Scottish 'skirmish line' quickly dispersed by English archers. This is the only record of such a manoeuvre, but it dose make very good sense. The Scottish archers, probably very much weaker than their English counterparts in number, would be very unlikely to inflict much in the way of casualties, but would serve to screen the main Scottish formations from the sort of massed archery which disrupted Wallace's schiltroms at Falkirk. It does, however, raise the question of what became of the English archers. It is possible that by the time the Scottish archers had been dispersed the schiltroms were close enough to the English archers that they were obliged to retire swiftly for fear of being over-run, on the other hand there is no record of the English archers impeding the advance of either the Scots or the major formations of the English army, despite the fact that the battle was joined very quickly after this exchange of arrows. Nonetheless, it would be rash to discard the *Lanercost* account out of hand. If, for example, the archers were only deployed on that part of the English front that was not confronted by the first Scottish formation to engage, it might easily have appeared to the 'eye-witness' that archers were deployed by both sides and across the whole of the front. Assuming that the 'eye-witness' was stationed in the main body of the English army it is most unlikely that he would have had a clear view of the whole of the battlefield:

Now when the two armies had approached very near to each other, all the Scots fell on their knees to repeat Pater Noster [the Lord's Prayer], commending themselves to God and seeking help from heaven; after which they advanced boldly against the English. They had so arranged their army that two columns were abreast in advance of the third, so that neither should be in advance of the other; and the third followed, in which was Robert. Of a truth, when both armies engaged each other, and the great horses of the English charged the pikes of the Scots, as it were into a great forest, there arose a great and terrible crash of spears broken and destriers wounded to the death; and so they remained without movement for a while. Now the English in the rear could not reach the Scots because the leading division was in the way, nor could they do anything to help themselves, wherefore there was nothing for it but to take to flight. This account I heard from a trustworthy person who was an eye-witness.

Here the *Lanercost* account fits perfectly with the other contemporary and near-contemporary descriptions of the fight. Although the Scots were heavily outnumbered, the constricted nature of the battlefield meant that only a portion of the English army was able to take part in the fighting, allowing the Scots to achieve numerical superiority at what modern military terminology calls 'the forward edge of the battle area':

> In the leading division were killed the Earl of Gloucester, Sir John Comyn, Sir Edmund de Mauley and many other nobles besides foot soldiers, who fell in great numbers.

The chronicler's 'eye-witness' offers a suggestion that is not repeated in other chronicle accounts. In this version of events, the division which was first to come into contact with the Scots consisted of both infantry and cavalry. This would be well within the scope of the normal operational practices of the early fourteenth century; indeed any other arrangement could be seen as atypical. The 'battles' or divisions of the English armies that fought at Halidon Hill, Poitiers and Crécy consisted of archers, spearmen and men-at-arms and thus consisted of both horse and foot. The fact that the men-at-arms deployed on foot does not indicate that they were infantrymen, but that they were dismounted cavalry. Similarly the mounted archers of Edward III's reign should not be considered cavalry, but mounted infantry; they were never deployed with the intention that they should fight from the saddle. Assuming that the chronicler's informant had observed this part of the engagement accurately it would seem that a major portion of the English army, a formation large enough to conduct independent manoeuvres and operations, fell on the leading Scottish formation but were unable to bring their advance to a halt:

> Another calamity which befell the English was that, whereas they had shortly before crossed a great ditch called Bannockburn, into which the tide flows, and now wanted to re-cross it in confusion, many nobles and others fell into it with their horses in the crush, while others escaped with much difficulty, and many were never able to extricate themselves from the ditch; thus Bannockburn was spoken about for many years in English throats.
>
> The King and Sir Hugh Despenser (who, after Piers Gaveston, was as his right eye) and Sir Henry Beaumont (whom he [Edward] had promoted to an earldom in Scotland), with many others mounted and on foot, to their perpetual shame

fled like miserable wretches to Dunbar Castle, guided by a certain knight of Scotland who knew through what districts they could escape. Some who were not so speedy were killed by the Scots, who pursued them hotly; but these, holding bravely together, came safe and sound through the ambushes to England. At Dunbar the King embarked with some of his chosen followers in an open boat for Berwick, leaving all others to their fate.

In like manner as the King and his following fled in one direction to Berwick, so the Earl of Hereford, the Earl of Angus, Sir John Segrave, Sir Anthony Lucy and Sir Ingleram de Umfraville, with a great crowd of knights, six hundred other mounted men and one thousand foot fled in another direction to Carlisle. The Earl of Pembroke left the army on foot and saved himself with the fugitive Welsh; but the aforesaid earls and others, who had fled towards Carlisle were captured on the way at Bothwell Castle, for the sheriff, the warden of the castle, who had held the castle down to that time for the King of England, perceiving that his countrymen had won the battle, allowed the chief men who came thither to enter the castle in the belief that they would find a safe refuge, and when they had entered the castle, took them prisoners, thereby treacherously deceiving them. Many also were taken wandering around the castle and hither and thither in the country, and many were killed; it was said also that certain knights were captured by women, nor did any of them get back to England, save in abject confusion.

Again, *Lanercost* is in agreement with the other accounts of the battle. It is not absolutely clear what the writer means when he tells us that the English had crossed the ditch of the Bannockburn 'shortly before'. It could be construed as an indication that the army had only crossed the Bannockburn that very morning, however it is surely safer to assume that the writer means that the army had crossed on the previous evening, given that the Scots started to advance early in the morning. An attempt to move the army across the Bannock Burn during the night would have been a very difficult task indeed, and one fraught with danger. It is apparent that the English commanders were concerned that the Scots would make a night attack, in which case attempting a river crossing in the dark in the close vicinity of the enemy would have been a rash undertaking, and one that might well have given rise to comment among contemporaries. Alternatively, had the English army made their crossing of the Bannock Burn early on the morning of the 24th the Scots would have had a tremendous opportunity to mount their attack at a point when the English were in an extremely vulnerable situation. The *Lanercost* description of the confused retreat of the English army raises an interesting, and perhaps very significant issue, and one that gives some credence to the claim that the account was based on the perceptions of one who took part in the campaign. The Bannock Burn is indeed tidal throughout its lower course, a piece of information unlikely to have been available, or to have seemed significant, to a monk at Lanercost.

Friar Baston

Friar Baston is unique among the contemporary and near-contemporary writers who gave accounts of the battle in that he was the only indisputable eye-witness. A Carmelite and a noted poet of the day, he had travelled north with the English army for the specific purpose of recording what was expected to be a great victory. He was denied the opportunity of composing a paean of praise for English arms and Edward II by the outcome of the battle, but he did get to write about a Scottish victory; indeed he had little choice in the matter, since he was taken prisoner and was obliged to write his account as part or all of the price of his liberty. Baston really has nothing to say of any value in terms of helping us to reconstruct the action, and the fragment printed here is no more than an indication of the style and content of Baston's work:

> The dry ground of Stirling sustains the first conflicts,
> Splendid is the attacking host, but it soon takes a downward turn,
> Great is the grief, grief enhancing grief ...

It is of course a great shame that Baston did not choose to give a blow-by-blow account of the course of the action, focusing instead on the fortunes, or rather the misfortunes, of the leading men of the day, but we should not assume that the nature of his presentation would have been radically different had the Scots been defeated. It was not his intention to analyse the fight, but to provide a glowing recognition of victory along the lines of Andrew Marvel's *'Ode to Cromwell on his Return from Ireland'* rather than the construction of a realistic account of the action.

Geoffrey Baker of Swinbroke

> To Stirling the King brought his forces with all the pomp usual at that date when the chivalry of England still fought on horseback, with curvetting chargers and

flashing armours, and when men, in their arrogant rashness were so confident that in addition to the necessary equipment of horses, arms and provisions, they brought gold and silver vessels such as are used at the banquets of the mighty of the earth in days of peace. Men of that day had never seen such an overweening array of chivalry, as that poor Carmelite, friar Baston, in his poem on the campaign, at which he was present and was taken prisoner by the Scots, bewailed bitterly. That night you might have seen the English – not angels – drenching themselves with wine and drinking healths; while the Scots kept watch and fasted. Next morning the Scots chose a fine position, and dug ditches three feet deep and three feet wide along the whole of their front from left to right, covering them over with intertwined branches, that is to say, hurdles, screened by grass, across which indeed infantry might pass if they knew the trick, but which could not bear the weight of cavalry.

Baker's account is the first to ascribe any tactical value to Scottish preparation of the battle site. Although his description of trenches covering the front of the Scottish army is highly detailed, it is also highly questionable. The construction of coverings that would bear the weight of a man, but not of a horse, would be both difficult and of doubtful effectiveness and it is very questionable that they could be concealed adequately. If true, it would indicate that Robert was so confident of the location the English would choose for their camp that he was prepared to devote a great deal of time and effort to the project. Despite the fact that his assertions about the trenches are a rather obvious attempt to explain (or perhaps excuse) a major defeat, several writers have chosen to give them credence. There are two very clear arguments against the existence of the trenches; one is that such a project would have been difficult, if not impossible to hide from the garrison of Stirling Castle, who would surely have passed that information to the English army on 23 June if not before. The other problem is that Baker's account very clearly implies that the Scots stood on the defensive behind these trenches. Although this might have stood the Scots in good stead from the point of view of bringing an English advance to a halt, merely denying the English the opportunity to advance would not have brought victory. Since it is clear from all of the other accounts that the Scots advanced against the English and drove them back into the Bannock Burn and the River Forth one has to wonder how they could have maintained their good order – crucial to the success of bodies of spearmen – as they passed over the trenches:

None of the Scots was allowed to mount their horses, and arrayed in brigades as usual they stood in a closely formed line behind the aforesaid cannily, I will not say deceitfully, constructed ditch. As the English moved from the west the rising sun shone on their gilded shields and helmets.

Baker's informant, assuming that he had one, would seem either to have misled the chronicler or was badly misunderstood by him. The route followed by the English army very clearly led to their deployment to the *east* of the Scots, not to the west. It is possible however that Baker misconstrued his information. As the Scots descended to the plain from the woods early on the 24th they would have had the sun in their faces, but their arms and armour would have reflected the sun back at the English lines. If Baker's informant complained about the glare of the sun it would not be unreasonable for the chronicler – in the absence of more detailed information – to assume that the English army had indeed been drawn up facing to the east, rather than the west:

Such a general as Alexander would have preferred to try conclusions on some other ground or other day, or at least would have waited till midday when the sun would have been on their right. But the impetuous and headstrong obstinacy of the English preferred death to delay. In the front line were the cavalry with their heavy chargers, unaware of the concealed ditch; in the second were the infantry, including the archers, who were kept ready for the enemy's flight; in the rear the King with the bishops and other clerics, amongst them that foolish knight, Hugh the Spenser.

The front line of the cavalry charged, and as the horses' legs were caught in the ditch through the hurdles, down fell the men and died before the enemy could strike; and at their fall on came the enemy, slaughtering and taking prisoners, and sparing only the rich for ransom. There died Gilbert, Earl of Gloucester, whom the Scots would willingly have saved for ransom, if they had recognised him, but he was not wearing his coat-armour. Many were killed by the archers of their own army, who were not placed in a suitable position, but stood behind the man-at-arms, whereas at the present day the custom is to post them on the flanks. When they saw the Scots charging fiercely on the horsemen who had fallen at the ditch, some of them shot their arrows high in the air to fall feebly on the enemy's helmets, some shot ahead and hit a few Scots in the chest, and many English in the back. So all yesterday's pomp came to naught.

Here Baker is on rather firmer ground. At least some portion of the English cavalry – Gloucester's formation – were deployed in front of the main body of the army and they did indeed charge the leading formation of Scots, however the absence of any description of Gloucester's men falling into concealed ditches from other sources strengthens the suggestion that there were no ditches to fall into. The issue of the trenches should not lead us to dismiss the rest of Baker's account, though there is very little else that he adds to the story, however his description of English archers having their view of the enemy obscured by the cavalry may be of value and has a certain ring of credibility. The sort of speculative shooting that he relates would be very likely to bring about as many casualties among the English as among the Scots. Placing archers in the second line of English formations does not invalidate either *Lanercost*'s description of a brief exchange of archery prior to the advance of King Robert's army or Barbour's account of Sir Robert Keith's charge against English archers on the flank of the main battle. There is no reason to assume that all of the archers in King Edward's army were concentrated in one unit; indeed that would be contrary to the general practice of English armies of the later Middle Ages, and is simply inconceivable in terms of common sense.

Trokelowe

Trokelowe's account, though very brief, is broadly in agreement with *Lanercost*, Barbour and the *Vita*, save on the question of the initial deployment of the English infantry.

Trokelowe obviously had access to some source material and was aware of King Robert's decision to fight on foot. He sees this as the morale-building gesture that it was, telling us that Robert and his lords dismounted to ensure that the danger of battle would be shared equally by nobility and commoners alike:

> The next day each army made ready for battle, and about the third hour they were drawn up in formidable array … The English leaders put in their first line their infantry, archers and spearmen; their cavalry, centre and wings, they drew up behind …
>
> … the Scots, inspired by the speeches of their leaders, resolutely awaited the attack; they were all on foot; picked men they were, enthusiastic, armed with keen axes, and other weapons, and with their shields closely locked in front of them, they formed an impenetrable phalanx … The cause of the disaster I do not know, unless it was that the English were too impetuous and disorderly; they

were tired and weak, both men and horses, because of their excessive haste, and they were hungry and had had no sleep. Also the Scots, knowing the ground, which the English did not, attacked sooner than expected in dense battle array.

It might be tempting to reject Trokelowe's account simply on the basis of his assertion that the English infantry were deployed in front of, not behind, the cavalry, which is the reverse of every other account, however this may be a matter of perception. If his information was gleaned from an eye-witness – even if it only reached Trokelowe by hearsay – we should consider the possibility that this was how the situation looked to that witness. If he was stationed to the rear of the main body of the army and was unaware of Gloucester's formation then his observation may have some validity. The assumption that *all* of the English cavalry were positioned to the front of the army is not substantiated by any of the contemporary material, indeed the accounts of *Lanercost*, Barbour and the *Vita* clearly have only one English cavalry formation to the fore – that of the Earl of Gloucester. Assuming that the English were divided into four formations – as they were for the Dunbar and Falkirk campaigns – an eye-witness might well see the English deployment as a great body of infantry to the fore and three cavalry formations, 'centre and wings', to the rear. This would make good tactical sense and would conform to Edward's declaration before the campaign that the Scots were going to be found in rough terrain where the cavalry would find it difficult to come to blows. Neither Edward nor his subordinates seem to have given any consideration to the possibility that the Scots might actually force battle; they expected to have to attack, and attack uphill into wooded terrain. Given the experience of Falkirk it would not be at all unreasonable if Edward had decided to put his infantry to the fore with a view to 'pinning' the Scots before the cavalry came into action. This would not of itself compromise those accounts that have Gloucester's formation in apposition in front of the rest of the army. The English command clearly thought it possible that the Scots might not offer or accept battle, but attempt to withdraw from the field; they had already done enough on the night of the 23rd to give Robert a major propaganda victory. It would have been prudent to have a strong mobile force to the fore which could either take advantage of any opportunity to disrupt the withdrawal of the Scots or to screen the main body of the army from a sudden advance if the Scots chose to attack.

In common with the other commentators of the period, Trokelowe is in no doubt that the Scots forced the pace of the battle by advancing to contact, telling us that they had formed an 'impenetrable phalanx' and that they advanced in 'dense battle array'. The English army was also deployed ready for battle, however the Scots advanced 'sooner than expected', and the general tenor of all the other accounts is that the English had expected that they, not the Scots, would take the offensive. This, and the fact that the English were tired and hungry after their rapid marches to Stirling, were the salient issues in Trokelowe's opinion.

Interestingly – and this is shared by all of the other medieval accounts – Trokelowe's interpretation gives no indication of the effect of pools or swamps on the course of the action, though clearly there might be practical difficulties in digging ditches in a morass. For Trokelowe the most significant issues would seem to have been the nature of the Scottish formations – that they advanced with their 'shields locked together' – and possibly that the English were undermined by their own impetuosity and lack of good order. A plausible interpretation of these factors is that the English army, though deployed for battle, was arrayed for an advance, not to receive an attack, and that they either failed to adjust their deployment quickly enough to withstand the Scots and were caught in the midst of reorganisation, or that they made no effort to redeploy and were forced to fight in an inappropriate formation.

Trokelowe points to one other factor of significance that has seldom attracted the attention of historians – that the Scots 'knew the ground' and made the best use of the terrain. It is difficult to know exactly what Trokelowe means by this assertion in the sense that once the armies were face-to-face on the plain there would be little advantage to be gained from knowledge of the ground. According to all of the contemporary material the main action took place on a dry, flat field. The English had been camped right next to the field since the previous evening and would have had ample opportunity to examine it. On the other hand, the Scots had the advantage of local knowledge in a rather wider sense and may have been able to move down to the plain, deploy for battle and commence their advance before the English command could complete steps to reorganise the army appropriately.

Trokelowe tells us that the battle started 'about the third hour', though one might wonder who would have been sufficiently detached to keep an eye on the time. The medieval day, like that of the Romans, was divided, nominally, into twelve equal portions regardless of the time of year. In Scotland at midsummer the nights are very short indeed, so an 'hour' of daylight for the medieval observer would equate – conservatively – to ninety minutes. This would imply that the battle commenced about four and a half hours after dawn or in the region of eight or nine o'clock. If this is correct then there had been plenty of time for Robert to make a detailed observation of the English army before leading his army to the battlefield, but there would also have been plenty of time for the English army to prepare for battle. It is possible, therefore, that instead of attacking at first light, Robert waited until the English army had formed up for an advance toward the Torwood and beyond and were therefore vulnerable to attack.

Failure to redeploy to more suitable formations may not have been a practical proposition for Edward's commanders in the time available once they had become aware that the Scots were going to force battle. If they were in columns for the march rather than lines for combat the business of reforming the units accordingly would be more than just a matter of moving individual formations from column to line. Each unit would require a great deal more 'frontage' space, and if they were to present an organised and continuous front to the enemy, units on the flanks of the army would very probably have to move some distance to the left or right to accommodate those in the centre. This would be a time-consuming business at the best of times, and the risk of serious disorganisation would be high even if the enemy were not present. Attempting to achieve a major redeployment as the enemy approached would be a very great gamble even if the troops were well trained, disciplined and in good heart, none of which applied to Edward's army. It is possible, therefore, that Edward and his subordinates saw the Scots descend to the field and assumed, initially, that they would halt and wait for the English attack. When they saw that the Scots were intent on advancing to contact they decided that the risk of joining battle in less than suitable formations was outweighed by the risks involved in attempting to redeploy in great haste. The maxim that 'order and counter-order leads to disorder' is, like most military clichés, based on sound observation and deduction and one that would have been well known to Edward and his lieutenants. It is important to bear in mind that neither Edward nor his senior officers were lacking in military experience and knowledge. Edward, admittedly, had not taken part in a battle of manoeuvre on this scale (nor had Robert), but several of his senior officers had been present at Falkirk or other large actions. We would be doing these men a great injustice if we were to presume that when they saw the Scots advance they failed to consider any steps to counter the attack, but it is a realistic possibility that their experience of battle led them to conclude that there was no time to make radical changes to the arrangement of the army.

The Meaux Chronicle

So the English and the Scots met on the plain of Bannock near Stirling, the English very confident in their strength and numbers, the Scots after confession and communion calling on God alone as their protector. The armies being arrayed against each other, the Scots put their foot in the front line, and the English their horse, and at the first onset gave victory to the Scots, and the English turned their backs and were slain … because iron spikes had been placed in hollows under the ground so that both horse and foot might trip.

Abbot Burton, the author of the Meaux chronicle, is as clear as all of the other writers about the time of the main action taking place on the 'plain'. He, too, agrees that the English army was quite confident that their superior numbers would be enough to ensure victory and that the English had deployed with their cavalry in front of the infantry whereas the Scots had deployed with the infantry to the fore. Unlike some of the other commentators he does not suggest that the entire Scottish army fought on foot, though he obviously understood that the majority did so, since he makes no reference to Scottish cavalry being engaged at all. Clearly, in Burton's view, the English cavalry had failed to make any great impression on the Scots and were forced to retire. His assertion that the Scots had placed iron spikes in 'hollows under the ground' is less than convincing. If the English retreated and were pursued by the enemy – which would have been absolutely vital if the Scots were to secure a major victory – then the Scots would have had to negotiate these traps during their advance. If iron spikes caused English troops 'both horse and foot to slip' they would have inflicted the same problems on the Scots. Burton stresses the importance of intercession by God, hardly surprising given that he was a cleric and would have put great value on the fact that the Scots had made confession, taken communion and put their faith in 'God alone as their protector'.

The Scottish Sources

John Barbour

Of all the medieval sources for Bannockburn, John Barbour's 'life' of Robert I, *The Bruce*, is by far the longest and most detailed. It is also the only account that contains anything much in the way of useful information about the Scottish army, and is therefore indispensable to medievalists with an interest in the subject. Barbour is not always completely reliable; there are many errors of date and some of location, but the sheer scale of his work probably makes this inevitable. Many of these errors are really quite insignificant. So long as the order of events is not compromised it is generally of little importance whether some incident occurred on the eve or feast day of a particular saint or festival. This does not mean that Barbour was always above putting the needs of his narrative above the demands of accuracy. For example, he asserts that Edward Bruce agreed to a pact that would allow a period of a full year for the relief of Stirling Castle by an English army. He may of course have been misinformed, or he may have misread his sources inadvertently, but there is every possibility that the year-long pact was a device to show the rash and impetuous nature of Edward Bruce and/or to enhance the achievement of victory.

Like any writer he was conditioned by the customs of his times. There were literary, political, social and theological implications to be considered. The first of these is also the easiest to recognise. Since the poem was probably intended – at least to some extent – as a performance piece it was important to maintain the rhythm of the words, and various phrases are used to 'fill up' space to avoid interrupting the flow of the narrative. Accordingly we find, for example, that individuals and groups are often described as moving from one place to another 'in hy' – at great speed – but generally the phrase has no real significance; we should not assume that medieval Scotsmen and Englishmen spent their lives in frantic haste.

We should also bear in mind the nature of Barbour's audience. Like Barbour himself they were, for the most part, members of the noble class and they were chiefly interested in the deeds of other nobles. We must also remember that there were significant political themes to be addressed or, in some cases, wilfully ignored. Barbour hoped to inspire his audience with the martial ardour of their forbears and to justify the actions of King Robert and his adherents, but he was also careful not to ascribe any value to King John or to the Balliol party generally. Naturally, Barbour devoted a good deal of space to relating the efforts of King Robert to heroic figures from scripture. The same approach to figures from antiquity gave him the opportunity to demonstrate the remarkable breadth and depth of his classical education.

Even so, *The Bruce* is a very valuable source; many incidents which get little or no attention in other accounts are more thoroughly aired by Barbour. David de Strathbogie's raid on King Robert's stores at Cambuskenneth and Keith's charge against the English archers are two such examples, with neither incident being described by any other author. Barbour wrote for an audience that was deeply immersed in war with England as an historical tradition. He could certainly afford to inflate or reduce the importance of specific events since there would have been very few, if any, who actually lived through the campaign of 1314 by the time Barbour wrote his poem. On the other hand, most of his audience would have grown up on a diet of hero-worship for King Robert, Moray and Douglas and on tales of the experiences of their fathers or grandfathers.

Since Barbour put pen to paper so long after the events but still maintains a remarkably sound chronology of the war years it is clear that Barbour did not compile his account from popular folk tales of the day, but from works that have not survived to the present day. Professor Duncan has examined the likely nature of Barbour's source material in his masterful presentation of *The Bruce*, which cannot be too highly recommended, not simply for the 'translation' of the work into modern English but for the invaluable introduction and exceptionally fine footnotes.

Barbour's Bannockburn account starts with Edward Bruce laying siege to the castle of Stirling, which was commanded by Sir Philip Moubray:

Thartill a siege they set stythly,
Thai bykyrrit oftsys sturdily,
Bot gret chivalry done wes nane.

[*They set close siege, and fought many skirmishes, but there were no great deeds of chivalry.*]

Barbour immediately shows his preoccupation with the actions of the noble classes. He does not suggest that the fighting itself was unproductive or ineffectual, but that the combat was not 'graced' by noble deeds performed by noble men. Naturally, since he was writing for an aristocratic audience, one imbued with romantic concepts of chivalry, he quickly passes on to the arrangements for the pact under which Moubray promised to surrender his charge unless relieved by an English army by midsummer. Barbour dates this arrangement to the summer of 1313, though it is clear from record evidence and other chronicle accounts that Edward Bruce laid siege to Stirling around the beginning of Lent, 1314. Barbour may have been influenced by a text that no longer exists, but which was available to Sir Thomas Grey, whose dating of the events leading to Bannockburn is, as Professor Duncan has pointed out, slightly ambiguous. Barbour goes on to criticise Edward Bruce for giving 'so outrageous a day' – such a long period – for the pact, emphasising the length of time that Edward II would have for the mustering of a great army and gives King Robert a speech in which he takes his brother to task:

The king said quhen he hard the day,
'That wes unwysly doyn, perfay.
Ik hard never quhar sa lang warning
Wes gevyn to sa mychty a king.'

[*The king said, when he heard the day* [agreed date], '*That was unwisely done, I never heard of such a long warning given to so mighty a king.*']

The precise date of the agreement has not survived, though it was clearly made shortly after the fall of Edinburgh and Roxburgh castles in the spring of 1314. Although Stirling could, in theory, be supplied by water, in practice the loss of the other occupation strongholds in Lothian and Fife must have given Robert effective control of the River Forth. It would, perhaps, have been possible to force a passage as far as Stirling, but that would hardly constitute a reliable means of re-supply, so Moubray's command was in a perilous situation. Professor Duncan has suggested that the siege was set toward the end of March and that Edward Bruce – Barbour does not refer to him as the Earl of Carrick – and Moubray made their pact around the middle of May, thus reducing the period of the pact from one year to six weeks. This is certainly a realistic and plausible analysis. Regardless of when the siege commenced, Edward Bruce was certainly absent from Stirling in the middle of April when he conducted a major raid through Cumbria, returning to Scotland about 18 April. Edward had, according to *Lanercost*, invaded England 'contrary to agreement' – that is to say in contravention of a truce. However the chronicle goes on to say that the Scots attacked because the community of Cumbria 'had not paid them the tribute that they had pledged themselves to pay on certain days'.

Although Barbour is often eager to portray Edward Bruce as a rash and intemperate man, the military situation at Stirling must be taken into account. If the surrender pact had not yet been made by the time Edward left to travel to Cumbria the garrison of Stirling would have had an opportunity to gather supplies from the vicinity unless Edward had left enough of a force to keep them contained. This would obviously have forced Edward to divide his force in order to provide a presence at Stirling and a mobile force to lead into England, a risky undertaking since the numbers of men available to him would not have been particularly large. Any foray into England was a risky business, so Edward would surely have endeavoured to have as large a force of men-at-arms as he could gather. This would compromise the size of force that he could afford to leave behind, a force that would have to include a strong heavy cavalry element to counter the men-at-arms element of the Stirling garrison. Despite Barbour's assertions, it is not clear that Edward Bruce was a rash commander, (though his death at the battle of Faughart may have been a consequence of over-confidence) and he had been entrusted by his brother with a number of independent commands which he had led with conspicuous success. It is therefore very possible that the pact had been concluded before Edward departed Stirling for Cumbria. Edward certainly took a force of some scale on his expedition, enough to make an attempt on Carlisle, possibly, as Professor Duncan suggests, to 'equal the chivalry of Moray and Douglas', whose successes at Edinburgh and Roxburgh had already contributed to the situation at Stirling.

Having set the scene with Edward Bruce's compact and the reaction of the king, Barbour goes on to describe the mustering of troops for the campaign:

Than all that worthi war to fycht
Off Scotland set all hale that mycht
To purvey tham agane that day,
Wapynnys and armouris purvayit thai
And all that afferis to fechting.
And in Ingland the mychty king
Purvayit him in a gret array
That certis hard I never say
That Inglis men mar aparaile
Maid than did than for bataill,
For quhen the tyme wes cummyn ner

He assemblit all his power
And but his awne chivalry
That wes sa gret it wes ferly
He had of mony ser counter
With him gud men of gret bounte
Of France, worthi chevalry

He had intill his company,
The erle of Henaud als wes thar,
And with him men that worthi war,
Off Gascoynne and of Almany,
And off the duche of Bretayngny
He had wycht men and wel farand
Armyt clenly bath fute and hand.

[*Then all the men of Scotland who were capable of fighting set themselves to the purchase of arms and armour and all that is needed for war. And in England, the mighty king made preparations for war on a grand scale. I am certain that the English never made a greater effort than for this battle. When the time* [for the campaign] *drew near he gathered all his power, and apart from his own chivalry* [in the sense of cavalry] *who were so numerous that it was terrifying, he had men of great ability from many other countries. He had great paladins from France in his army and the Earl* [Count] *of Hainault also was there, and with him worthy men of Gascony and Almayne and from the Duchy of Britanny he had strong men, well armed* [armoured] *on hand and foot.*]

Barbour's objective was to show the extensive resources of Edward II when compared to Robert I, however he was not above gilding lilies. It would be remarkable if no one from Edward's extensive French possessions served at Bannockburn, but there is no reason to expect that any large body of foreign troops took part in the campaign. Barbour is certainly mistaken in his assertion that the 'Earl' (Count) of Hainault joined Edward's force, though the count did join Edward III for the disastrous Weardale campaign of 1327. Barbour adds further contingents:

All Wals als wiuth him had he
And off Irland a gret mengne,
Off Pouty Aquitane and Bayoun
He had gret mony of renoune,

And off Scotland he had yeit then
A gret menye of worthy men.

[*He* [Edward] *also had with him all of Wales and a large company from Ireland. He had many men of great prowess from Poitou, Aquitane and Bayonne and also from Scotland he still had a great company of worthy men.*]

Like any chronicler worthy of the name, Barbour is at pains to 'talk up' the scale of the armies, particularly – for obvious dramatic and patriotic reasons – the English host:

Quhen all thir sammyn assemblit war
He had of fechtaris with him thar
Ane hunder thousand men and ma
And fourty thousand war of tha
Armyt on horse bath heid and hand,
And of thai teit war thre thousand
With helyt horsing plate and mailye
To mak the front of the batailye,
And fifty thousand of archeris
He had foroutyn hobelar,
And men of fute and small rangale
That yemyt harnays and vittaile
He had sa fele it wes ferly.

[*When all of these were gathered together he had with him 100,000 and more fighting men, and forty thousand of these were on horseback, armoured on head and hand, and of these three thousand were on horses armoured with plate and mail to form the front of the battle. And he had fifty thousand archers apart from hobelars and so many footmen and men to carry harness and rations that it was terrifying.*]

Clearly Barbour's estimates of the English army can only be accepted as literary, not literal, figures. No European medieval army ever amounted to anything like 100,000 men, on the other hand, the figure of 3,000 men of 'covered' horses may not be too far from the mark, though it is almost certainly something of an exaggeration. Bernard de Linton, who, unlike Barbour, was around at the time and may even have been present at the battle, tells us that Edward's army included 3,100 men on covered horses and was very probably one the sources of Barbour's information. Barbour has the entire English army muster at Berwick – though some proportion of it actually gathered at Wark – where, on the advice of his chief officers, Edward divided his army into ten divisions:

In alkane war weile ten thousand
That lete thai stalwartly suld stand

In the bataile and stythly fycht
And leve nocht for that fayis mycht.
He set ledaris til ilk bataile
That knawn war of gud governaile,
And til renownyt erls twa
Of Gloysster and Herfurd war tha
He gaf the vaward in leding
With mony men at thar bidding
Ordaynit into full gud array
Thai war sa chivalrous that thai
Trowyt giff thai come to fycht
Thar suld na strength withstand thar mycht.
And the king quhen his mengne
Divisit intill batallis ser
His awne bataill ordanyt he
And quha suld at his bridle be,
Schir Gillis Argente he set
Apon a half his reyngye to get,
And of Valence Schir Amery
On other half that wes worthy

[*In each battle* [division] *there were at least* 10,000 *men who would stand and fight fiercely in battle, and not flee from the enemy's power. He set leaders to each battle that were known as good leaders and to two famous earls, Gloucester and Hereford he gave leadership of the vanguard, with many well-armed and drilled men under their command. They were so chivalrous that they believed that if they had to fight no power could withstand them. And the king, when his army was divided into separate commands, organized his own battle, and who should be at his bridle. He set Sir Giles d'Argentan on one side to hold his reins and on the other he set Sir Aymer de Valence, a worthy* [knight].]

Barbour's assertion that the English army was divided into ten formations has, perhaps, been taken too literally by scholars. Like the gross inflation of the army sizes (both English and Scots) this is probably more a matter of the demands of literature than any realistic appraisal; of the order of battle adopted by Edward and his officers, however, there is a possibility that Barbour is conflating different pieces of information. The divisions (battles) of a medieval army frequently consisted of both horse and foot. The infantry were enlisted for one of two functions, spearmen or archers, and we should expect – unless there is pressing evidence to the contrary – that each 'battle' would contain both. It is very rare to find a description of a medieval army that consisted of more than three battles, but the cavalry element of English armies often comprised four formations, the largest of which would normally include the royal household arrayed for war and be commanded – nominally at least – by the king himself. If we consider that each of three 'battles' was divided into a body of spearmen and one of archers it might well seem to an observer that there were in fact six formations, not three formations with two subdivisions in each. These, with the addition of four cavalry formations might well present the appearance of ten separate formations, though in fact they might be only three 'battles', each with contingents of spearmen, archers and cavalry and a 'tenth' unit comprising the king's cavalry formation.

Barbour leaves the English as they depart from Berwick and turns to the Scottish army, listing Robert's senior officers – Edward Bruce, Douglas, Randolph and Walter Steward – as well as:

Outakyn other mony barounys
And knychtis that of gret renowne is
Come with thar men full stalwartly.
Quhen thai war assemblyt halely
Off fechtand men I trow thai war
Thretty thousand and sumdele mar,
Foroutyn carriage and petaill
That yemyt harnays and vitaill.
Our all the ost than yeid the king
And beheld to thar contenyng
And saw thaim of full fayr affer.
Off hardy countenance thai wer,
Be liklynes the mast cowart
Semyt full weill to do his part.

The king has sene all thar having
Thai knew him weile into sic thing,
And saw thaim all commouinall
Off sic contenance and sa hardy
Forout effray or abaysing.
In his hart had he gret liking
And thoucht that men of sa gret will

Gif they wlad set thar will thartill
Suld be full hard to wyn perfay.

[... *many other barons and knights of great renown* [who] *stalwartly brought their own men. When they were all gathered together I swear there must have been thirty thousand fighting men and more as well as carriage-men and lesser people that carried harness and rations. The king inspected the whole army, and saw that they bore themselves well. They were of stern countenance and even the most cowardly looking seemed like he would play his part very well. In his heart he had great joy, thinking that men of such great will, if they should set their will to it* [combat] *would be very hard to defeat.*]

Again, Barbour's figure of 30,000 (and somewhat more) combatants is not to be taken seriously. His intention is to show the reader – or listener, since the poem was probably written with performance in mind – that King Robert had gathered a very powerful force, though clearly very much smaller than that of Edward. Barbour tells us that Robert was happy about his situation, and then moves on to a discussion between the king and his senior officers:

... And callyt his consaile preve
And said tham, 'Lords, now ye se
That Inglismen with mekill mycht
Has all disponyt thaim for the fycht
For thai yone castel wald reskew.
Tharfor is gud we ordane now
How we may let tham of thar purpose
And sua to thaim the wayis clos
That thai pas nocht but gret letting.
We haf here with us at bidding
Weill thretty thousand men and ma,
Mak we four bataillis of tha

And ordane us on sic maner
And quhen our fayis cummys ner
We to the New Park hald our way,
For that behovys thain need away
Bot gi that thai will beneath us ga
And our the merrais pass, and sua
We sall be at avantage thar
And me think that rycht spedfull war

To gang on fute to this fechting
Armyt bot in litill arming,
For schup we us on hors to fycht
Sen our fayis ar mar of mycht
And better horsyt than ar we
We suld into gret perell be
An gyff we fecht on fute perfay
at avantage we sall be ay,
For in the park amang the treys
The horsmen alwayis cummerit beis,
And the sykis alssua that ar thar-doun
Sall put thaim to confusione.

[*He called his privy council and said to them, 'Lords, now you see that the English seek battle with great strength, and want to relieve that castle. Therefore it is wise that we should decide now how we are to deny them their objective, closing the roads so that they cannot get through without great loss. We have here thirty thousand men and more under our command. We will divide them into four divisions and deploy in such a way that when our enemy approaches we hold our position in the New Park, for they will probably have to come that way, but if they go below us and cross over the morass we shall be at an advantage. Also, I think that it would be best to go to battle on foot, and with little armour, for if we mount our horses for the fight, when our enemy is stronger and better-horsed than we, we should be in a lot of trouble. And if we fight on foot, we shall always have an advantage, for in the Park, among the trees, the horsemen will be less manoeuvrable, and the streams down below* [on the plain] *will disrupt them.*]

Evidently Barbour believed that King Robert, though not necessarily committing himself to a major engagement, was prepared to fight if the circumstances seemed promising. The relief of Stirling Castle is presented as the chief objective of the English army, but Robert's decision to station his own forces in the strong position of the New Park – where it would be very difficult for the English cavalry to make an effective attack but where he would still be able to intervene should the English try to approach Stirling 'below' the high ground on which the Park was situated – does rather indicate that he believed the 'real' objective to be to force battle. Presumably this was actually self-evident, not only to the king, but to the army generally. Whatever the strategic and political significance of Stirling Castle, Edward cannot have believed that the retention of one fortress was so important that it was worth the expense of raising a large army. Realistically, unless he could bring the Scots to battle – and defeat them – the relief of the castle would be of little value. He could not keep an army in being for very long due to the enormous expense and the high rate of desertion typical of armies of the day. As soon as the army disbanded, the Scots would be able to renew the siege. The streams across the plain were obviously expected to cause problems for the English, but it is not certain that the streams in question ran across the English position. Barbour may simply mean that the courses of the Bannock and the Pelstream would prevent the English army from adopting the optimum formation for battle or would prevent them from moving to out-flank a Scottish advance.

King Robert's instruction to his men to be 'armyt bot in littil arming', though an important piece of information, does not imply that the Scots went to battle without armour, just that they should dispense with some of the heaviest pieces, perhaps exchanging great barrel helms – which were in any case going out of use – for the lighter, and much more fashionable, bacinet. In practice this would only really apply to the men-at-arms. The rank and file would, in the main, wear armour of cloth and leather. With the leaders appointed and the army divided into four formations of infantry, Barbour goes on to describe the planned deployment, with the King taking the rearguard:

He said the rerward he wuld ma
And evyn forrouth him wald ga
The vaward, and on ather hand
The tother bataillis suld be gangand
Besid on sid a litill space,
And the king that behind thaim was
Suld se quhar thar war mast myster
And releve thar with his baner.

[*He said he would take the rearguard, and straight in front of him would be the vanguard, and on either side, a little distance apart, would go the other two divisions, and the king, who was behind them should see where there was the greatest threat and relieve them with his banner.*]

The deployment of the four main formations – for there were also archers and cavalry present – was planned well before the arrival of the English army. Barbour's description could mean that the Scots adopted a 'diamond' forma-tion, however the term *vaward* (vanguard) should not be interpreted strictly and simply to mean that that formation should always form the leading edge of the battle on their own. Barbour does not actually say that the vanguard was ranged in front of the other units, only that two other formations were deployed a little distance on either side with the king's formation directly to the rear of the vanguard, so that he could see what was going on and commit his force where it would do the most good. This may indicate a little wishful thinking on Barbour's part. If we are to assume that each of these formations was some-thing in the region of 200 metres wide – and they can hardly have been very much less – it would be extremely difficult for the king to identify the most pressing need unless one or other of the formations to his front was utterly overwhelmed. Further, should that occur, the only really practical option would be to move his own formation to the left or right to face the enemy, unless of course it was the *vaward* that was defeated, in which case preventing his own formation from panicking and taking to their heels would surely present an insuperable challenge, even for a leader of King Robert's calibre.

Training a large body of men to move forward in unison is not that great a challenge, but changing the direction of their advance by inclining on the march is very difficult to achieve without losing the uniformity of 'dressing' (the intervals between the men) which would be vital to the success of a force of spearmen.

Having decided on his order of battle, Robert set his men to the task of preparing the 'pots' that figure so prominently in accounts of the action. The army spent the whole of the Saturday night digging and heard mass early on Sunday morning, at which point the combatants were ordered to arm them-selves for battle, while the carters, farriers, lorimers, blacksmiths, cooks and other ancillaries were ordered to move away from the main body of the army:

Syne all the smale folk and pitail
He send with harnays and vitaill

Intil the park weill fer him fra
And fra the bataillis gert them ga
And als he bad went thar way
Twenty thousand weile ner war thai.
Thai held thar way til a vale

[*Then all the ancillaries, with stocks of equipment and food, were sent some distance into*
the Park, well away from the fighting formations. They obeyed his [the King's] *orders.*
There were nearly twenty thousand of them, and they made their way to a valley.]

These, of course, were the 'small folk' – the porters, craftsmen, cooks, grooms
and servants – that were a vital component of any medieval army, and who, so
Barbour tells us, joined the battle at a crucial juncture to help secure Robert's
victory on the Monday morning. It is easy to dismiss their involvement,
particularly since they do not appear in any of the other contemporary or
near-contemporary accounts, however this may be a matter of the perception
of those whose observations formed the basis of the other depictions of the
battle. *Lanercost's* 'reliable eye-witness' may not have been in a position to see
the advance of the 'small folk' since at that point he was, presumably, either in
the thick of the fighting or attempting to escape with his life. He would, in
any case, have the main body of the Scottish army between himself and the
'small folk'. Their absence from the *Scalacronica* account is, perhaps, more telling. Sir Thomas Grey senior was certainly present, but that does not mean that
he had an unobstructed view of the action, though, if the intervention of the
'small folk' were of any significance, he would surely have become aware of it
in the aftermath of the fight. Alternatively, he – or Thomas junior, who wrote
the account – may have known of the intervention but considered that it was
either unimportant or that it would not be of interest to an audience. Given
his preoccupation with the deeds of 'noble knights', it may just have held no
interest for him personally. Having disposed of the ancillaries, Barbour turns
his attention back to the king and the army:

The king gert thaim all buskit be
For he wyst in certante
That his fayis all nycht lay
At the Fawkyrk, and syne that thai
Held towart him the way all straucht
With mony men of mekill maucht.

Tharfor til his nevo bad he
The erle of Murreff with his menye
Besid the kyrk to kepe the way
That na man pas that gat away
For to debat the castel,
And he said himself suld weill

Kepe the entre with his batail
Giff that ony wald assale,
And syne his broder Schyr Edward
And young Walter Steward
And the lord of Douglas alsua
With thar mengne gud tent suld ta
Quhilk off thaim had of help myster
And help with thaim that with him wer.

[*The king ordered them all to prepare themselves, for he knew that his enemies had camped at Falkirk for the night, and were moving against him with many men of great might. Therefore he ordered his nephew, the Earl of Moray, with his troops, to guard the road that passed beside the church to ensure that no man could pass that way to the castle, and he said that he would guard the entry with his own division in case the enemy advanced by that direction. And his brother, Sir Edward, and young Walter the Steward and the lord of Douglas should pay close attention as to which of them* [the king or Moray] *should be most in need of support.*]

There were only two approaches to the castle that were practical proposi-tions for the English army; the road through the New Park or across the low ground to the east of the Park. The location of the Park is beyond dispute, though the exact course of the road, and therefore the location of the Entry, cannot be identified precisely. In general, historians have assumed that the 'kyrk' beside the road that Moray was to guard was St Ninians. Professor Duncan has pointed out that the only possible alternative to St Ninians would be the chapel of Larbert, which lay to the east of the Falkirk–Stirling road and a little to the southeast of the Torwood. This would place Moray's action against Clifford and Beaumont several kilometres away from the New Park. This is not impossible, but it would mean that elements of Robert's were widely separated, surely too far apart to allow Robert to observe the advance of the English and instruct Moray to take the field to prevent them reaching the castle. The distances involved would have made it virtually impossible for Edward Bruce, Douglas and the Stewart to bring their troops into action in support of either the king or Moray. If they were close enough to support one formation, they would be far too far away to intervene in support of the other. The conclusion must be that Barbour had St Ninians in mind:

> The king send than James of Douglas
> And Schyr Robert the Keyth that was
> Marschell off the ost of fe
> The Inglismennys come to se,
> And thai lap on and furth thai raid
> Weile horsyt men with thaim thai haid,
> And sone the gret ost haf thai sene
> Quhar scheldis schynand was sa schene
> And basynetis burnyst brycht
> That gave agayne the sone gret lycht.

[*The king then sent Sir James Douglas and Sir Robert Keith, who was the marshal of the army by heritable right, to observe the English. They mounted and rode off with well-mounted men and soon saw the great army, whose shiny shields and burnished bacinets reflected the sun brightly.*]

Robert's decision to send men to observe the approach of the English army was unremarkable, failure to do so would have been positively negligent, however this passage gives us two scraps of useful information about the nature of the Scottish army. Sir Robert 'the' Keith – 'the' is inserted to meet the demands of the meter of the poem – held the post of Marshal of the king's army, which was a hereditary office, a normal practice of the time. The precise nature and extent of his responsibilities cannot be ascertained, but obviously he was the most senior officer in a formal and customary command structure of some antiquity in the cavalry element of Scottish armies. The other significant point relates to the nature of Scottish noble cavalry. Barbour tells us that the party that Keith and Douglas led was 'well-horsed', an expression which appears from time to time in a variety of contemporary documents. One of the first references to William Wallace refers to him as a leader of men who were all 'well-horsed', a clear indication that his party consisted of men-at-arms. A minor point is Barbour's reference to 'bacinets'. This might be construed as an example of a writer using observations of the military practice of his own time when describing events of an earlier period, such as Bower's description of the English army (see below) being equipped with cannon. Although generally assumed to be a development of the 1340s, there are many references to bacinets dating from the early years of the fourteenth century. In 1316 Edward obtained a grant of one infantryman from every villa in England that stipulated that each man should have a bacinet as part of their equipment; an indication that the bacinet was no longer the preserve of fashionable gentlemen. Antiquarians and historians may have been misled by what we might call 'artistic' evidence, primarily funeral brasses and statuary. Bacinets do not become common in effigies before the 1340s, but we should bear in mind that most of these effigies are of men who died of natural causes. The armour depicted may have involved a deal of 'artistic licence', but the wide variety of styles surely indicated that some at least were in fact taken 'from life' – that they were genuine depictions of the armour owned by that particular individual in their soldiering days, and may therefore be representative of the style of armour worn in their youth, not at the time of their death.

Keith and Douglas observed the English army, and returned to the king:

Towart the king thai tuk thair way,
And tauld him intil prevete
The multitude and beaute
Off thair fayis that come sa braid
And off the gret mycht that thai haid.
Than the king bad thaim thai suld ma
Na contenance that it war sua
Bot lat thaim into commouine say
That thai cum intil evyll array
To confort his on that wys,
For oftrsys thou a word may rys
Disconford and tynsail with-all
And throu a word als weill may fall
Conford may rys and hardyment
May get men to do thar intent.

[They returned to the king and told him privately of the great strength and power of the enemy. The king told them that they should not spread that information, but rather to let it be known that the enemy was approaching in very poor order, which would be a comfort to

the troops, for often defeat can come from one word, but confidence and determination can be enhanced by another, inspiring the men to do their duty.]

Control of the 'news agenda' is not, apparently, a modern phenomenon. Robert manipulated the information that would pass through the army with the clear intention of bolstering the morale of the troops as the English approached:

And quhen thai cummyn war sa ner
That bit twa myle betwixt thaim wer
They chesyt a joly company
Off men that wicht war and hardy
On fayr coureris armyt at rycht
Four banrentis off mekill mycht
War capitaynis of that route,
The Syr the Clifford that wes stout
Wes of thaim all soverane leidar
Aucht hunder armyt I trow thai war.
Thai war all young men and joly
Yarnand to do chivalry,
Off best of all the ost war thai
Off contenance and off array.
Thai war he fairest company
That men mycht find of sa mony,
To the castell thai thocht to far
For gif that thai weill mycht cum thar
Thai thocht it suld reskewit be.
Forth on thar way held this menye
And towart Streviine held thar way,
The New Park all eschewit thai
For thai wist weill the king wes thar
And newth the New Park ghan thai far
Weill newth the kyrk intill a rout.

[*… and when they* [the English] *had come so close that there was only two miles between the armies, they chose a brave company of men that were strong and brave, whose chargers were strong and well armoured. Four bannerets of great prowess led this force, and Clifford was the officer in command. I believe that there were eight hundred of them. They were all brave young men, eager to perform acts of chivalry. They were the finest troops that could* *be found in the whole army in skill and equipment. They intended to pass to the castle, for if they could get to it, it would be relieved. This company made their way toward Stirling. They kept away from the New Park because they were aware that the king was there so they passed well below the New Park and below the church in one body.]*

Evidently Barbour believed that the objective of Clifford's command was to effect a formal or technical relief of the castle. This would indeed be a chivalrous deed, since it would involve passing the entirety of the Scottish army. Even if Clifford's force amounted to 800 – Grey, whose father served in that formation, gives a figure of 300 – this would still be the sort of achievement that brought honour to the participants.

Strictly speaking the castle would have been technically relieved if the English army came within three miles, but that would not have the social cachet of a relief by a 'joly' company of men-at-arms. Barbour does not name the four bannerets whose commands made up Clifford's force, though presumably one of them was Sir Henry Beaumont. The force may have consisted of brave men, but Clifford was not a rash commander. Aware that Robert – with the main body of the army – was in a strong position in the New Park, he kept to the open fields below the Park and toward St Ninians Church. Their progress was observed by the king, a clear indication that the ensuing action occurred within a relatively modest distance of the king's position at the Entry, since it was Robert who brought their advance to the attention of Moray, who promptly led his men to bar their way:

The Erle Thomas that wes sa stout
Quhen he saw thaim sa ta the plane
Ingret hy went he thaim agane
With five hunder foroutyn ma
Anoyit in his hart and wa
That thai sa fer wer passit by,
For the king haid said him rudly
That a rose of his chaplete
Was fallyn, for quhar he wes set
To kep the way thai men were passit
And tharfor he hastyt him sa fast
That cummynin schot tyme wes he
Tro the plane filed with his menye,
For he thocht that he suld amend

That he trespassit had or than end
And quhen the Inglismen him saw
Cum on foroutyn dyn or aw
And tak sa hardely the plane
In hy thai spoed thaim him agane

And strak with spurs the stedis stith
That bar thaim evyn hard and swith.
And quhen the erle sa that menye
Cum sa stoutly, til his said he
Be nocht abaysit for that schor
Bot settis speris you befor
And bak to bak set all your rout
And all the speris poyntis out
Suagate us best defend may we
Enveronyt with thaim gif we be.

[*When Earl Thomas, who was so staunch, saw them take the plain he moved against them in great haste with no more than five hundred men, angered in his heart that they had gone as far, for the king had rebuked him, saying that a rose had fallen from his chaplet, for the enemy was passing the place where he had been stationed. He quickly led his men to the plain filed for he felt that he must make amends for his negligence, and when the English saw him coming on without fear and so bravely take the plain they quickly moved against him, using their spurs on the chargers that bore them. And when the Earl saw them advancing bravely he spoke to his men 'Do not be afraid of their appearance, but put your spears before you, and arrange yourselves so that all your spears point outwards, that we may defend ourselves if we are surrounded by them.'*]

Moray, then, had failed to fulfil his orders. Clifford's force had been able to cross most of the low ground to the east of the Torwood and was well on its way to effecting a relief of the castle. The fact that the king was able to observe Clifford and rebuke his nephew, but that there was still time for Moray to gather his troops and lead them out to obstruct the enemy, is a strong indication that the Scottish army did not have a very extensive front, but was relatively concentrated. Moray's speech to his troops is almost certainly a product of Barbour's pen – his troops should have needed no instruction about the value of their formation as they had, after all, been at Stirling for some weeks, training for exactly this sort of situation. Barbour continues with a stirring and graphic account of the ensuing action, describing the inability of the English cavalry to break into the Scottish formation, until, frustrated and desperate, they began to throw their weapons at the Scots in the hope of disrupting their ranks. The struggle continued for some time, prompting Douglas to ask permission from the king to go to Moray's aid. Initially this was refused; in part, because the king was not prepared to have his plans disrupted, and in part to allow Moray to have the undiluted honour of scoring a significant victory with only his own command. However, the king eventually relented, and Douglas led his men down onto the plain, where he drew to a halt to observe the progress of the fight. While all this was going on, the king was faced with another problem – the earls of Gloucester and Hereford, at the head of a strong company of men-at-arms, were attempting to force a passage into the New Park:

> The vaward, that wist na thing
> Off this arrest na his dwelling
> Raif to the Park all straucht thar way
> Foroutyn stinting in gud array,
> And quhen the king wist that thai wer
> In hale bataill cummand sa ner
> His bataill gert he weill array.
> He raid apon a littil palfrey
> Laucht and joly arayand
> His bataill with ane ax in hand
> And on his bassynet he bar
> Ane hat of quyrbolle ay-quhar,
> And thar-upon into taknyng
> Ane hey croune that he wes he king

[*The English vanguard, who knew nothing of this reverse, made their way straight to the Park in good order and when the king became aware of them, he put his division into good order. He was mounted on a small palfrey, directing the troops, axe in hand. On his bacinet he wore a cap of boiled leather and on top of that a crown to show that he was the king.*]

Robert's choice of mount – a palfrey – has been construed as evidence that the Scots did not have access to the more muscular destrier, but is really a matter of having the most appropriate mount. He clearly did not expect to be taking part in the action himself. This was nearly his undoing as Sir Henry de Bohun, riding somewhat in advance of Gloucester and Hereford's force, saw the king and saw an opportunity to perform a great act of chivalry. Barbour describes the encounter in some detail and relates how the king's success gave heart to his troops. The English, on the other hand, were seriously demoralised:

And quhen the kingis men thaim saw
Sua in hale bataill thaim withdraw
A gret schout til thaim gan thai mak
And they in hy tuk all the bak,
And thai that folowit thaim ha slane
Sum off thaim that they hat ourtane
Bot thai war few forsuth to say
Thar hors fete had ner all away
Bot how-sa quhoyne deyt thar
Rebutyt foulily thai war

[*When the king's men saw them withdraw in a single body, they gave a great shout and they* [the English] *retreated quickly, and those* [Scots] *who pursued them killed some that they had overtaken. Those killed were few in number, and the rest were taken away speedily by their horses, heavily defeated.*]

The number of casualties incurred by Gloucester and Hereford's force must have been quite small. Barbour would not miss an opportunity to regale his audience with talk of large numbers of English dead, but the action was a significant boost to the confidence of the Scots. This was a superstitious age, and the troops would be likely to take the king's successful duel as a good omen.

The attack at the Entry had been repulsed, but Moray's men were still in action near St Ninians when Douglas's formation approached:

The Erle Thomas wes yet fechtand
With fayis apon athyr hand
And slew of thaim a quantite
Bot wery war his men and he
The-quhether with wappynnys sturdely
Thai thaim defendyt manlely
Quhil that the Douglas come ner
That sped him on gret maner,
And Inglismen that war fechtand

Quhen thai the Douglas saw ner-hand
Thai wandyst and maid ane opynnyng.
James of Douglas be thar relying

Knew that thai discumfyt wer
Than bad thaim that with him wer
Stand still and pres na forthyrmar.
'For thai that yonder fechtand ar,'
He said 'ar off sa gret bounte
That thar fayis weill sone sone be
Discumfyt throu that awne mycht
Thocht na man help thaim for to fycht
And cum we now to the fechting
Quhen thai ar at discumfyting
Men suld say we thaim fruschit had,
And sua suld thai that caus has mad
With gret travail and hard fechting
Los a part of thar loving,
And it wer syn to les that prys
That of sa soverane bounte is.
And he throu plane and hard fechting
Has her eschevyt unlikly thing

[*Earl Thomas was still fighting foes on either side, and killed many, both he and his men were very tired, but still wielded their weapons manfully, until Douglas approached with speed and power, and the English that were fighting, when they saw Douglas close by, they hesitated and drew back. Douglas could tell from their retreat that they were close to defeat and told his men to halt and not to press any further forward. He said, 'those that are fighting over there are so brave that they will shortly overcome the enemy through their own efforts, though no man aids them in their fight. And if we join the fighting now, when they [the English] are already being defeated, men should say that we had beaten them, and those who have achieved this with hard work and fighting would be robbed of the honour they deserve.*]

After a hard fight the English troops, realising that they could do no more, withdrew, leaving the field to the earl's force, and having incurred – according to Barbour – only one fatal casualty, an unnamed yeoman.

At this juncture Barbour has the army gather together to hear a rousing speech from the king in which he leaves the decision of whether or not to fight on the following day to his troops. This is unlikely to say the least, but there is evidence to suggest that Robert was not yet fully committed to giving battle against the whole English army. His troops had acquitted themselves well and he could, perhaps, have avoided battle without serious political consequences. True, the castle would be relieved, but so long as Robert kept his army intact, Edward would not be able to take the risk of splitting his troops to carry out operations to impose his lordship, and the retention of one castle would be a poor prize for the effort and expense of leading a large army into Scotland. Naturally, Barbour has the army react in a positive way, cheering the king and declaring their willingness to fight. Although Barbour's main narrative of the first day's action limits participation to the 'battle' of the king and 500 men under Moray, when he comes to sum up the events of the day, he introduces another element, informing us that Edward Bruce – and presumably at least some proportion of his command – joined the action at the Entry in the pursuit of Gloucester and Hereford. This might be dismissed as a product of Barbour's imagination, since none of the other accounts mentions Edward Bruce's intervention, but it is hard to see what motive he could have for inventing an episode to show Edward Bruce in a good light, and it is perfectly possible that he could have joined the fight without anyone in the English army being aware that he had done so. The English were making a hasty retreat by that time, and probably had more pressing matters in mind than questions about who was or was not involved in the action. In a sense, it is not an important issue – the Scots had defeated the English in the action at the Entry. However it may have been a matter of some importance to the men involved. If Edward Bruce's division took any part in the fighting it would mean that at least half of the Scottish army had been engaged in successful actions on the Sunday evening. Furthermore, Douglas's command may not have actually been in action, but his men had witnessed Moray's fight at St Ninians. Both of the engagements had demonstrated the power of confident infantry when attacked by unsupported cavalry and there must have been a morale dividend for Robert's troops equal to or greater than the damage to the confidence of the English.

Important as they undoubtedly were, the two actions on Sunday night were hardly such significant defeats as to persuade Edward II to abandon his plan to bring the Scots to battle, so the English army made camp for the night and Edward consulted his staff officers:

The king with his consaill preve
Has tane to rede that he wald nocht
Fecht or the morne bot war he socht,
Tharfor thai herberyd thaim that nycht

Doune in the Kers, and gert all dycht
And maid redsy thar aparaill
Agayne the morne for the bataill,
And for in the Kers pulis war
Housis thai brak and thak bar
To mak briggis quhar thaim mycht pas,
And sum sayis that yeit the folk that was
In the castell quhen nycht gan fall
For thai that knew the myscheiff all
Thai went full ner all that thai was
And duris and wyndowys with tham bar,
Swa that thai had before the day
Briggyt the pulis swa that thai
War passit our everilkane,
And the hard feld on hors has tane

[*The king* [Edward], *with his privy council, has taken advice that he would not fight before morning unless forced to, therefore they camped that night down in the Carse and prepared their arms for battle the following morning, and, because there were streams in the Carse they demolished houses and took the thatch to make bridges where they might pass* [over the streams]. *And there are those who say that after dusk almost all of the men in the castle, knowing the problems* [of the terrain] *carried doors and windows, so that before daybreak they had bridged the streams and moved onto the hard field on horseback.*]

This passage has led historians to reach an untenable conclusion that has bedevilled the study of this battle. There are two specific issues. Firstly, a misunderstanding of the word 'Carse', frequently misinterpreted as 'swamp' or 'marsh' and secondly the word 'pulis', often translated as 'pools' for obvious, if incorrect, reasons. A carse is not a marsh, but an area which, though wet and difficult in the winter, is hard ground in summer. We might take note of the work of another Scottish poet, Samuel Colville who tells us that in spring the ground is like '… toasted breid /and through the Carse a man may reid (ride).' The term 'pulis', far from indicating stagnant water, actually means streams or burns.

Covering these 'pulis' with thatch from houses in the vicinity and with doors and windows from the castle is therefore a more practical proposition than one might expect. The object of the exercise was to make bridges that would allow the English army to cross on to the 'hard feld' where they would spend the night. They would be 'All reddy for till gif batale/Arayit intill thar apparaill' (all ready to give battle/arrayed in their equipment), an observation which accords perfectly with the *Scalacronica* account, in which Grey tells us that the English cavalry 'stood to' all night with their horses 'bitted'.

It would seem, then, that the English army passed an uncomfortable night on the 'hard feld', while the Scots were able to rest in whatever bivouac arrangements they had had over the preceding weeks. These were hardly likely to be sophisticated tents and pavilions – other than for the wealthy – but they surely enjoyed much better conditions than the English. This is a matter of some significance, especially when we remember that the English army had performed two hard marches on the Saturday and Sunday. Having brought the English to the battlefield, Barbour turns his attention back to the Scots:

The Scottismen quhen it wes day
Thar mes devoutly gert thai say
Syne tuk a sop and maid thaim yar
An quhen thai all assemblit was
And in thair battaillis all purvayit
With thar braid baners all displayit
Thai maid knychts, as it afferis
To men that usit thai mysteries,
The king made Walter Stewart knycht,
And James of Douglas that wes wycht
And other als of gret bounte
He maid ilkane in thar degree.
Quhen this wes donyne that I you say
Thai went all furth in gud array
And tak the plane ful apertly,
Mony gud man wicht and hardy
That war full of gret bounte
Intill thai routis men mycht se.

[*When it was day, the Scots devoutly heard mass and took food and prepared and when all their divisions were arrayed with banners unfurled, knights were made, as is proper for men to such men. The king made Walter Stewart a knight, and the valiant James Douglas and others of great prowess. He knighted each in appropriate degree. When what I tell you was completed, they set out in good order and quite openly took the plain.*]

The most significant piece of information from this passage is that the Scots 'ful apertly' left the higher, wooded ground of the New Park, a clear indication that Robert had decided, not to accept battle, but to force it. The act of 'making knights' was something of a tradition on the eve of battle, and what is interesting is that James Douglas was one of the recipients of the accolade. Barbour's assertion that the recipients were knighted 'in thar degree' had led to the assumption that Douglas was in fact being promoted to a banneret, however that puts a lot of weight on a slender piece of evidence. Douglas was not, apparently, a knight in the spring of 1307, when he approached an unnamed officer of the occupation government and 'begged to be received' into King Edward's peace, though he quickly changed his mind and plumped for the Bruce party. It would not be surprising if Robert had knighted him at some point over the next seven years, though he was definitely not yet a knight at the time of his earliest appearance as a witness to a royal charter in April 1308 (*RRS*, v, pp.295–6). It is not clear that King Robert had made many knights before Bannockburn, though there is a strong possibility that he was the unnamed Scottish magnate who knighted William Wallace in 1297/8. The King, or Douglas, may have felt it appropriate to wait for a suitably dramatic occasion.

The Scots, then, were carefully deployed for the fight, but Barbour contradicts himself when describing the English. Having already declared that they had made themselves ready for battle, he now tells us that Edward's army:

War nocht arayit on sic maner
For all thar bataillis samyn war
In a schiltrum, but quhether it was
Throu the gret straitens of the place
That thai war in to bid fechting
Or that it was for abaysing
I wat nocht, but in a schiltrom
It semyt thai war all and sum,
Outane the vaward anerly
That rycht with a gret company
Be thaimselvyn arayit war.

[*... were not arrayed in that manner, for all their divisions were in one schiltrom, but whether that was due to the narrow space in which they were ordered to fight or whether it was to make a daunting appearance I do not know, but it seems that they were all in one body, save for the vanguard alone, which was arrayed in a great body by themselves.*]

From the perspective of the Scots, then, the English army appeared to be divided into two bodies of troops, including the vanguard, which was separate from the rest of the force and – presumably – to their front. Barbour has set the stage for the battle, but before the action can commence, he relates a conversation between King Edward and Sir Ingram de Umfraville. Umfraville suggests that the English withdraw their camp in good order, confident that the discipline of the Scots would not withstand the temptation to break ranks and loot the tents and wagons of the English army. They would therefore be vulnerable to an attack by the cavalry. Edward, however, rejects the proposal, since he feels a victory over 'sic rangale' (such rabble) through a stratagem would not be so honourable as a straight fight. Ever keen to show the importance of piety, Barbour describes the Scots kneeling for a brief prayer, which Edward interprets as a plea for mercy and an overture to surrender, but which Umfraville tells him is simply the Scots putting their trust in God.

This whole episode might be dismissed as Barbour's desire to attribute victory to God's help were it not supported by the *Lanercost* account. However inspiring the power of prayer, there may have been a very sound practical military value to the business of having the army kneel. The business of marching large linear formations down to the plain would have led inevitably to some loss of order. If the rank and file of the formations were to kneel down, even for just a couple of minutes, the formation commanders and their subordinates would have an excellent opportunity to identify and rectify any irregularities that had developed during the descent from the Park. If what we would nowadays call the 'junior leaders' remained standing while the rest of the troops prayed they would be able to see, and therefore remedy, any gaps or deficiencies in the dressing of the formation. Both armies were now committed to battle:

Thuis war thai boune on ather sid,
And Inglismen with mekill prid
That war intill thar avaward
To the Bataill that Schyr Edward
Governyt and led held straucht thar way

The hors with speris hardnyt thai
And prikyt apon thaim strudely,

And thai met thaim rycht hardely
Sua that at thar assemble thar
Sic a fruschyng of speris war
That fer away men mycht it her.
At that meting foroutyn wer
War stedis stekyt mony ane
And mony gude man borne doun and slayne,
And mony ane hardyment douchtely
Was thar eschevyt, for hardely
Thai dang on other with wapnys ser.
Sum of the hors that stekyt wer
Ruschyt and rely rycht rudlye,
Bot the remanand nocht-forthi
That mycht cum to the assembling
For that led main na stinting
Bit assemblyt full hardely,
And thai met them ful sturdily
With speris that were scharp to scher
And axys that weile groundyn wer.
Quhar-with was roucht mony a rout.
The fechting wes thar sa fell and stout
That mony a worthi man and swicht
Throu fors wes fellyt in that fycht
That had na mycht to rys agane.

[*So on both sides they were ready, and very proud English men in their vanguard made straight for the division of Sir Edward Bruce. They put their spurs to their horses fiercely and they met them* [the Scots] *with such vigour that there was such a breaking of spears that men might hear it from a great distance. At this clash many horses were undoubtedly killed, and many men were brought down and killed, and many brave deeds were performed, for they attacked one another fiercely with various weapons. Some of the horses that were stabbed fell down hard where they were, but the others pressed on into the fight. And they* [the Scots] *met them in a determined manner with spears sharp enough to cut and well-ground axes. That fight was hard and fierce, and many worthy and brave men were killed that had no strength to get up.*]

This, then, was the first major clash of the battle. The Scots advanced toward the English lines and were counter-attacked by cavalry, but were able to maintain the integrity of their formation.

As the fight developed, Moray brought his formation into action; not, apparently, just the 500 men who had fought the previous evening, but one of the four divisions which Barbour allots to the Scottish army for the main battle:

And Quhen the erle of Murref swa
Thar vaward saw sa stoutly ga
The way to Schyr Edward all straucht
That met thaim with full mekill maucht,
He held hys way with his baner
To the gret rout quhar samyn wer
The nyne battailllis that war sa braid.
That sa fele banereis with thaim hald
And of men sa gret quantite
That it war wonder for to se.
The gud erle thidder tuk the way
With his battail in gud array
And assemblit sa hardily
That man mycht her that had bene by
A gret frusch of the speris that brast,
For that fayis assmblyt fat
That on stedis with mekill prid
Come prikand as thai wald our-rid
The erle and all his company,
Bot thai met thaim sa sturdily
That mony of thaim sa till erd thai bar,
For mony a sted was stekyt that
And mony gud man fellyt under fet
That had na hap to rys up yete.
Thar mycht se a hard bataill
And sum defend and sum assaile
And mony a reale romble rid
Be roucht thar apon ather sid
Quhill throu the byrnys bryst the blud
That til the erd doune stremand yhude.

[*... and when the Earl of Moray saw their* [the English] *vanguard advance on Sir Edward who met them with such strength, he made his way with his banner toward the great force of the nine formations which, with their many banners and great force of men, were a wonder to see. The good Earl made his way there with his formation in good order, and attacked so fiercely that men who might be near at hand could hear a great breaking of spears, for their enemies attacked very quickly on horseback with great confidence, spurring* [their horses] *as though they would ride over the Earl and his company. But he met them so fiercely that many of them were dashed to the ground, for many a horse was stabbed there and many good men who fell under their feet had no hope of rising up again. Men could see a great battle there, with some attacking and some defending, and many great combats were performed by each side until blood burst through their armour and streamed down to the ground.*]

Here Barbour repeats his assertion that the English army was divided into ten formations, one of which had already engaged with Edward Bruce's formation. Although he refers only to the English cavalry, it is by no means clear that he wants the reader to believe that all of the ten formations consisted of mounted men, but that the cavalry were to the fore of the rest of the army – a credible possibility in the light of the other accounts of the battle. It is perfectly possible that the English commanders were confident that the cavalry would be able to deal with the Scots, or that with the cavalry occupying all or most of the English front line, it was not possible to bring the infantry into action. It cannot be over-emphasised that the battle had developed quite contrary to English expectations, and that Edward II and his subordinates had assumed, on the basis of their lengthy experience of fighting the Scots, that they would be mounting an attack, not coping with one. Once again, the English cavalry proved unequal to the task of breaking into the Scottish formations and were soon in difficulties:

The erle of Murreff and his men
Sa soutely thaim contenyt then
That thai wan place ay mar and mar
On thar fayis the-quhether thai war
Ay ten far ane or may perfay
Sua that it semyt weill that thai
War tynt amang sa gret menye
As thai war plungyt in the se.

[*The Earl of Moray and his men then contained them* [the English] *so fiercely that they pushed their enemies back more and more though I am sure that they were outnumbered ten to one or perhaps more until it seemed that they were immersed among that great crowd just as if they were plunged into an ocean* [of their enemies].]

Many historians have interpreted the last two lines of this section as an indication that the Scots stood still, surrounded by their opponents like rocks in the sea, however Barbour tells his readers that the Scots pressed forward 'more and more', forcing the English backwards. There are several problems with that proposition. The first is the undoubted difficulty of achieving a steady advance to the plain with a body of perhaps 2,000 men in a circular formation; not impossible, but certainly very challenging. The second, and perhaps more crucial question, would be why the English cavalry commanders, having failed to break the Scots at the first onset, made no effort to lead their men westward, past the Scots. This would have allowed them to regroup behind the Scots and allowed the English infantry to engage. If we accept the interpretation of Barbour to the effect that the four Scottish formations were deployed in one line, once the cavalry had passed around Moray's formation – and the same applies to Edward Bruce's troops – they would be in no immediate danger.

Given Barbour's careful description of Moray's troops in action on the Sunday evening, it would be a curious thing if he neglected to mention that the Scots had formed circular schiltroms on the Monday morning. The third question, inevitably, must be 'how could the Scots achieve victory without advancing?' If they were motionless, Edward II and his officers would have been able to redeploy their troops, but, more importantly, they would only need to draw back a matter of a couple of yards to be safe from the Scottish spearmen. We cannot seriously consider that the Scots stood firm and that the English simply threw themselves onto Scottish spear points until the sheer weight of their casualties drove them to despair and flight. It is reasonable to assume that peer pressure and the physical courage and martial enthusiasm of men imbued with the chivalric values of the fourteenth century could spill over into recklessness, but not into mass suicide.

Barbour's description of the clash, that it was as if the Scots had been plunged into a 'sea' of their enemies, may lie at the root of a popular image of the battle – a great round mass of Scottish spearmen surrounded by waves of English cavalry, however neither Barbour nor any of the other accounts of the battle suggest that the Scots deployed in ring formations.

Barbour concludes this segment of the poem with a dramatic relation of the exploits of Edward Bruce and Moray's formations then passes to the next Scottish formation, that of the Stewart and Sir James Douglas.

> Quhen they twa first bataillis wer
> Assemblyt as I said you er,
> The Stewart Walter that than was
> And the gud lord als of Douglas
> In a bataill in gud array,
> And assemblyt sa hardely
> Besid the erle a litill by
> That thar feyis feld that cummyn wele,
> For with wapynnys stalwart of stele
> They dang upon with all thar mycht.

[*When those two formations were engaged as I said before, Walter, who was then the Stewart, and also Sir James Douglas, when they saw how the Earl and his formation attacked so stoutly, led their men in one formation and in good order, and met the enemy a little way from the earl, and made their presence felt, for with strong steel weapons they struck them with all their might.*]

Although Barbour believed that the Scottish army had been divided into four formations arrayed in a lozenge or diamond, he clearly shows the Scottish army advancing 'en echelon', bringing one formation into action at a time – Edward Bruce, then Moray, then the Stewart and Douglas, each joining the fight to the flank of the preceding formation:

> That tyme thar thre bataillis wer
> All syd be sid fechtand weill ner.

[*By that time the three formations were fighting nearly side by side.*]

Barbour's description is clear: as each formation came into action, the Scottish line was effectively lengthened by the width of each one, thus denying the English the opportunity to envelop the open flank of each formation as it approached. Any attempt to mount an attack around the Scots would have to be mounted while another Scottish formation was approaching the exposed flank of the would-be attackers. This description is less incompatible with that of *Lanercost*'s 'eye-witness' than one might at first think. *The Lanercost Chronicle*, in common with the other contemporary accounts of the action, has the Scots divided into three formations rather than four; even if we assume that Barbour is correct we cannot assume that the *Lanercost* witness was wrong – he may not have been able to see a fourth Scottish division. Furthermore, it might not have been apparent to the *Lanercost* witness that the Scots were, in fact, 'en echelon,' as Barbour describes it, rather than deployed with two formations abreast in advance and a third in the rear.

With three of the formations engaged, Barbour turns to the English archers, who were now starting to make an impression on the Scots:

The Inglis archeris schot sa fast
That mycht schot haff ony last
It had bene hard to Scottismen
Bot King Robert that wele gan ken
That thar archeris war perilous
And thar schot rycht hard and greous
Ordanyt forouth the assemble
Hys marschell with a gret menye,
Five hunder armyt into stele
That on licht hors war horsyt welle,
For prik amang the archeris
And sua assaile thaim with thar speris
That thai na layser haiff to schut
This marscell that Ik off mute
That Schyr Robert of Keyth was cauld
As Ik befor her has you tauld
Quhen he saw the bataillis sua
Assembill and togidder ga
And saw the archeris schoyt stoutly,
With all thaim off his company
In hy apon thaim gan he rid
And ourtuk tham at a sid,
And ruschyt amang thaim sa rudly
Stikand thaim sa dispitously
Ands in sic fusoun berand doun
And slayasnd tham foroutyn ransoun

That trhai thaim scaylit everilkane,
And fra that tyme furth thar wes nane
That assemblyt schot to ma.

[*The English archers shot very quickly, and if they had continued it would have been hard
on the Scots, but King Robert was well aware of how dangerous their archers were; that the
wounds they inflicted were hard and grievous, so he sent out a party from the main army;
namely his marshal with a great force, five hundred men, well armoured in steel, and well
mounted on chargers, to attack the archers strenuously with their spears to prevent them
from shooting. This marshal was Sir Robert Keith, as I have told you before. When he saw
the formations go into action and saw the archers shoot stoutly, he rode steadfastly toward
them with all his men and attacked them from the flank, breaking among them so fiercely
and striking them pitilessly, slaying them without quarter, that the whole body took to their
heels, and from then on no one tried to gather men for more shooting.*]

It has been suggested that this entire episode is a product of Barbour's imagination, largely because it is not an incident that figures in any of the other
accounts of the battle, and perhaps because British medievalists struggle to
accept the possibility that archers might be defeated by unsupported cavalry
in light of the great longbow victories – Dupplin Muir, Halidon Hill, Crécy,
Poitiers and Agincourt. There are, however, several problems with that analysis. At Dupplin and Halidon, the English archers were faced by attacks from
infantry, not cavalry. The target threatening them was a slow one. More significantly perhaps, each of the longbow victories mentioned above consisted
of attacks made on carefully deployed troops facing their opponents, not an
attack on archers who were already engaged in a different direction. Finally,
in all of these examples the archers were deployed uphill of their opponents.
There was a world of difference between marching steadily uphill under a rain
of arrows and galloping across flat ground into the flank of a body of archers
with no close-combat troops in support.

Despite the promise at the start of his work that he would put in 'suthfast
wryt' (accurate writing) the career of King Robert, Barbour was not above
embroidering his account for the sake of providing the audience with an exciting tale, and, given the experiences of the Scots with English archery, tales of
English archers being swept away would have gone down well with his readership, however this would probably have been too significant an incident to
invent if he wanted to remain credible in the eyes of his readers. Barbour could
relate or inflate or just plainly invent noble deeds of King Robert – especially

those claimed to have occurred when he was 'in the hills' – with impunity, but would need to have taken some care over the depiction of events that were close to people's hearts. If Keith rode down the English archers and was not accorded his place in Barbour's narrative, we can be confident that Keith's descendants would be less than pleased. If, on the other hand, Keith's attack was an invention, we can be sure that the descendants of other men would be concerned that their ancestor's worth was not receiving due attention.

A question raised by this passage is 'where did Keith's force come from?' Barbour is quite emphatic about the Scots being divided into four formations, and that all those formations fought on foot. He makes no reference to an independent command for Keith until he is ordered to lead an attack against the English archers. There are several possible explanations. Keith may have had command of a distinct element within one of the Scottish formations – presumably that of the king, since the other three were already engaged. This would imply that either Keith's men were mounted or that their grooms were nearby, ready to bring the chargers to the troops as required. Alternatively, Keith's troops may have formed a small unit, quite separate from any of the main formations, charged with intervention in the wake of either victory or disaster. King Robert may have decided to fight on foot for reasons of policy and morale, but we should not assume that he was absolutely determined to conquer or die. If the battle was going badly, Robert might well be glad of a body of men-at-arms. None of this really compromises the assertion in the other accounts that the Scottish army fought on foot. There can be no real doubt that almost all of them did, and that it is what the witnesses recalled about the nature of the fighting, but we should bear in mind that the witnesses – the *Lanercost* source and Friar Baston – were rather probably more pre-occupied with the business of staying alive than of recording their experience of the battle. Other writers, after the way of time, focus almost exclusively on the deeds – or deaths – of the aristocracy, and perhaps had little mind for the thousands of common infantry.

In addition to giving us the only account of Keith's attack, this passage probably lies at the root of the tradition that Scottish armies fielded 'light' cavalry throughout the wars of the Middle Ages. Barbour tells us that Keith's men were 'on licht hors', but we should not ask one word – 'lycht' – to bear too much weight. Barbour tells us, in the same line, that they were 'horsyt welle'; or that they were 'well-horsed', a term exclusively used at the time to describe men-at-arms with good quality mounts suitable for war. A reasonable interpretation would be that Barbour only means to tell us the Scots, or most of them anyway, did not have destriers of the first order, or at least did not use them for his engagement. The riders are described as 'armyt into stele' and were clearly men-at-arms.

Keith's attack was a resounding success, and Barbour returns to the Scottish archers:

Quhen Scottis archeris saw that this sua
War rebutyt thai woux hardy
And with all thar mycht schot egrely
Amang the horsmen that thar raid
And woundis wid to thaim thai maid
And slew of tham a full gret dele
Thai bar tham hardely and wele
For, fra thar fayis archeris war
Scaylit as I said till you are
That ma na thai war be gret thing
Sua that thai dred nocht thar schoting.

[*When the Scottish archers saw that they* [the English archers] *had been defeated, they became bolder, and shot eagerly and with all their might against the* [English] *horsemen that were riding there, giving them wide wounds and killing many of them. They were confident and bold, for since the other archers, who were much more numerous, had all run away as I told before, they* [the Scots] *did not fear their shooting.*]

All this seems to have occurred before the King took his own formation into battle, which would certainly facilitate drawing a portion of troops from his own direct command and entrusting them to Keith. In Barbour's account, then, at this juncture there were three Scottish formations in the fight, with King Robert's formation in the rear. Again, this does not really clash with the other accounts very significantly. To the *Lanercost* witness the horizon must have been seemed with wide bodies of hostile approaching Scots with another great body of more Scots in the rear – whether the front line of the Scottish army consisted of two units or three was probably not an immediate concern. What is not clear from Barbour's account is the location of the Scottish archers. The English archers would seem to have been drawn together on a flank where they could enfilade the Scottish spearmen, and we might reasonably assume that King Robert might station his archers to the flanks of his army to provide a degree of cover to his close-combat troops, however

Barbour does not give us that information. The *Lanercost* account however describes an exchange of archery before the first contact between Edward Bruce and Gloucester's formations in which the Scottish are defeated by what we can reasonably assume to be a greater force of English archers. Given that the main body of the Scottish army closed quickly on their opponents it is quite possible that the exchange took place as *Lanercost* describes it, and that both English and Scottish archers were forced out of the way by the advance of Edward Bruce and of Gloucester's cavalry, and then by Moray, forcing a confused concentration of English archers to the extreme flank of the Scottish army. Most historians have chosen to locate Keith's action on the left of the Scottish army, based on the assumption, perhaps, that Edward Bruce led the right-hand formation and was first into action, followed by Moray on his left, however Barbour does not make this absolutely clear. If the Scottish advance started from the left flank rather than the right, the archers of both sides might find themselves pushed toward Bannockburn rather than the Pelstream. If the Scots advanced with two formations abreast, as Sir Thomas Grey tells us, the effect need not be any different. Even if the two Scottish formations were in perfect alignment, there is no reason to assume that the English army had a flat front line. Other accounts suggest that Gloucester's formation was detached from the rest of the army even before his advance to contact. He evidently attacked, and with no support on his flank there would have been, however briefly, a space between the other Scottish formation(s) and the main body of the English army. Edward Bruce's formation seems to have marched with the Bannock Burn (or possibly the Pelstream, if he was on the left flank of the army) protecting their flank, so the easiest apparent route to safety – or at least away from the current melee – would be to move away from the burn and Edward Bruce's Scots.

The dispersal of the English archers greatly encouraged their Scottish counterparts but did nothing to help the morale of the rest of the army. 'Nakyt' (unarmoured), they fled from the 'armyt' Scottish cavalry:

Thai scaylit thaim on sic maner
That sum to that gret bataill wer
Withdrawyn thaim in full gret hy
And sum wer fled all trely,
Bot the folk that behind thaim was,
That for thar awne folk had na space

Yheyt to cum to the assembling
In again smartly gan thai ding
The archeris that thai met fleand
That then war maid sa recreand
That thar hartis war tynt clenely.

[*They fled in such a way that some escaped into the great body* [of the English army]
and some fled utterly, but the men who were behind them, who had no space for manoeu-
vre and had yet to be engaged, came right up against the archers who were running away,
and were so discouraged that they, too, lost heart completely.]

Keith's action, then, had had a major impact on the flow of the battle. The
English archers had been prevented from making any great impact on the fighting and had also been thrown back onto the main body of the English army,
causing confusion and demoralisation among those who had not yet fought.
Seeing that all is going well, Robert gives a short speech to the effect that if the
Scots press their advantage home, they will achieve a great victory. Barbour has
all four Scottish formations in line, pushing against an English army that has lost
its cohesion and any separation between commands since they had now been
pushed into one great heaving formation, 'Thai than war in a schiltrom all'.
Barbour gives us a lengthy description of the bravery of the Scots and of the
martial prowess of their leaders, and the battle is clearly won, but he has other
episodes to relate. The first of these is the story of the 'sma' folk':

In this tyme that I tell of her
At that bataill on this maner
Wes strykyn quhar on ather party
Thai war fechtand enforcely,
Yomen and swanys and pitaill
That in the Park to yeme vittaill
Wart left, quhen thai wist but lessing
That thar lordis with fell fechting
On that fayis assembyt wer'
Ane of thaimselvyn that war thar
Capitane off thaim all thai maid,
And schetis that war sumdele braid
Thai festnyt in steid of baneris
Apon lang treys and speris,

And said that thai wald se the fycht;
And help thar lordis at thar mycht.
Quhen her-tilall assentyt wer
In a rout thai assemblyt er
Fyfteen thousand thai war or ma,
And than in gret hy gan they ga
With thar baneris all in a rout
As thai had men bene styth and stout.
Thai come with all that assemble
Rycht quhill thai mycht the bataill se,
Than all at abys thai gave a cry,
'Sla! Sla! Apon thaim hastily!'
And thar-withall cummand war thai,
Bot thai were wele fer yete away.
And Inglismen that ruschyt war
Thouch for of fycht as I said ar
Quhen they saw cummnad with sic a cry
Towart thaim sic a company
That thaim thocht wele als mony war
As thai wes fechtand with thaim thar
And thai before had nocht thaim sene,
That wit ye weill withoutyn wene
Thai war abaysit sa gretumly
That the best and the mast hardy
That was intil thar ost that day
Wald with thar mensk haf bene away.

[*At this point in the battle, I tell you, just as the fight was being pursued furiously by both sides, men and boys who had been left in the Park to look after food, aware that their lords were heavily engaged with the enemy, chose one of their number to be their captain, and they fastened broad sheets to long poles and spears and said that they would see the battle and help their lords to the best of their ability. When they had all agreed to this they gathered together in one body, fifteen thousand of them or more with their banners, and then they went to a place where they could have a good view of the battle. Then all at once they gave a shout 'Kill! Kill! Attack them quickly!' And then they started to advance toward the fighting, though they were still a good distance away. The English, who were exhausted by the fighting as I said before, saw them coming on with a great cry and thought them to be an even greater company than those that they were already fighting, and one that they had not seen before. You can be sure that they were so downcast that even the best and most hardy men that were in that army that day wished they could be somewhere else and preserve their honour.*]

Once again, it is difficult to accept the possibility that this was an episode that Barbour invented; the bones of the episode might be found in many other medieval battles. Once it becomes clear that the enemy are beaten, the various ancillaries of the army – grooms, porters, farriers, drivers, cooks and servants – might gravitate to the locations of the fighting in search of plunder, or just out of morbid curiosity. Although he was keen to give the camp followers their due, Barbour's narrative does not indicate that they were crucial to victory; the English are already exhausted, demoralised and disorganised and are being pressed back steadily. King Edward sees that the day is lost, and leaves the field:

And quhen the king of Ingland
Saw his men fley in syndry palce,
And saw his fayis rout that was
Worthyn sa wycht and sa hardy
That all his folk war halyly
Sa stonayit that thai had na mycht
To stynt thar fayis in the fycht,
He was abaysit sa gretumly
That he and his company
Fyve hunder armyt all at rycht
Intill a frusch all tok the flycht
And to the castell held thar way.
And yeit haiff Ik hard som men say
That of Valence Schir Aymer
Quhen he in the feld saw vencsyt ner
Be the reyngye led awy the king
Agane his will fra the fechting.
And quhen Schyr Gylis the Argente
Saw the king thus and his menye
Schap thaim to fley as spedyly,
He copme rycht to the king in hy
And said, 'Schyr, sen it is sua
That ye thusgat your gat will ga
Havyn gud dayt for agayne will I,

Yeit fled I never sekyrly
And I cheys her to bid and dey.'

[*And when the King of England saw his men deserting in various places, and saw that his enemy's army was so stout that they had stunned his own people so much that they were unable to fight, he was so downcast that he, and his company of five hundred men-at-arms ran off in a mob and made their way to the castle. And I have heard men say that when he saw defeat was near Sir Aymer de Valence took the king's rein and led him away from the fighting against his will. And when Sir Giles d'Argentan saw the king and his followers prepare for flight he came right up to the king and said 'Sir, since you think to get away, have a good day, for I shall return [to the fight], indeed, I never fled, and I choose to stay here and die.'*]

Edward's exit was an acknowledgement of defeat, and an indication to the English army that any who could still do so should do their best to escape. For those who could see what was going on and who had the opportunity to do so, the best plan was to join the king's party if possible. A strong body of well-mounted men-at-arms would have a good chance of making their escape from the battlefield, and one could hardly be accused of desertion if one was in the company of the king. If the worst came to the worst and the Scots were able to force Edward's surrender, it would be no worse than falling prisoner in any other action, and one could hope that some help might be available in one's ransom negotiations. The Scots continued to press forward, continually reducing the space available to the English army, who, seeing the king disappear toward the castle, scattered before the enemy:

And fled sa fast rycht effrayitly
That of thaim a full gret party
Fled to the water of Forth and thar
The maist part of thaim drownyt war.
And Bannokburne betwixt the brays
Off men and hors sua stekyt wais
That apon drownyt hors and men
Men mycht pass dry out-our it then.

[*And fled in such terror that a great many fled to the waters of the Forth and most of a great party of them were drowned there. And the Bannock Burn was so stuffed between its banks with drowned men and horses that a man might cross over it dry.*]

Claims that men could have walked dry-shod over a stream or river because it was overflowing with bodies are not unknown in chronicle accounts; similarly streams that ran red with blood for three days after a battle. Literary flourishes should not be taken too literally, but there can be little doubt that English casualties were heavy. Interestingly, Barbour is very clear that the retreating English soldiers were pressed back toward the Forth as well as the Bannock Burn, an indication perhaps that the army scattered and fled in whatever directions seemed to offer a better prospect than the battlefield itself.

King Edward had escaped the field, but his situation was still bleak; his army had been destroyed and he had to seek shelter in the nearest haven, Stirling Castle. Any shelter there would have been most hazardous, as the governor, Sir Philip Moubray explained:

> The king with thaim he with him had
> In a rout till the castell rad
> And wald haiff bene tharin, for thai
> Wyst nocht quhat to get away,
> Bot Philip the Moubra said him till
> 'The castell, Schyr, is at your will,
> But cum ye in it ye sall se
> That ye sall sone asssegyt be
> And thar sall nane of Ingland
> To mak you rescours tak on hand
> And but rescours may na castell
> Be haldyn lang, ye wate this wele.
> Tharfor confort you and rely
> Your men about you rycht starkly
> And haldis about the Park your way
> Knyt als sadly as ye may,
> For I trow that nane sall haff mycht
> That chassys with sa fele to fycht.'
> And his consail they haff doyne
> And beneath the castell went thai sone
> Rycht be the Rond Table away
> And syne the Park enveround thai
> And towart Lythkow held in hy.

[*The king, and those with him, rode in a close formation to the castle, and would have entered, for they did not know what road to take to escape, however Sir Philip Moubray spoke* [to the king] *'Sir, the castle is at your disposal, but if you enter you will see that you will soon be besieged. No one from England can undertake your relief and you know that no castle can be held for long without relief. Take comfort; and rally your men close around you. Make your way round the Park, as close-knit as you can be, for I am sure that none who might pursue you will have the strength to attack* [such a strong party].*' They took his advice and shortly rode below the castle, past the Round Table and around the Park before making their way toward Linlithgow.*]

Edward was doubtless further demoralised by Moubray's advice, but the situation was clear. The English army was in no fit state to renew the fight and there was no realistic possibility of a new army being raised to come to Edward's rescue, certainly not within the period that the castle garrison might be expected to hold out. Technically, Sir Philip was not obliged to surrender the castle at all. An English army had arrived in the vicinity of the town within the period stipulated in the agreement that Moubray had made with Edward Bruce, but surrender was the only realistic option.

King Edward made his escape, pursued by Douglas at the head of a small body of men-at-arms, less than sixty in number according to Barbour. Not all of the English leadership was as fortunate. Gloucester, Clifford, Comyn and many others were dead on the field – Hereford escaped, apparently with a strong company, and sought safety behind the walls of Bothwell Castle, one of the few strongholds still in Plantagenet hands, only to be taken prisoner by its commander, Sir Walter Gilbertson (or FitzGilbert). Interestingly, Gilbertson was English by birth, but had lived in Scotland since before the invasion of 1296 and was one of a small number of English soldiers to decide that their career in Scotland was more important than allegiance to their king.

The English army left the field in several directions, but a large number of them, perhaps trying to follow King Edward's example, found their way up through the town to Stirling Castle, where, unable to gain entry, they congregated around the castle rock:

Bot to the castell that wes ner
Off Strevilline fled sic a mengye
That it war winder for to se,
For the craggis al helyit war
About the castell her and thar

Off thaim that for strenth of that sted
Thidderwart to warand fled,
And for thai sa fele that war
Fled under the castell war
The King Robert that wes witty
Held his gud men ner him by
For dred that ris agayne suld thai
This was the caus forsuth to say
Quharthouch the king of Ingland
Eschapyt hame intill his land
Quhen that the feld sa clene wes maid
Off Inglismen that nane abaid
The Scottismen sone tuk in hand
Off tharis all that ever thai fand,
As silver gold clathis and arming
With vescahll and all other thing
That ever mycht lay on thare hand.
So gret a riches thair thai fand
That mony man mychty wes maid
Off the riches that thai thar haid
Quhen this wes donyne that her I say
The king send a gret company
Up to the crag thaim til assaile
That war fled fra the gret battail,
And thai thaim yald foroutyn debate
And in hand has tane thaim fute-hate.

[*A great number, so many that it was a wonder to see, fled to the castle of Stirling which was nearby. The rocks around the castle were covered in men that had made their way there, trusting to the strength of the place. So many of them gathered at the castle that King Robert, who was aware [of this] kept his troops close at hand for fear that they [the English] would re-group. Truth to tell, this was the way that the King of England was able to escape home to his own land; once the field had been completely cleared of Englishmen, the Scots soon set themselves to looting every thing that they could lay their hands on; silver, gold, clothing, armour, vessels and everything else. They found such great wealth that many a man was 'made for life' from the riches they seized there. When this was done, the king sent a large company to the Castle Rock to attack those who had fled there from the battle, and they surrendered immediately and were quickly taken into custody.*]

The men assembling on Stirling Castle rock, though evidently a large body of troops, probably did not really pose much of a threat to King Robert's army. They could hardly depend on the castle garrison for water, food and any necessary replenishment of arms or ammunition. They had endured a long march followed by two sharp defeats on Sunday evening and then another crushing defeat on the Monday morning. The majority of them were bound to be tired, demoralised and hungry as well as leaderless. Robert could have chosen to starve them off the rock or he could have let them make their own way home – either course would call for a continued deployment of troops. The English refugees could be bottled up on the heights of the castle or they could be pursued out of the country, but they could not be allowed to wander freely, foraging their way home.

Barbour turns back to the battlefield briefly, mentioning various prominent English lords who had been killed in action, and the only two prominent Scottish fatalities, Sir Walter Ross and William Vipont, before going on to discuss the only success of the day for King Edward's army. Ross was a dear friend of Edward Bruce, but not as dear as Ross's sister, the love of Edward's life. He loved her more than he did his own wife, Isabelle of Atholl. Isabelle's brother, David de Strathbogie, Earl of Atholl, had been a member of Edward II's occupation government until the spring or summer of 1312, when he defected to the Bruce party. He abandoned the Bruce cause when his sister was spurned by Edward in favour of his mistress. He may not have actually joined Edward II's forces so much as taken action for his own reasons, but he conducted a night-raid on Cambuskenneth Abbey on 23/24 June.

> ... apon Saynct Jhonys nycht
> Quhen bath the kingis war boun to fycht,
> In Cammyskynnell the kingis vitaill
> He tuk and sadly gert assaile
> Schyr Wilyam of Herth and him slew
> And with him men ma than ynew
> Tharfor syne intil Ingland
> He wes bannyst and all his land
> Wes seyst as forfaut to the king
> That did tharoff syne his liking

[*... on St John's night, when both the kings were prepared for battle, he* [Atholl] *captured the king's stores and fiercely attacked Sir William Aird, and killed him and many others.*

Therefore he was banished to England and all of his land was forfeited to the king, who used it as he saw fit.]

Atholl's raid on the night dividing the two days of the battle had no significant effect at the time, either militarily or politically, however his fracture with the Bruce leadership would become an issue in the 1330s, when Atholl would be one of the mainstays of Edward Balliol's attempt on the kingship. Residual local loyalty to the Strathbogie family would make him a power to be reckoned with in the northeast between the battle of Dupplin Muir in August 1332 and his death at the battle of Culblean in November 1335.

Professor Duncan has suggested that the stores kept at Cambuskenneth consisted of foodstuffs for horses and that Atholl, recently appointed as King Robert's constable, would be aware of this. That does not, however, explain why stores of any kind should have been deposited at Cambuskenneth. Elsewhere (see above) Barbour writes of the men who were sent to a valley during the main action, and that they were responsible, among other things, for food. King Robert's army was certainly a very impressive force by Scottish standards, and would have needed enormous quantities of bread, meat, oats and hay on a daily basis. It might well have been convenient to have supplies delivered to a secure location and then carried to the army for consumption, in which case the Abbey of Cambuskenneth was conveniently situated and would probably have been enclosed with a precinct wall which would ease security against thieves, though, clearly, not against a party of men-at-arms.

Barbour returns to the king once again, relating the tales of Sir Marmaduke Twenge, who surrendered in person, and Sir Philip Moubray, who came to surrender at the castle, before telling the reader of Douglas's pursuit of King Edward:

Than cum Sir Philip the Mowbra
And to the king yauld the castell,
His cunnand has he haldyn well,
And with him tretyt sua the king
That he belevyt of his dwelling
And held him lely his fey
Quhill the last end off his lyf-day
Now will we of the lord of Douglas

Tell how that he folowit the chas.
He had to quhone in his company

But he sped him in full gret hy,
And as he throuch the Torwood fur
So met he ridand on the mur
Schyr Laurence off Abernethy
That with four scor in company
Come for till help the Inglismen
For he was Inglisman yet then,
Bot quhen he hard how that it wes
He left the Inglsi-mennys pes
And to the lord Douglas rycht that
For to be lele and tru he swar.
And or the king of Ingand was
Passyt Lythkow thai come sa ner
With all the folk that with him wer
That weill amang thaim schout thai mycht,
Bort thai thocht tham to few to fycht
With the gret rout that thai had that
For five hunder armyt thai war
Togidder sarraly raid thai
And held thaim apon bridill ay,
Thai wat governyt wittily
For it semyt ay thai war redy
For to defend tham at thar mycht
Gif thai assailyt war in fycht.

[*The Sir Philip Moubray came to yield the castle to the king, keeping his word. He and the king accorded so well that he joined the king's household and served him loyally to the end of his life. Now we tell of the Lord of Douglas, and how he followed the chase. He had very few in his company, but pursued in great haste, and, as he passed out of the Torwood he met Sir Laurence Abernethy riding on the Muir, who had come with a company of four score [eighty] to help the English, because he was then still an Englishman, but when he heard what had happened, he left the peace of the English and he swore to Douglas that he would be loyal and true. Then they both followed the chase, and, before the king of England reached as far as Linlithgow, they [Douglas's party] came near enough that they could shout at them, but they thought themselves too few to fight with the great crowd of them there, for there were five hundred men-at-arms riding in close order with their reins held short. They were well led, for it seemed that they were always ready to defend themselves with all their might if they were forced to fight.*]

Moubray, of course, had little choice but to surrender the castle to King Robert, and the ease of his acceptance into the Bruce party perhaps indicated that this was part of the price for the surrender pact in the first place. Douglas, meanwhile, was still in pursuit of Edward II, but with too small a force to engage Edward's party. As he passed out of the Torwood he encountered Sir Laurence Abernethy at the head of a party of eighty men. Abernethy quickly embraced the Bruce cause and added his force to that of Douglas. Clearly Abernethy's troops were men-at-arms. Their number was far too few to make any sort of valuable contribution to Edward's army, so presumably they were not spearmen or archers. Equally clearly, they joined the pursuit and were able to keep up with the fleeing English, some 500 men-at-arms mounted on sound, if tiring, chargers. Since Barbour has already told us that King Edward rode around the New Park to escape, we might reasonably conclude that he passed behind the main body of the Scottish army, that is on the west side of the New Park, and not between the high ground and the western end of the battlefield. In this case, Douglas may have been able to close the gap between him and his quarry by travelling through the New Park, possibly emerging in the vicinity of the Entry before heading for Linlithgow, having met – and recruited – Sir Laurence Abernethy 'riding on the muir'. Douglas did not feel his company was strong enough to force a fight, but he was determined to pursue Edward as far as possible:

> And the lord Douglas and his men,
> How that he wald nocht schaip him then
> For to fecht with thaim all planly,
> He convoyit thaim sa narrowly
> That of the henmaist ay tuk he,
> Mycht nane behin his falowis be
> A pennystane cast na he in hy
> Was dede, or tane deliverly
> That nane rescours wald till him ma
> All-thocht he luvyt him never sua.
> On this maner convoyit he
> Quhill that the king and his menye
> To Wenchburg all cummyn ar.
>
> Than lychtit all that thai war
> To bayt that hors that wer wery,

And Douglas and his cumpnay
Baytit alsua besid thaim ner.
Thai war sa fele withoutyn wer
And in armys sa clenely dycht
And sua arayit for to fycht,
And he sa quhone and but supleyng
That he wald nocht in plane fechting
Assale thaim, bot ay raid thaim by
Waytand hys point ay ythandly.
A litill quhill thai baytyt thar
And he was alwayis by thaim ner,
He leyt thaim nocht hhaff sic layser
As any water for to ma,
And giff ony stad war sa
That he behind left ony space
Seysyt alsone in hand he was.
Thai convoyit thaim on sic a wis
Quhill thai the king and his rout is
Cummyn to the castell of Dunbar
Quhar he and sum of his menye war
Resavyt rycht weill, for yete than
The Erle Patrik was Inglisman.

[*The lord Douglas and his men could not attack them openly, but he shadowed them so closely that he could take any who fell behind, so a man could not even be a stone's throw from his companions but he would be killed or taken prisoner instantly, for none could help him, however beloved he might be. In this fashion, he [Douglas] pursued the king and his party as far as Winchburgh. Then they [the English] all dismounted to rest their horses, which were very weary, and Douglas and his company rested nearby. They were so strong in number, so well equipped and so well arrayed for battle, and he so few and without hope of reinforcements, that he could not attack them, but rode close to them, seeking a favourable opportunity. They rested there for a short while, then mounted and went on their way, but he was always close to them. He would not let them so much as halt to pass water, and if any were left behind, even a short distance, he was quickly taken prisoner. They accompanied them in this way until the king and his party came to the castle of Dunbar, where he and some of his party were made very welcome, for at that time Earl Patrick was an Englishman.*]

From the very outset of the pursuit of King Edward Barbour makes a point of the weakness of Douglas's force and the strength of the English; allegedly little more than 100 Scots – including Abernethy's men – against 500 English. Given that the pursuit was so aggressive, one might well ask why the English did not turn and fight. First and foremost, there was the presence of King Edward. His company were, doubtless, well armed and brave, but if there was an engagement, anything might occur – the king might even be killed or captured, in which case the political situation would have plunged from bad to dreadful. The king would have to be ransomed at enormous financial and diplomatic cost; anything that remained of his royal prestige in the wake of the defeat at Bannockburn would be lost. There is also the question of fitness to fight. The men around King Edward had already witnessed or taken part in three separated defeats in less than twenty-four hours, been effectively refused entry to Stirling Castle, and then performed a long retreat under close pressure from the enemy, losing many comrades along the way as horses became exhausted. Their morale cannot have been in good condition, either physically or mentally, for combat. The two forces halted briefly at Winchburgh to let their horses rest before pressing on toward Dunbar. Major fortress as it was, Dunbar Castle could not possibly accommodate all of Edward's party, so the king, and a few of his party, entered the castle, where they were well received by Earl Patrick, an English adherent since the invasion of 1296 and a crucial prop to the occupation government in Roxburghshire, Berwickshire and East Lothian. As Barbour tells us, 'The Erle Patrik was Inglisman'.

The arrival of King Edward's party put Patrick in a difficult position. The occupation government had been failing for years, but the location of Patrick's estates – regardless of his political preferences – meant that he could not afford to entertain any sort of rapprochement with the Bruce party without exposing his property to retaliation from English forces, particularly the garrison of Berwick. It might seem that he now had a golden opportunity to put King Robert in his debt forever, since he could take King Edward prisoner, however this may not have been a practical proposition. Even if he entered the castle with just a handful of his closest associates, Edward would still probably have a couple of dozen men-at-arms at his back. It would be remarkable if the Earl had more than a modest handful of men able to fight at all. Additionally, the Earl had to take a long view of the situation. Robert was proving capable of defeating the English on the battlefield and might well prove capable of achieving the diplomatic and political victories he needed to put his kingship beyond doubt, but what of his successor? English kings were plainly capable of invading and destroying the southern counties of Scotland, even if the conquest of the whole nation was beyond them. At some point in the future, Earl Patrick – or his successors – might well have to find a way into the 'peace' of another English king, who might not be disposed to accept the allegiance of a man who had handed Edward II to the Scots.

Fordoun

The most remarkable aspect of Fordoun's account of Bannockburn is that he has so little to say about it. The actual process of the campaign and the engagements themselves receive virtually no attention whatsoever, but the importance of divine intervention, or, more significantly perhaps, the trust that King Robert reposed in God, form the basis of Fordoun's few words on the topic. Beyond telling us that Edward II brought a large army of horse and foot to the battle and that the Earl of Gloucester and many other English nobles were killed or taken prisoner, Fordoun tells us that victory fell to the Scots through Robert's reliance on God rather than numbers. He then claims – quite wrongly, as he himself must have been all too aware – that from Bannockburn onwards the Scots enjoyed continual victories over the English and that the country 'overflowed with boundless wealth'. In fairness, there was probably some truth in this in the sense that a good number of Scots certainly benefited from the spoils of war on a number of levels. The ransacking of the English baggage train and the ransoms of English nobles certainly brought considerable wealth to some, and the campaigns that King Robert mounted in the northern counties of England over the next decade doubtless improved the financial status of a good many more.

Even so, Fordoun must have been aware of the military and economic blows suffered by the Scots in the 1330s and 1340s, indeed Fordoun's chronicle – though brief on any topic – is an important source for the wars of David II and Edward III. Fordoun's brevity on the subject of Bannockburn is something of a curiosity. Though much less partisan in his accounts than Bower, Fordoun's chronicle does have a rather nationalistic theme and one might have expected that such a great victory might have brought more from Fordoun's pen than assertions about the importance of divine endorsement to the Bruce cause. He might have avoided giving an account of the fighting for any one of a number of reasons. As a cleric, he may have felt that his lack of specialist knowledge and experience prevented him from giving a useful description of the action, though that does not seem to have been an issue to most ecclesiastical chroniclers. He may have considered that the story of the fighting had been so thoroughly taken to heart by the Scots that there was no value in going over it again. Alternatively, he may have been of the opinion that the nature of the armies, the terrain and the tactics were simply not as important as the decision of God to award victory to King Robert:

> Edward II, king of England, hearing of these Glorious doings of King Robert's and seeing the countless losses and endless evils brought upon him and his by that king, gathered together in revenge for the foregoing, a very strong army, both of well-armed horsemen and of foot – crossbowmen and archers, well-skilled in war-craft. At the head of this body of men, and trusting in the glory of man's might, he entered Scotland in hostile wise; and laying it waste on every side, he got as far as Bannockburn. But King Robert, putting his trust, not in a host of people but in the Lord God, came, with a few men against the aforesaid king of England, on the Blessed John the Baptist's day, in the year 1314, and fought against him, and put him and his to flight, through the help Him to whom it belongeth to give the victory. There the Earl of Gloucester and a great many other nobles were killed; a great many were drowned in the waters or slaughtered in the pitfalls; a great many, of divers ranks, were cut off by divers kinds of deaths; and many – a great many – nobles were taken, for whose ransom not only were the queen and other Scottish prisoners released from their dungeons, but even the Scots themselves were, all and sundry, enriched very much. Among these was also taken John of Brittany, for whom the Queen and Robert, bishop of Glasgow, were exchanged. From that day forward moreover, the whole land of Scotland not only always rejoiced in victory over the English, but also overflowed with boundless wealth.

The only military element to be considered here is Fordoun's assertion that many English soldiers were 'slaughtered in the pitfalls'. To what extent Fordoun relied on the work of other writers or on contemporary popular belief is open to question, but clearly he thought that 'pitfalls' were an important aspect of the battle; important enough to be the only tactical application that is mentioned at all in Fordoun's account. We should not, however, automatically accept that the pitfalls – assuming that these should be equated with the 'pots' of Barbour's epic – had a significant impact on any part of the action. Fordoun may mention them for no better reason than that they were not a normal part of the tradition of Scottish war. The other elements – spearmen, archers and men-at-arms – may not have struck Fordoun as being worthy of any description since these would all have been perfectly familiar to his readership. He may mention the pitfalls simply because he was aware that they had been dug, though the term itself surely suggests sizeable traps for man and horse rather than modest holes in the ground, as Barbour describes them. Naturally, the digging of traps does not guarantee that anyone will fall into them; there is no evidence to indicate that pots or pitfalls had any effect whatsoever on the main battle.

Bower's *Scotichronicon*

Bower was more passionately nationalistic than the author of Fordoun's chronicle, but he, too, had remarkably little to say about the course of the battle, though he was certainly aware of Barbour's account, referring to 'The book which the archdeacon of Aberdeen composed in the mother tongue.' He may have felt that a full description of the fighting was not necessary since Barbour had already produced one, but he was, in any case, more interested in the trust that the Scots put in the power of God's intervention. Bower opens his account with a list of the countries from which Edward drew support:

> ... from every part of the kingdoms of England, Scotland, France and Germany, Wales and Ireland, Flanders and Gascony, Boulogne and Brittany, Gueldres and Bohemia, Holland, Zeeland and Brabant.

He then returns to the value of faith and divine intervention:

> Thus the King of England trusted in his military power; King Robert trusted only in the help of God alone. The first took his stand with excessive confidence: the other remained suitably fearful.

Bower's chronicle includes a poem by the Abbot of Arbroath, Bernard de Linton, one of King Robert's most trusted advisors and probably the man who framed much of the king's diplomatic correspondence, including the Declaration of Arbroath. Sadly the abbot's lines offer nothing much beyond assertions of English arrogance and overconfidence, and the worthiness of the Scots for putting their trust in God, but does not forget Bruce propaganda needs:

May the assembly of the Scots flourish, abounding in valour;
And may the king rejoice, turning tears to joy,
Now that the English have been cast down in all directions and routed
And made prisoner
'May the king be praised for his goodness!'

Inasmuch as Bower discussed the fighting at all, there must be some suspicion that Bower is merely rehearsing his knowledge of the equipment kit needed for war in his own day, not that of King Robert. Accordingly he ascribes weapons to the English that had yet to be invented; his account of Edward's army included:

> … petraries and mattocks, trebuchets and mangonels, ladders and engines, pavilions and awnings, slings and cannons, and other engines of war.

There is no evidence to suggest that Edward brought a siege train at all. He did not expect to have to attack Stirling or Bothwell and there were very few other castles of any significance that were still intact. Whatever else Edward may have brought to the battlefield he most certainly did not bring cannons of any description:

> After the king of Scotland had had them [the English army] reconnoitred, he caused pits to be made with sharp stakes fixed in them and covered over so that they could not be noticed: and he advised his men to make confession and hear masses devoutly, and that they should all take communion in the sacrament of the body of Christ, and to put their trust in God alone.

The influence of Barbour is clear; Robert makes preparations to the field, but his chief ally in the fight is to be God. Recognition of the importance of divine intervention is not limited to the Scots. In an episode lifted from Barbour's account, Bower describes the confidence of the English but shows the wisdom of an older head among their ranks:

> [The English] began to shout 'Look! All those Scots have surrendered to us with trembling hearts.' An older English knight, Ingram de Umfraville, formed a sounder understanding and replied to them saying 'You are right, that they are surrendering, but to God, not to you.'

The battle rages, but Bower has nothing of significance to add to Barbour's depiction of the fighting, though he his keen to show the reader the extent to which God favoured the Scots:

> On the English side two hundred knights were killed, besides the Earl of Gloucester and innumerable others. On the Scottish side two knights fell, namely William de Vieuxpont and Walter de Ross.

Bower does, however, cite Friar Baston's poem. Baston asserts the English 'spend the night in braggartry and revelry with Bacchus', and clearly believes that arrogance and failure of religious observation lay at the heart of the defeat, but once again there is little information about the battle. Knights mount steeds, and esquires leap up 'to put the bridle ready to hand', but we are offered little about the deployment for battle or the progress of the fighting:

> The Scottish king ranges and arranges deadly battle-lines.
> Cavalry and foot-soldiers are there: what a marvellous assemblage.

Baston's words here could be seen as a contradiction of the chronicle accounts in which all of the Scots fight on foot. Clearly there is evidence that some of the Scottish army served on horseback, but Baston's line is probably more a matter of the needs of the poem than an attempt to show the nature of the army.

Baston was at least present and it would be unreasonable to assume that he somehow managed to avoid seeing the battle unfold; quite the reverse. A good deal of the poem is focused on the deeds and reputations of the aristocracy and the deaths of famous men-at-arms, notably the fall of Sir Giles d'Argentan: 'I scarce retained my senses when I saw you drop.'

The *Pluscarden Chronicle*

Compiled in 1461, the relevant material in the *Pluscarden Chronicle* is largely a condensed amalgam of Bower and Fordoun, and, like them, puts much more emphasis on the hand of God than the approach to, and conduct of, battle:

> Edward, the new King of England, burning with rage on seeing the countless evils brought upon him and his by King Robert, and brooding over his glorious deeds and achievements, roused himself to avenge them; and having got his

whole forces together, hastened to levy war afresh against Scotland. He collected troops from all sides, from England, Wales, Ireland, Cornwall, Normandy, Picardy, Flanders, Almayne, Gascony, Gueldres, Brabant and Holland, and from amongst the rest of those who favoured his cause, and, together with his Anglicised Scots, effected a hostile entrance into the country, a brave show, with every appliance of settling in the country forever, and tilling it with his husbandmen.

Pluscarden puts the English army at 300,000 men-at-arms, with all the 'unarmed followers and traders and husbandmen and settlers on foot'. Obviously this is a huge exaggeration, even over Barbour's claims. Once again the failure to trust in God is presented as the most important factor in the defeat of the English, while simple faith is the most important factor in the Scottish victory:

Accordingly, surrounded by this proud host and trusting in the glory of man's might, he got as far as a place called Bannockburn and pitched his tents. But trusting in the lord and making God his strength and asking the blessed apostle Andrew and Saint John the Baptist to help him to deliver the wretched people of Scotland from undue bondage, King Robert, with an army small in comparison with the multitude of the said King of England, fought a deadly battle with him and, by the help of the Most High, to whom it belongeth to give the victory, and in whose hands are all the ends of the Earth, put him to flight with all his pomp and countless forces. Here the Earl of Gloucester and many nobles of England fell slain; some were killed in the pitfalls which the Scots had made; some again, thinking to save themselves, were drowned in the Firth of Forth; some lost their lives in the confusion of the crowd while escaping, some fled, some were taken, some were slaughtered, overtaken by sundry kinds of death, and were destroyed without number with the edge of the sword.

Among these was captured John of Brittany, for whom the captured Queen of Scotland was exchanged, for it would have been absurd to hear of a Queen being a prisoner. For him too was exchanged the Bishop of Glasgow, a venerable man of great age, who had been in like manner kept in prison by the tyrant. Note that this war began between Edward Bruce, the King's brother, and Philip Mowbray, commander at Stirling on behalf of the King of England, who the said Edward besieged, the former promising that, if that castle were not relieved by the King of England in one year's time from then, he would without further delay surrender it into his hand for behoof of the King of Scotland. But the King rebuked his brother for this, telling him that he had behaved most foolishly in having trysted with that most powerful King of England to fight at the aforesaid term of a year and a day.

The *Pluscarden* writer repeats what is surely Barbour's tale of a year's notice being allowed for the relief of Stirling Castle, and likewise King Robert's displeasure at Edward Bruce's contract with Sir Philip Moubray. However, Edward Bruce was a very experienced soldier and his 'rash' temperament may well be nothing more than a device used by Barbour to enhance the measured wisdom of the King. There is nothing in English record or narrative evidence to indicate that a pact of one year's duration had been made, though Moubray would surely have been dismissed for such dealings. The Bruce–Moubray compact strongly suggests that the strong garrison at Linlithgow pele had proved incapable of preventing the Scots from laying siege to Stirling, but the pele was still operational in August 1313. It is possible that the complement of men-at-arms at Linlithgow had dwindled to the extent that they were incapable of mounting operations against the Scots at all.

5

Brave Companies:
The Armies of the English
and the Scots

The Scottish and English men-at-arms, spearmen and archers who served their kings in the thirteenth and fourteenth centuries were largely indistinguishable from one another. Field armies raised in either country consisted of the same troop types, though not necessarily in similar numbers or proportions. To a considerable degree this is a matter of scale rather than national capabilities. Scottish kings could not call on the numbers of men-at-arms available to the Kings of England simply because England was a very much larger state. On the other hand, although English kings could, if they chose, raise much larger numbers of infantry than their Scottish equivalents, they would struggle to keep them fed and paid for any length of time. If we are to have any understanding of medieval battle in general, and the Bannockburn action in particular, it is useful to form some idea of the strengths and weaknesses of the different arms of service – how they were recruited, trained, led, and their roles on the battlefield.

The Cavalry: Knights and Men-at-arms

The term 'man-at-arms' is one that demands explanation. Any man serving in the heavy cavalry role was a 'man-at-arms' (the 'homines ad arma' of Plantagenet muster rolls and pay records), though several other terms – vallet, socius and esquire – appear frequently in contemporary records.[1] The precise nature of the level of equipment required to serve as a man-at-arms is never really discussed in great detail by the writers of the late thirteenth and early fourteenth centuries, presumably because there was a broad – even universal – understanding of what was meant by the term. A man-at-arms would be expected to have adequate armour, sword, spear, shield and, most importantly, a horse suitable for cavalry service. Effectively this actually meant a minimum of two horses, since the loss, injury or illness of one's mount would, naturally, compromise one's ability to serve in the cavalry. There are examples of men who rose from obscurity to serve as men-at-arms, but the majority of the heavy cavalry were drawn from the nobility – the people who could afford to serve.

They were not all lords of great estates or knights of the royal household. The majority were men of rather humbler station, holding estates that consisted of a handful of farms or the brothers and sons of such men. These estates were not, as a rule, held in exchange for armed service alone, but rather for a range of services including administrative and court duties, and an obligation to provide advice and support for one's superior in political and social affairs. There might also be a cash element or an obligation to offer a token recognition of the fact that landholding was based on leases, not outright purchase. Some of the 'token' rents which appear to be trivial might actually be regarded as rentals protected against inflation. A burden of – for example – a pound of cumin[2] might be valued at 2d for the purposes of accounting, but that value need not bear any real relationship with the actual cost of a pound of cumin at a given moment in time. Whether by policy or accident, the burden of man-at-arms service falls into the category of rentals hedged against the changing value of money. A man undertaking to give forty days' knight service in exchange for land in the early twelfth century[3] would need to provide himself with suitable arms, armour and mount, undoubtedly an expensive business, but the level and quality of equipment and horseflesh required to qualify as a man-at-arms in 1300 was considerably better than the standards that had been expected a century and a half before.

To a great extent this increase in the demands placed on prospective men-at-arms was offset, or even outstripped, by the general economic improvement that Scotland – like the rest of western Europe – had experienced throughout the same period. It is even possible that economic growth had eclipsed the increasing cost of military service to such an extent that the increased burden passed unnoticed over the six or seven generations concerned.

The absence of any recorded resistance to the increasingly heavy burdens of military obligation on tenants should not, however, be interpreted as sure evidence that they were necessarily content with the situation. Very little in the way of personal writing has survived from the late Middle Ages, and only a tiny portion of that emanates from the lesser nobility, the people who would have been most seriously affected. Another major consideration is the experience of war among the Scots of the late thirteenth century. For three generations war had been virtually unknown in Scotland. There had been a handful of minor crises and a couple of rather modest expeditions to confirm the suzerainty of Alexander II and Alexander III in the West Highlands. There had even been an invasion. A Scottish army conquered the kingdom of Man in 1275[4] but there was no longer – if there ever had been – very much demand for regular active service from the political classes across the nation. It is possible, therefore, that the men who served King John in the early stages of the Wars of Independence were not, in fact, equipped to quite the standard that was expected of men-at-arms – their equipment was slightly old-fashioned and their horses of a slightly lesser quality.

Against this, we should bear in mind that the opening of hostilities in March 1296 had not been unexpected. Some proportion of the class who served as men-at-arms must surely have thought it wise to ensure that their kit was up-to-date and their horses adequate for the business of fighting. A number of men, such as Simon de Horsburgh and Richard de Siward served in Edward's army in 1296 and must surely have had suitable mounts and arms.[5] Furthermore, there had been a real risk of a general civil war between the Bruce and Balliol parties after the death of Alexander III and again after the death of Margaret, Maid of Norway. Even if many Scottish men-at-arms at Dunbar in 1296 were seriously under-equipped, it is abundantly clear that many of them were able to bring themselves up to the required standard in a very short space of time. By 1298 there were several Scots serving as men-at-arms in English garrisons such as Edinburgh, Stirling and Dundee on exactly the same basis as their colleagues from England, France and Ireland and some Scots were present in the army that defeated Wallace at Falkirk.[6] This does not appear, however, to be evidence that the Scots in question had necessarily acquired better kit very recently. The early appearances of William Wallace show him as the leader of a small band of men-at-arms, 'all well-mounted',[7] that is to say, with horses appropriate for cavalry action, not just beasts fit to transport the men from A to B. Wallace's men may have acquired suitable mounts in the recent past, but it is probably safer to assume that the men of his company were members of the gentry and minor aristocracy who had not served at all in the summer of 1296 and whose equipment and chargers were therefore still available.

In the years after Wallace's defeat at Falkirk, the Scots avoided general engagements with the armies of Edward I, but operations did not come to an end.[8] The general practice of war became one of local domination through mobile forces, rather than of confrontation between large field armies.

There were certainly actions, but they were, almost without exception, cavalry affairs, though they have not all been seen in that context by chroniclers or historians. The battle of Roslin illustrates this perfectly. Of the contemporary and near-contemporary writers, Bower and Blind Harry alone describe a vast 'all-arms' battle of manoeuvre with thousands upon thousands of men committed to the fight and a great open-field victory for the forces of King John, but these men were writing more than a century after the event. The rest of the chroniclers and all of the record material points in a very different direction.

A cavalry force was assembled at Berwick to mount an operation into Scotland. Grey tells us that the intention was to raise a Scottish siege of Linlithgow.[9] There is no suggestion in English records that Linlithgow was under threat from the Scots at all, let alone under siege, though an entry in Bain's *Calendar of Documents*,[10] does show that two men were paid considerable sums to carry out a reconnaissance to locate the Scottish army in that vicinity, which suggests that there was a perceived threat of some magnitude.

Whatever the intended target, the English force — including a contingent of Scottish men-at-arms in the following of the Earl of Dunbar — was caught by surprise by a force of Scottish men-at-arms under the Guardian, John Comyn, and were roundly defeated. There is nothing to suggest that this was an engagement of more than a few hundred men on either side, but it was an important victory for the Scots. It was good for morale at home, but it was also good for the reputation of the Scots in the diplomatic arena. This is an important point about medieval battles in general, and perhaps particularly in the relatively small-scale context of the wars between England and Scotland. The size of the engagement is not always a useful guide to the political significance of the event. The fight at Roslin has probably received more attention from historians than the battle of Culblean in November 1335, though Culblean was almost certainly a much larger action, and unquestionably more significant.[11]

The primacy of the heavy cavalry in the thinking of Robert I is clear from the early days of his campaign for kingship. It was also very nearly his undoing. In the wake of his inauguration in March 1306 he attempted to gather an army to expel the English from Scotland. It is almost axiomatic that his intention was to bring about a battle at an early opportunity and wage a conventional war of manoeuvre against Edward I. This is further taken, very often, as evidence that Robert I was immature and unrealistic, which would certainly be the case had that been his plan. It does, however, rather fly in the face of what we know of Robert's experience before 1306. His knowledge of the events of the past ten years and his own roles in both the English and Scottish military structures must have made him aware that he could not hope to raise men-at-arms in anything like the quantity that Edward could. Even so, the striking arm of Robert's small army at Methven was definitely the men-at-arms element of his force. The same applies to his adversary. An English document of the time[12] indicates that there were over 70 knights and men-at-arms, nearly 2,000 archers and 140 crossbowmen in De Valence's force, however Scottish men-at-arms from areas under English control would also have been called upon to discharge their military obligations.[13] This does not mean that Robert necessarily chose to rely exclusively on the heavy cavalry of the nobility, but that those were the men available to him. There are also social factors to be considered of course. If Robert was to make good his claim to the throne, he would need the support of the political community, and the sort of service that they could provide was chiefly that of men-at-arms. Additionally, his prestige as king would be impaired if he was not surrounded by men of substance, men with a stake in the country. In the eyes of his contemporaries Robert would have been little more than a successful brigand if he could not command the support of such men.

Equally, the Bruce cause could provide a vehicle for advancement for such men and also for men of more humble origins. If a man could acquire the relevant equipment and skills he could reasonably expect to be accepted into the *comitiva* of one or other of the greater lords. Gib Harper, an associate of Edward Bruce, Earl of Carrick, who was killed in action at Faughart, would appear to have been a man of 'low birth',[14] but he certainly served as a man-at-arms and had probably ascended the social order through military service.

Despite his close relationship with Edward Bruce, Harper does not appear to have become a knight, probably because of his social status, however we should not assume that knighthood was necessarily an impossible career ambition for men of his background, nor should we assume that men of greater status necessarily became knights at a given age or at a specific point in their career. According to Barbour (see 'sources' above), James Douglas was not knighted until the eve of Bannockburn, though he was certainly of the right class, had the right sort of experience and had even established a reputation as a paladin. It is widely assumed that Douglas was not knighted at Bannockburn, but that he was promoted to the status of banneret.[15] This may not have been the case since there are a number of factors which might have prevented him from becoming a knight at an earlier point of the war. In 1314 Douglas had yet to become a magnate; his career prospects rested on his fame as a soldier and he was not a person of any great political status. He may have felt that knighthood should be postponed to an auspicious moment and the eve of battle was a traditional juncture for making knights. Alternatively, it may have been a matter of royal policy. There is nothing to indicate that Robert had made many, if any, knights before 1314. He, too, may have been waiting for a dramatic moment.

The value of giving heavy cavalry service was not limited to development, retention or confirmation of political status. For some men the lure of adventure would probably have been sufficient motivation in itself, but for others there were the attractions of profit and of building a chivalrous reputation. As Dr MacDonald puts it,[16] 'There can be little doubt that financial gain through warfare was important to the Scottish magnate, as it was to his English and continental counterparts.' The most significant possibilities for financial gain lay in the possibility of gaining land grants or offices through successful military service or from the ransoms of prisoners. The social/military ethos of chivalry was also an important motivating factor, though not in isolation. To quote Dr MacDonald again, it was a crucial element in the 'mental world of the secular and clerical aristocracy'. Proving that nobles fought precisely because of the chivalric ethos is, however, a rather different matter.[17] Although it may have been the single most important issue for a few individuals, for most men it was only one part of a complicated set of social values, pressures and traditions.

Dr Michael Brown[18] has demonstrated that successful service and leadership in war could be a useful political career vehicle in the 1330s and 1340s. To some degree, the personal career aspect may have been less significant in 1314, when the most pressing issue was national political independence. This does not mean that the supporters of King Robert were any less ambitious than their successors, but if they – and their heirs – were to retain the gains they made under Robert, they would have to ensure that his kingship was established beyond doubt. This still applied in the early years of David II's reign. If Bruce kingship had been extinguished they would be in a very precarious position. However, once it became clear that Edward III and Edward Balliol were not capable of achieving their objectives, personal ambition came to fore. William Douglas of Lothian could afford to murder Alexander Ramsay of Dalhousie – a rival for local prominence – despite the fact that Ramsay enjoyed the support of King David. This was partly because Douglas was aware that David could not afford to lose Douglas's support, but also because Douglas was confident that the Bruce dynasty was no longer at risk of being destroyed through English intervention.

It is apparent that by 1314 the majority of the political and armigerous class of Scotland had come to see the Bruce party as the best prospect for career advancement, but this had not been the case in the early years of his kingship and he had to compete with the occupation government to gain the allegiance of such men. Initially he was at a considerable disadvantage. Men who opted to join the Bruce party in 1306 faced a very real risk of permanent forfeiture should Bruce fail to impose his rule. In addition to that risk there was also the attraction of serving in the occupation garrisons and English field armies for pay. Edward I and Edward II both faced cash-flow problems that made it difficult to ensure that wages were paid regularly and on time, but the men who served in the garrison could be reasonably confident that they would receive their money eventually.

Despite the prospect of pay and the fact that men who lived in areas under English rule were expected to discharge the military obligations attached to their properties, the occupation government often toiled to find the scale of cavalry service that was needed to counter Bruce expansion. As early as the summer of 1306 Henry Percy, Edward's lieutenant for Wigtonshire, Dumfriesshire and Ayrshire, informed James Dalilegh that he could not attract men to the king's service unless he could offer to pay them.[19]

Obviously landholders in these areas owed military service for their properties, but could not be persuaded to discharge that service – at least beyond their accustomed obligation – without compensation. Further, if they were not in receipt of pay the risks of being on campaign were substantially greater in that they would not have their horses valued for 'restauro', and would therefore not be entitled to compensation for chargers lost in action. Percy went on to order Dalilegh to pay wages to the men who were serving in his company and to make similar provisions for men-at-arms in the companies of Sir Robert Clifford and Sir John de St John. It is clear from many other documents that there was a perennial shortage of men-at-arms for both field and garrison service in Scotland, but Percy's instructions would also suggest that local men-at-arms could be found if funds were forthcoming for their wages and expenses.

There is no record material relating to the retinues of Scottish lords and magnates in the service of Robert I, but this does not imply that such material did not exist. Fortunately, there are several instances of the retinues of Scottish lords in English service and some of these records relate to specific garrisons. Sir Archibald Livingstone, for example, served as the commander of Livingstone Peel and later of Linlithgow with a retinue of ten men-at-arms, all of whom were Scots and probably tenants of Sir Archibald.[20] Others relate to field service formations. In 1306–07 a force under Sir John de St John included the retinue of Sir Roger de Kirkpatrick with five chargers and Sir John de Campbell with two, along with Dougal and Fergus McDowal.[21] Clearly knight service was not limited to what some historians have described as 'Anglo–Norman' or Feudal Scotland. We find that Sir John de Moubray was paid 200 marks for 'keeping lands between the mountains and the Orkneys' with thirty men-at-arms between August 1307 and February 1308.[22] It is, of course, possible that some portion of these men were not Scots, though in the same period (and document) we find Sir Richard Siward serving with twenty men-at-arms in Dumfriesshire and Ingram de Umfraville leading a retinue in Galloway under the command of Sir John de St John. Evidently Umfraville's force was considerable and surely included English soldiers, but it is difficult to imagine that there was not a sizeable Scottish contingent in their ranks. Umfraville was an important Scottish landholder who would have been due a substantial quantity of service from his tenants.

In October 1313 the garrison of Lochmaben had several small retinues of Scottish men-at-arms, including Sir Roger de Kirkpatrick with another knight and four 'esquires' (in this period the terms esquire, vallet and man-at-arms all meant the same thing – an armoured cavalryman with a covered or barded/barbed charger) and William Herries and Sir Thomas Torthorald with one esquire each.[23] It would seem most likely that the esquires who served in these retinues were the tenants of Kirkpatrick, Herries and Torthorald, however the fact that a man held land from a lord in Plantagenet allegiance is not a secure guide to his allegiance. Some men surely favoured the Bruce (or, in 1296–1304, Balliol) cause to the extent that they were willing to risk all in the expectation that they would be restored at the close of the war. Many landholders, however, were tenants and vassals of more than one superior. A man who held his more important property from a Bruce adherent, or whose chief property lay in an area of Bruce dominance, might well join the Bruce party even though he also held land in occupied territory.

The military and political significance of the armigerous class is clear from both record and narrative sources, but not all soldiers who served with horses were men-at-arms. English and Scottish armies both contained a troop-type known as 'hobelars'. The hobelar was a mounted soldier, but hobelars did not normally fight in a mounted capacity. Less heavily armoured, and less well mounted than a man-at-arms, the hobelar could not, as a rule, take a place in the cavalry force during a general engagement, but would serve as infantry in battle. However, general engagements were something of a rarity during the Wars of Independence, and the hobelar could carry out several different functions in the army. As light cavalry, they had an obvious reconnaissance role. They could generally expect to be able to take their horses into difficult terrain to evade opposing men-at-arms or to simply outrun opposing foot soldiers. They could be used to 'pad out' bodies of men-at-arms for raiding, foraging and interdiction of the enemy's reconnaissance.

By the second half of the fourteenth century the distinction between men-at-arms had become somewhat blurred, at least in the context of English garrisons. The commander of Berwick in the 1320s pointed out that it was unfair to pay the hobelars under his command half of the rate paid to men-at-arms when there was little, if any, difference in the quality of either their mounts or their armour. By that point the hobelar had become an established part of the military structure of England, but in 1314 they were rather few and far between. In 1313, the garrison at Lochmaben included fourteen men-at-arms and sixty-five archers, but only one hobelar, presumably retained as a scout or messenger rather than a one-man unit.[24]

There is no evidence to suggest that hobelars had a mounted role at Bannockburn or in the campaign generally, though Barbour and Bower both tell us that there were many mounted English soldiers present apart from the men-at-arms. They had certainly been employed in earlier English armies. In 1296 the Earl of Ulster, Richard de Burgh (father of Robert's queen, Elizabeth), brought 266 light cavalry to Scotland and supplied 391 for the campaign of 1301.[25]

There is a widely held belief that Scottish men-at-arms were substantially less well equipped and less well mounted than those of England or France, however contemporary material would indicate that there was no real disparity in overall effectiveness. Beyond the acquisition of a decent hauberk, helmet, shield and so forth, greater expenditure on armour gave only a marginal benefit to the wearer, but the investment was well worthwhile if that margin was potentially life-saving. The money invested in horseflesh varied enormously, but for practical purposes the performance parameters of a mount that cost £5 – which seems to have been the minimum acceptable value for the charger of a man-at-arms – was not that much inferior to a very expensive destrier. The additional benefit of a costly horse made more of a difference to the rider than to his opponent and was probably more a question of stamina and prestige than of battlefield effectiveness. From the point of view of the target there would have been very little difference between an adversary with a £5 horse and one with a £50 horse.

At least one writer has stated categorically that Scottish 'knights' rode lighter horses that could carry the same weight as destriers, but could not achieve the same speed, and that 'the reduction in speed meant that they did not ride with couched lances'. In the total absence of any medieval chronicle evidence or modern analysis to support this contention, and more particularly, the fact that the pay rolls and horse valuations of the occupation governments of Edward I, II and III make no distinction whatsoever between Scottish and English knights and men-at-arms, would suggest that this is purely an invention of Victorian and later historians.

This does not mean that Scottish armies, chiefly, if not exclusively, those operating in England, did not contain a large proportion of men who served with light horses, but it is important to bear in mind the distinction between cavalry and mounted infantry. The rank and file of the armies led by Douglas and Randolph into Northumberland, Cumberland, Westmorland, Yorkshire and Lancashire did indeed travel on 'hobins', but the wealthier strata of Scottish society, the earls, barons, knights and men-at-arms, were mounted and armed to much the same standard as the English or French nobility. The practice of ensuring that the entire force was mounted was a matter of strategic mobility, not of tactical practice. The men might ride to battle, but they dismounted to go into action. The battle of Myton is a case in point. Douglas and Randolph's men moved across the country on horseback, but when the opportunity arose to join battle, they dismounted and – according to the *Lanercost Chronicle*:

… came together in one schiltrom, and having done so, all together, they gave a mighty shout, terrifying the English, who, when they heard it, at once turned to flight.

The Templars

Over recent years a good deal has been written about the intervention of the Templars at Bannockburn. Immediately after the suppression of the order in France, a Templar fleet disappeared from La Rochelle and shortly thereafter it turned up in Argyll, where they were offered sanctuary by Robert I, repaying his generosity by throwing themselves into the fight at a crucial juncture. There are several problems with this story. Naturally, the complete absence of any supporting contemporary material whatsoever is an issue. The tale seems to have originated in Paris at the beginning of the eighteenth century, but did not become popular until the later years of the twentieth century when several pseudo-historians incorporated it into conspiracy-theory novels. Many of these works included assertions about the connection between the Templars and Roslin Chapel, a collegiate church founded in the middle of the fifteenth century, more than 100 years after the Templar order had been dissolved in Scotland.

Realistically, there is not the slightest speck of evidence to suggest that King Robert would have had any interest whatsoever in offering sanctuary to the Templars. The Templars were suppressed at the instigation of the King of France, Philip the Fair, and given that French recognition of his kingship was an important, even crucial, aspect of his foreign policy, it is quite unimaginable that Robert would have risked giving offence to King Philip for the sake of gaining the services of a handful of men-at-arms. Similarly, it is most unlikely that Robert would have chosen to do anything that might further complicate his relationship with the papacy. Although King Philip had been the prime instigator in suppressing the Templars, he could not have done so without the acquiescence of the Pope. In 1314 Robert had been an excommunicate for some time, and was eager, even desperate, to be readmitted to the church – an act that could not be brought about without papal sanction.

By the time of Bannockburn, the Templars had long lost their military *raison d'etre*. The last toe-hold of the Crusader kingdoms had been lost in 1291, and the Templars had become little more than an international land conglomerate. Far from being 'battle-hardened veterans' the Templars had largely become 'conference hardened property dealers'. It is of course quite possible that men who had, at one time, been Templars did serve on either side at Bannockburn, but there is nothing to suggest that there was any such thing as a formed body of Templars anywhere in 1314, let alone in Scotland. It is true that there were a great many Templar properties in Scotland, but we should not equate that with any great number of actual knights; most of these properties probably never saw a Templar from one year to the next. The granting of lands to the order did not signify that Templars took up residence in those locations, merely that the rents and other incomes generated passed to the order, ostensibly for the support of their operations in the Holy Land and elsewhere.

The imagined role of the Templars at Bannockburn has been fiercely defended by enthusiasts, however it is notable that not one of the many talented scholars who have studied the Wars of Independence in great detail – Professors Barrow, Nicholson, Duncan, Prestwich and Doctors Watson, M. Brown, Barrell, Ayton and King and many others – has made any reference to the intervention of the Templars. Various writers – particularly on websites – have claimed that the story is supported by contemporary material, though none, as yet, have actually produced any references to medieval record or narrative evidence, presumably because it does not exist. Absence of evidence is not the same thing as evidence of absence, but it is difficult to see where the rationale for Templar involvement comes from given that there is no mention of their role in any of the contemporary accounts.

The Infantry

Robert's return to the Scottish mainland in 1307 marked a change in his approach to warfare. Before 1306 his career as a soldier had been passed in a traditional 'knightly' environment, but for the first year and more of his campaign to impose his kingship he relied heavily on men recruited from the western seaboard and the Isles.

Securing the northeast gave him control of areas that could provide him with men-at-arms to complement his Hebridean infantry, and the capture of Inverness and Aberdeen gave him access to the European market. This was not simply a matter of access to arms and armour, but also of acquiring the means of exporting the most important Scottish cash crop, wool. In 1309–10 his campaigns were focused on extending his area of control within Scotland, but by 1311–12 he had begun to mount extensive raiding operations into the north of England. These had two useful aspects. The ability of northern English counties to make war against the Scots was severely compromised, but, more importantly, they provided Robert with very significant sums of money and allowed him to keep substantial forces under arms for rather longer than the traditional forty days of service.

It is not clear that West Highland troops continued to be the mainstay of Robert's armies after 1309–10. As Robert extended his rule into Tayside, Perthshire and Fife he was able to gather troops and income from some of the more densely populated and prosperous parts of the country. In practice, the Highland troops of Robert's early campaigns probably only comprised a few hundred men at any one time and could therefore be replaced relatively easily once he had established his rule north of the Rivers Forth and Clyde.

There is no specific record of Highland men serving in large numbers at Bannockburn, though equally, there is no reason to assume that they did not. Only Barbour offers any information about the geographical origins of Robert's army, and then only of the king's formation. Robert's immediate command consisted of men from Carrick, Argyll, Kintyre and a contingent of men from the Isles whose lord was Angus Og, though Barbour does not actually say that Angus was present himself. Professor Duncan[26] has pointed out that this is surely an anomaly, since the Earl of Carrick was not the King, but his brother Edward. The balance of the army consisted of men from the 'plane land' or Lowlands.[27] This virtual exclusion of Highland troops may be a reflection of Barbour's personal outlook – as a lowland man himself he may have had some prejudice against Highland people. Alternatively the army may have been drawn chiefly from those areas with most to lose from an invasion. However successful he might be in battle, Edward II was unlikely to be able to carry his campaign into the far north and west of Scotland in the near future.

Although English and Scottish troop-types were more or less interchangeable, an exception might be made for the followings of Angus Og MacDonald and the other West Highland lords who served in the Bruce cause. They certainly differed from their comrades and their enemy in language and, probably, dress, but there is no suggestion in any of the contemporary accounts that they were different to the close combat infantry of either the Scottish or English armies, or indeed those of any other west European country in terms of application. In the context of a field engagement, they were spearmen first and foremost and therefore were as much bound by the practical realities of spear tactics as anyone else. Such evidence as has survived of the military community of the medieval West Highlands – the Kilmartin stones for example – clearly indicates that the prevailing military fashions of the late thirteenth-century Argyll were not radically different from those of the rest of Europe. They depict men wearing chainmail and fabric armour bearing the same style of swords that we find in the art and archaeology of France, Belgium and England.

Where West Highland lords differed from their counterparts elsewhere in Scotland was in the obligation to provide military service at sea, or at least on water. For obvious geographical reasons the communities of the West Highlands were, inevitably, less focused on the horse than those of eastern Scotland. A severe limitation of pastureland made horse ownership more expensive and the shortage of good land routes meant that many journeys could be made more easily and more quickly by water. This should not be taken as an indication that the lords of the west coast were not capable of fighting on horseback, but rather that cavalry service was not a normal part of the lives of most of their tenants. It is unlikely, for example, that a man as prominent as Angus Og would not have learned the skills of mounted combat, and the same would apply to the men who would have formed his immediate military entourage. But the overwhelming majority of the men available to highland lords served as infantry and as crew for birlinns, the galleys that formed a mainstay of warfare on the western seaboard, and the Isles. Nusbacher's description of northern lords as the 'chiefs of highland tribes'[28] is somewhat patronising and misleading. They were the lords of a highly developed society.

We should not expect that there was very much operational distinction to be drawn between Highland and Lowland troops. According to their means, men would equip themselves with spear, sword, armour and helmet and fight in the same manner wherever they came from. The belief that Highland men armed, dressed and fought differently to their Lowland brothers is not founded in narrative or record evidence, but in Gothic literature and modern nationalist romance. It would be easy to assume that Highland warfare lagged behind the times, but the first curtain wall castle in Scotland was not built in the more prosperous east, but in Argyll.[29]

Spearmen

It is a long-established maxim of medieval military history that the prime function of infantry in battle was to act as cannon-fodder (or arrow-fodder). There are several fairly obvious drawbacks to that view. First and foremost, there is the concept of 'cannon-fodder' itself. It is a concept widely understood amongst historians, journalists, novelists and the general public, but utterly unknown to military theory. There is no such thing as 'spare' soldiers in war any more than there is 'spare' money in accountancy. As a matter of common sense, it is evident that the infantry must have been seen as having a vital function or they would not have been recruited in the first place. As a general rule the major field armies of the later medieval period throughout Europe were 'infantry heavy'. This was more evident in Scottish armies than English ones, but not by a very great margin. If we accept that King Robert's army at Bannockburn was in the region of 7,000 men, of whom 500 served on horseback, we might conclude that the cavalry element of a late medieval Scottish army was likely to be no more than ten per cent of the whole force, however this would be very misleading.

It is possible that the men-at-arms who normally formed the *comitiva* of Douglas, Moray or the king's household all served under Sir Robert Keith during the main action, but it is not probable. When the king and the great lords fought on foot they surely did so in the company of their tenants and associates. There was nothing particularly innovative about men-at-arms dismounting to fight, though clearly the preferred option was to fight on horseback. Even so, the majority of King Robert's army, like that of his adversary, were most certainly infantrymen. If they were not considered a vital part of the business of battle, one has to ask why they were recruited at all. Admittedly Robert did not always have to pay his troops regular wages, but he did have to feed them, and that would have been a major burden. At the time of the battle, Robert's force – even excluding the non-combatants – would have been one of the largest concentrations of human beings in the country, larger than any town in Scotland, with the probable exception of Edinburgh.

In part, the idea that the infantry had no real battlefield function is a product of the social attitudes of chroniclers. The ethos of the day held that the most significant acts on the battlefield were those carried out by armoured cavalrymen, an element of the army largely drawn from the political community. It should be stressed that this was a literary and social convention, not an observation by the military thinkers of the day. The concentration on the martial deeds of the nobility was in part a product of the social prominence of the individuals concerned. This should come as no surprise to the celebrity-obsessed society of the twenty-first century. Our newspapers are filled with gossip relating to the actions of people who are already well known to the wider public, the misdemeanours of the obscure are of generally little or no interest compared to the crimes of the famous.

This was equally true in the Middle Ages. The defection of a minor land-holder or burgess was not considered as crucial to the processes of politics or war as that of a senior lord or prelate. Also, the chronicles of the medieval period were not written for the general public. An ecclesiastical chronicle such as *Lanercost* might be complied for the edification of the members of the monastery or abbey, but other accounts – *Scalacronica* or Barbour's *Bruce*, were written for the entertainment and education of the noble class. It would be surprising if a noble audience was as concerned with the actions of men of the lower ranks of society as they were with those of their social equals. Further, medievalists do rather tend to focus on the significance of lordship and kingship to the exclusion of other factors. This is as much a feature of political history as of social history.

As an example of this we might look to a major development in Scottish society during the fourteenth century. At the close of the reign of King John servile status, though in decline, was still commonplace. Before the end of the reign of David II it seems to have disappeared.[30] It is certainly true that servile status was falling into desuetude across Europe generally, but there is no evidence to suggest that it was declining as rapidly as seems to have been the case in Scotland. There seems to be no clear rationale for the early disappearance of serfdom in Scotland, however the fact that the last act of manumission for a Scottish serf dates from the 1360s does indicate that it was no longer part of the normal fabric of Scottish society. There are a number of factors that we might consider relevant – a degree of social dislocation engendered by the wars, or the difficulty of preaching the cause of national political liberty to men who were not personally free – but none of these issues was unique to Scotland. Other nations suffered decades, even generations of war; other nations engaged in great campaigns to achieve or recover political independence.

What is not in doubt is that members of the non-noble portion of society could and did develop political views and that those views were of interest to the senior members of the political community. In May 1307 Edward I received a report from an officer at Forfar (possibly Sir Alexander Abernethy, see above) telling him that:

> … if Robert Bruce comes over the mountains now he will find the common people more at his will than ever.

This report implies a number of things that may not be immediately apparent. First of all, Edward's officer was clearly of the opinion that his king would be interested in the climate of opinion amongst the lower orders. This in itself rather undermines the traditional view of medieval kingship. All men might be vassals of the king, but that evidently did not mean that the king assumed that all of the people necessarily shared his own political view. The report gives us some insight into the widest political issue of the day, or at least, one officer's view of how the wider population saw that same issue. Had the report come from an officer in the southwest, where the Bruce family had long-established traditions of lordship, it would be no surprise that popular opinion in that area favoured the kingship of Robert Bruce. However the report came from the northeast, an area in which the Bruce family held neither great estates nor senior office. Evidently the people of the northeast were more inclined to accept the kingship of Robert Bruce than of Edward Plantagenet. Quite why that should be the case is open to question. It may be that the Plantagenet occupation was seen – rightly or wrongly – to be intolerably harsh, or that the people of the northeast believed that they were not being governed effectively, but it is difficult to accept that simple nationalism (or xenophobia) was not a significant aspect. The relative novelty of the Plantagenet administration may also have been a factor. In Lothian or Roxburghshire, the occupation had been a reality for little more than a decade by the time Edward I received his report. There had been alarms and crises – such as William Wallace's march to Haddington in 1297, or the action at Roslin in 1303 – but the administration had not been eclipsed at any point.

This was not the case in the northeast. Edward I had marched as far north as Elgin in 1296, but for most of the period between then and the Strathord armistice of 1304, the northeast had been under the control of the Balliol party. The mere presence of Plantagenet garrisons in the castles and towns of Kincardineshire and Aberdeenshire may have been seen as provocative and burdensome regardless of whether or not they really made any difference to everyday life. The final point to make in relation to this report is that the writer tells Edward the Scots would be more 'at the will' of Robert than they had been in the past. This strongly indicates that Robert had enjoyed a deal of support in a 'past' which

A medieval highland fantasy. Great swords of this style did not come into use until long after Bannockburn and were never a common weapon compared to the spear.

can only really refer to his brief kingship in the spring and early summer of 1306, since he spent the autumn and winter of 1306–07 in hiding.

Popular support for the Bruce cause in Carrick or Annandale might reasonably be attributed to a lengthy tradition of Bruce lordship, however the Bruces had no great tradition of lordship in the northeast. Clearly the inhabitants of the lands north of the Mounth were motivated by something more than considerations of the local political arena. Whether they were moved by the cause of Robert's claims to kingship or by the cause of Scottish kingship more generally is impossible to say, but evidently they were prepared to take a stand against the administration of Edward II, indeed, given that his reign was only a year old, it is probably more realistic to see the adoption of the Bruce cause as a reaction to Edward I, not to his son. Moreover, there is little evidence to suggest that the Plantagenet administration of the early 1300s was really very much different to that which Robert I put in place, or that which had existed under Alexander III or King John, in which case we must surely question the extent to which the nature of the administration was an issue for the political community beyond the question of its nationality.

Evidently some non-noble Scots had developed a degree of political awareness that was not simply a product of support for their lord. This is an important issue, since without wide support among the common people, Robert would have toiled to recruit the troops he needed to make good his claims to the throne. His campaigns of 1307–08 – and possibly beyond – may have depended on the services of troops raised in the Hebrides, but he could not hope to recover Scotland without very much greater resources than could be provided by Angus Og and other Highland magnates. Apart from the very obvious question of manpower – how many men could be provided for and for how long – there would also be a risk of alienating the very people to whom he would have to appeal to make his kingship a reality. There is no reason to assume that the inhabitants of the south and east of Scotland would have happily accepted a Bruce dynasty imposed at the point of Highland swords any more than a Plantagenet dynasty imposed with English ones.

Interestingly, neither Edward I nor Edward II seems to have made any serious attempt to exploit the military service due to the crown from the common populace in the regions which lay in their control. One draft writ survives from March 1304[31] in which Edward instructs the sheriff of Stirling to bring all of the forces, both horse and foot, of his bailiwick, including the baronies in it, but excluding those from 'any part of the earldom of Lennox'. Although this document was not, so far as we are aware, actually issued, there are a number of elements in it that give us some indication of the nature of service obligations and, perhaps, of the limitations of English administrative power in the region as perceived by Edward and his advisors. The call for both horse and foot indicates that Edward expected the sheriff to call out those men who owed cavalry service which, broadly speaking at least, we can equate with knight service due for landholding. This was not an innovation since individual land-holders and burgesses in several counties – notably Lothian, Dumfriesshire, Roxburghshire, Berwickshire, Aberdeenshire and Lanarkshire – can be identi-fied as serving in English garrisons and field armies throughout the period 1296–1304, however Edward's call for infantry service from Stirling would seem to be the only example of its kind.

Edward's writ makes it clear that he expected the sheriff to ensure that men were conscripted from the baronial franchises as well as from other proper-ties in the county. This might be construed as an attempt to go over – or perhaps under – the heads of the barons by appealing directly to their tenants, thus gaining their service regardless of whether the barons themselves were in Plantagenet or Balliol allegiance. It is possible that, if the writ had actually been issued, it would have been more an exercise in 'testing the waters' than an attempt to swell the ranks of the army.

The writ was drafted on 20 March, less than two months after the Strathord agreement had brought hostilities to an end. One might question what Edward would actually have wanted these troops to do, given that the only current operations were the siege of Stirling Castle where the defend-ing garrison was still holding out, and the hunt for William Wallace. Clearly Edward had sufficient forces to conduct the siege, and infantry would have been of little use in tracking down Wallace's small and highly mobile band of men-at-arms. Rather than a genuine attempt to raise troops, the writ may have been more an exercise in testing whether the acceptance of his lordship stretched beyond the nobility into the wider community. The spe-cific exclusion of the earldom of Lennox from the call for men is worthy of note. On 11 March 1304 Edward sent instructions to the earls of Lennox, Strathearn and Menteith to ensure that the 'fords of Forth and country around be guarded with horse and foot' and thereafter to attend him in par-liament. Clearly the writ excluded men from the Lennox because they were already called to service under the earl, but there is a possibility that Edward was confident that existing traditional leaders would be able to demand army service from their tenants and other men over whom they enjoyed customary military authority.

Quite why the writ was never issued – and it would seem that no efforts were made to conscript infantry from any other part of the country, other than through the agency of local lordship – is open to question. It is possible that Edward came to the conclusion that the writ would be widely ignored, in which case his prestige and lordship might be badly undermined or, more prosaically, he may have decided that he had no immediate need for more troops. The latter is certainly a strong possibility, given the military situation in the spring of 1304, but it is curious that neither Edward I nor Edward II, nor indeed Edward III in the 1330s, tried to make use of the military obligations of the common people in their campaigns to impose their kingship in Scotland. Apart from the obvious advantage of swelling their own forces, conscription would have helped to starve the armies of King John and King Robert of infantry. Shortage of foot soldiers does not seem to have been much of an issue for either the Balliol or the Bruce parties, even after the disaster at Falkirk in 1298.

Regardless of exactly why Scots embraced the Bruce cause is, naturally enough, less important than the fact that they did. They did not do so immediately, nor were there a vast number of supporters. The establishment of Robert's authority took many years of active campaigning and was still some way from completion in June 1314. His power was, however, sufficiently well established to allow him to recruit a major army to meet Edward II at Stirling and the bulk of the manpower certainly consisted of men of common origin. Almost all of these men served as either spearmen or archers, but we would be wrong to assume that they were ill-equipped, impoverished peasants. There is no surviving legislation defining the military liabilities of Scottish commoners as applied in the reigns of Alexander III or John or for the earlier part of the reign of Robert I, so it is impossible to give cast-iron declarations about the extent or nature of armament they carried. On the other hand, Barbour informs us that many of the men who volunteered for Robert's army in 1314 were turned away for want of adequate arms and armour. Also, we should consider King Robert's 1318 legislation on the subject.[32] All men with lands to a value of £10 or goods to a value of £40 per annum should acquire a spear, an iron cap, armoured gloves and a 'haubergeon'. This last was presumably a thick quilted coat or jacket, stuffed with raw wool at the very least or, more probably, a short chainmail hauberk. This was exactly the sort of level of equipment commonplace among the infantry of all European countries, but was clearly beyond the reach of the poorest members of society. These people – men with goods to the value of a cow – were obliged to equip themselves with a spear or a bow and arrows. It would be reasonable to

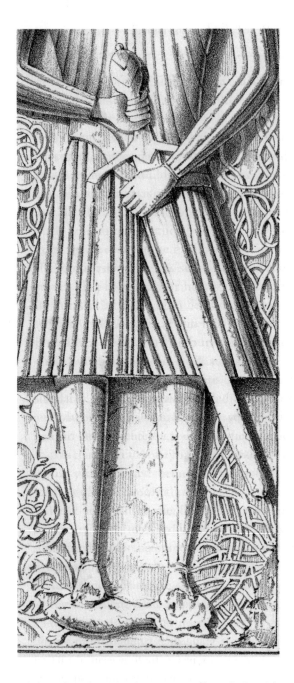

Clockwise from above: An ornate stone effigy of a Scottish nobleman from the Western Isles or West Highlands.

Scottish foot soldiers of the late thirteenth century as depicted in an English manuscript.

Scots manning a catapult at the siege of Carlisle.

conclude that the latter group were not expected to serve in war as a general rule, but were only called upon in times of great danger. Their more affluent colleagues – the £10/40 men – were not the lowest rung of the social ladder, but farm tenants, tradesmen and the majority of burgesses. The more successful burgesses were more likely to fall into the category of men-at-arms which, though it involved significant expense, could help to establish one as a member of the political community. The legislation of 1318 may have been an innovation on the part of Robert I's government, but it is equally, if not more likely, that it was more an exercise in defining responsibility more closely. It is unreasonable to assume that this prosperous class of men had, in the past, been ignored for the purposes of army service.

Scottish armies were not alone in being formed, chiefly, out of close-combat infantry. The army that Edward II led to Bannockburn probably consisted of at least 15,000 men. Of these, about 2,000 to 3,000 were men-at-arms and perhaps something in the region of 3,000 to 5,000 were archers. Rationally, therefore, we should conclude that somewhere in the region of 7,000 to 10,000 of the men who served did so as close-combat infantry. Some no doubt carried polearms and axes of different kinds, but the majority would most surely have carried spears. Victorian illustrators and writers were inclined to ascribe quite a variety of polearms to medieval Scottish and English infantry, but contemporary accounts uniformly refer to spears as the primary infantry weapon, not 'Jeddart' axes or bills.[33]

Clearly the spear was the normal weapon for close order infantry, but it was not the only weapon carried. The *Vita* author, among others, refers to the Scots as carrying sharp axes as a subsidiary arm. At least one modern author has suggested that the use of axes was forced on the Scots through their poverty; that swords were too expensive and too hard to come by, however swords were undoubtedly easily available in Scottish markets, even in the immediate aftermath of the campaign of 1296.[34] The Plea Rolls (court martial records) of Edward's 1296 army include a reference to the theft of seven swords from a shop in Perth. A more plausible explanation rests in the operational application of weapons. In a tightly packed formation of spearmen, a sword would be a difficult weapon to wield effectively when compared to the humble axe.

The spear itself was more than a stick with a sharp piece of metal at one end. The shaft had to be strong enough to withstand the shock of contact, though clearly this was not always the case. Barbour is not alone in relating the noise of breaking spears. This would be more common in combat between infantry and cavalry formations. Most horses would come to a halt before contacting the front rows of the enemy's spearmen, but some – through the forcefulness of their riders, the pressure of other animals behind or through panic – would make contact, and the weight and impetus of the horse might well cause a breaking of spears. It would also undoubtedly cause severe wounds to the horse, which in turn would cause it to shy and attempt to escape.

If there was no real difference between Scottish spearmen and English ones, it is reasonable to ask why the Scots should have enjoyed such success at Bannockburn, since the majority of their enemies were armed and armoured to the same standard. There are several tactical factors that apply to the main action – exhaustion, hunger, low morale – and the distraction and dismay caused by seeing Gloucester's cavalry worsted by the infantry of the enemy. There is, however, one factor that is more crucial than any other – training. The English army had started to assemble in early June, and therefore elements of the army may have been embodied for as much as two weeks before marching on Scotland. The army had left Wark and Berwick in June and had spent virtually all of the period between leaving Northumberland and arriving at Stirling performing major marches. There can have been very little time for personal weapon training, and even less time for training in formation.

The Scots, on the other hand, had been mustering at Stirling since about the end of May. No doubt a large proportion of them did not arrive until nearer the date of battle, but it is very much easier to incorporate unskilled people into existing workplace routines and disciplines than to 'start from scratch' which, regardless of the number of men with some experience in Edward's infantry, would have been very much the case for his army as a whole. There must surely have been English men who had served in the army in previous campaigns and some who had served in a major battle, although only Stirling Bridge and Falkirk would qualify as 'major' engagements. They might have had very good personal skills, but the formations in which they served in 1314 cannot have been drilled to any great standard on the march from Northumberland.

Edward definitely believed that his infantry would have an important role to play in the battle that he hoped would ensue from his offensive, but he probably envisaged a rather wider role as well. If the Scots could be beaten – and both Edward and his troops seem to have been confident that this could be achieved – the infantry could then be used to re-impose English administration, partly through their assignment to garrisons, but also just by the act of marching them through the countryside to impress the locals with the power of English kingship.

The issue of training with the spear is not one that has received much attention from historians; understandably, given the shortage of medieval writing
on the topic. We should not, however, assume that spear training was limited to the acts of stabbing and parrying. It would be useful to have a better
understanding of the dynamic of the unit. It is easy, for example, to assume
that when common spearmen and men-at-arms were arrayed in a single unit,
the men-at-arms formed the front rank of the formation. This is superficially
attractive in that the men-at-arms would, all in all, be better armoured than
their comrades, but there are problems with such an analysis. If men of the
noble class served alongside their tenants, we might expect that they would
be entrusted with a 'junior leader' role, accepting responsibility for maintaining the dressing of the troops in their immediate vicinity. It is more than just
a challenge to see how this role could have been discharged effectively whilst
in the front rank of the action. Further, it is difficult to see how service in the
front rank could be anything more than a death sentence if the combat lasted
any length of time. One possibility is that well-trained units could apply 'introduction' – a process of having the rear ranks pass through to the front of the
unit, thus rotating the men at the 'sharp end'. This was a normal practice for
musketeers in the seventeenth century since it enabled the unit to maintain a
steady, continuous fire. There is no obvious reason to assume that the required
standard of drill could not be achieved in the fourteenth century.

It would also be very useful to have some idea about the preferred depth of
formations. Classical observers disagreed about the value of excessively deep
formations, some arguing that only the front ranks could be brought into
combat, others arguing that the rear ranks bolstered the confidence of the men
to their front, while simultaneously discouraging flight. No doubt the same
arguments raged in the medieval period. In the absence of such information,
historians are unable to make valid observations about the depth, and therefore the frontage, of a unit of a given size. We might reasonably assume that
each man in the front rank would need about a metre to fight in, but even this
cannot be clearly demonstrated. Observations of re-enactors in training would
seem to suggest that a slightly greater allowance of frontage might allow more
men of the supporting ranks to engage.

Manoeuvring these units was far from easy. Men can achieve much better
march distances if they are arrayed in columns rather than lines, and can put
more men into the fight if they are in line rather than column, so an army on
the march faced with the prospect of battle would need to turn columns of
march into lines of battle. The simplest way to achieve this is by wheeling the

column to the left or right until the entire column has changed direction, then halting the unit and turning it to face the enemy. Unless the unit is arrayed on a flat field, this is a difficult thing to achieve without causing some degree of confusion in the ranks unless the troops have been trained to a reasonable standard of foot drill. The Scots had had several weeks to learn and perfect such evolutions, but the English had not. More crucially, whilst the English army cannot have had much time to rehearse these or any other manoeuvres at all, there is little chance that they had been rehearsed in anything like battlefield conditions; even if they had been trained, they had not been exercised. There is a very real possibility that the English army formed up on the morning of 24 June with the intention of marching toward the Scots and may therefore have been deployed in columns. If so, the advance of the Scots would not have been ideal circumstances for a change of formation. Converting from column to line would have been difficult enough, and more so when threatened, but it would also have been complicated by the fact that several other formations would have been trying to do the same thing in a very limited space, and all at the same time as Gloucester's cavalry were being repulsed by the Scots. We should not assume that the cavalry would have been prepared to collide with the infantry in their efforts to regroup for another charge, nor that the infantry would let themselves be brushed aside by their own horsemen, but the potential for accidental interference would have been very great.

If the arms and practice of Scottish and English close-combat infantry were effectively identical, can we say the same for their enlistment and terms of service? In both countries men were selected for service by agents of the crown – specific officers for the purpose in England, and sheriffs, earls and barons in Scotland. In both cases, we should expect to find a degree of dishonesty, with men bribing officials to avoid enlistment. This may have been a more difficult thing to achieve in Scotland. The population was much smaller and more widely distributed, and the liability for military service probably less common for the sort of army raised for service in England than those mustered for home defence. In an emergency, all males between the ages of sixteen and sixty might be liable for service, but the majority of such men would have been poorly armed and poorly armoured, hence Robert's insistence that only properly equipped men should be accepted into the army. Description of the Scottish army as 'simple labourers and ploughmen' or 'tribesmen and common husbandmen' cannot be taken at face value, the implication being that the Scottish army's rank and file was composed of the lowest orders of society.

While this is attractive to a certain Scottish sentimental tradition, it bears no real resemblance to the social composition of Robert's forces. The majority of the men who served were not impoverished farm labourers, but men of some substance in their immediate locality – burgesses and other town dwellers formed some part of the whole, but the bulk of Robert's spearmen and archers would have been the tenants of farms, not landless peasants. They were men who could afford the burden of purchasing arms and armour, but also men whose tenancy of a property obliged them to give military service at the behest of their landlord or sheriff.

Archers

The adoption of the longbow as a crucial and integral part of English military practice had yet to occur in 1314. It is certainly true that English armies had included archers since time immemorial, but in the past there had been many crossbowmen, and the archers were still considered more an ancillary to the spearmen and the cavalry than a combat group in their own right.

The first battle in which the bow played an important part in the defeat of a Scottish army was Falkirk in 1298. Edward I managed to steal a march on the Scottish army, forcing Wallace to accept a defensive battle. Initially the fighting favoured the Scots, who were able to hold their own against Edward's knights and men-at-arms. Once it had become apparent that the English cavalry were not capable of bursting through the ranks of Wallace's spearmen, the archers were deployed to disrupt the schiltroms until they had been sufficiently disrupted to allow the men-at-arms to penetrate their formations. There was little change, if any, in the status of the archers over the next quarter of a century, though archers were recruited for service in Plantagenet garrisons in Scotland. Examination of muster rolls and pay-records shows that a significant portion of these archers were in fact Scots, indeed it seems much more likely than not that the entire garrison of Livingston Peel in the early 1300s comprised Scotsmen.[35] Since the military activity of the Plantagenet garrisons was largely confined to raids and patrols by the men-at-arms, and since none of the bowmen were either described or paid as 'mounted' archers, it is surely the case that the chief role of these men was the defence of the castle, peel or town in which they were stationed.

In addition to the widely held notion that Scottish archers employed a short bow, there is a common belief that Scottish archers were recruited almost exclusively from the Forest of Ettrick. Quite why this belief has acquired such currency is hard to say, though the efforts of romantic novelists may have had a considerable influence. In practice, Robert I, and very possibly his predecessors, enlisted archers from wherever they might be found. Professor Duncan[36] suggests that Robert I may have issued charters which would have provided him with at least 100 archers, and possibly many more. Of all the charters that demand archer service, the heaviest burden is that of Kilsyth, which required thirty archers from the property holder. King Robert seems to have valued archery highly in that he chose to convert several military tenures from knight service to archer service obligations.[37] As Professor Barrow has pointed out,[38] Robert did not ignore knight service; it was still a crucial component of the Scottish military system. He may, however, have been prevented form extending the conversion of knight service to archers by the conservative nature of medieval society. Most, if not all, of the conversions applied to properties whose characteristics were being changed in other ways – generally by division into two or more distinct entities, suggesting that the King found it difficult to change the existing burdens on properties that were re-granted as a single fief.

A conspicuous absence from the Scottish military scene is the crossbowman. Professor Duncan has identified one charter that may demand the service of a crossbowman,[39] but even this is not certain. This does not mean that Scottish kings and lords were unaware of the power of the crossbow, or that crossbows could not be purchased or constructed locally. The accounts of Scottish castles in the reign of Alexander III are not sufficiently detailed to allow a viable analysis of the weapons available to the minute garrisons they housed, but it would be unreasonable to assume that crossbows were not available. Crossbows were certainly in use in Plantagenet garrisons and Edward I would appear to have hired a company of mounted crossbowmen for his campaign in 1298.[40] The absence of such men in later English armies may be an indication that they were too expensive or that they were not seen as having fulfilled a useful role, though it is also possible that crossbowmen were recruited for field service in the armies of Edward I and Edward II, but that they were not recorded as specific units.

Another weapon that is seemingly absent from the Scottish medieval arsenal is the sling, though a number of authors have chosen to include slingers in their accounts of the battle of Bannockburn.[41] There is, however, no mention of slingers in any of the contemporary narrative or record material save in a recitation of equipment (including cannon) ascribed to the English army in

Bower's *Scotichronicon*. It would be rash, however, to assume that nobody, on either side, used a sling. A staff sling is a remarkably powerful weapon, easily capable of projecting a two-ounce stone over a distance of 200 yards and more at the sort of velocity that could easily inflict a major wound.

We might give some thought to the reasons behind the apparent lack of interest in archery in Scotland when compared with England, however it is easy to conflate rather different situations. The armies of Edward III generally included large numbers of archers compared to those of Edward I and Edward II. This would seem to have been the result of a deliberate policy of fostering archery in general and of preference recruiting, that is to say that recruiters in the middle of the fourteenth century were under more pressure to recruit archers than other types of soldier.

This does not mean that the shires of medieval England were filled with budding expert bowmen waiting to be enlisted, but rather that a larger proportion of men were issued with bows and arrows. The act of providing a man with archery equipment does not, of itself, produce an expert archer, but that may not have been as significant as one might at first expect. The power of the bow as a battlefield weapon – and the same is true of the spear – rested on the deployment of large numbers. If the body of archers was sufficiently large and could be persuaded that the safest course of action in battle was to confront the enemy with steady shooting rather than to take flight, heavy casualties could be inflicted, even if the quality of the shooting was poor.

The efficacy of concerted archery would be demonstrated at the battles of Dupplin Muir, Halidon Hill, Crécy and Poitiers in the 1330s and 1340s, but the power of the bow had not yet been demonstrated in 1314. In fact, the archers did not even have an accustomed line-of-battle role in the English army, since there was not yet a 'typical' or 'traditional' English infantry policy. The value of archery was not in doubt. Edward I was clearly well aware of the power of the infantry in general and the archers in particular; he did not recruit infantrymen by the thousand without good reason. However he did not formulate a general plan of action for their deployment, but instead committed them to the fight as and when required.

It is important to remember that even in the great longbow victories, archers were only ever part of an army destined for general engagements. Edward I and his contemporaries were well aware of the concept of 'combined arms' as the route to victory. Even when deployed in strength, the archers were still very vulnerable to attack unless well supported by men-at-arms and spearmen.

If they could not be deployed in good time they could be charged down by even a relatively modest force of men-at-arms – as happened at Bannockburn – but they were also vulnerable to the weather. Rain would be an obvious problem; indeed, at the battle of Agincourt, English archers unstrung their bows so that they could protect their strings from a shower of rain, but even a slight breeze – whether tailwind, crosswind or headwind – would compromise the value of archery severely by reducing accuracy and/or velocity. If the archers were deployed in sufficiently large numbers, impeding the accuracy of their shooting might not be a matter of great significance, but any reduction in velocity would have dire implications for the effectiveness of the force. Given the relatively low weight of an arrow compared to its surface area, any amount of headwind would reduce the impetus of the projectile considerably, and therefore its effectiveness against armoured men.

Articulation

Little or nothing is known about the nature of practical articulation in the Scottish armies of the fourteenth century, but we can make some observations about the administrative structure of the English infantry. Under Edward I – if not before – there was a system of major and minor constituent units. The lowest level of articulation was based on junior leaders described variously as vintenars – a title derived from the French word *vingt* – corporals and petty officers. Each of these officers was responsible for a body of twenty men. To what extent this was a tactical unit and to what extent an administrative unit is unknown, but there were undoubtedly very few occasions where a twenty-man unit was deployed as a discrete formation on the battlefield. Certainly, none have been mentioned in chronicle or record sources. The next level of command rested with the centenars who presumably had charge of five vintenars. The centenars came under the authority of the millenars who must have been men with responsibility for ten of the companies led by the centenars. These units were certainly entrusted with a degree of operational responsibility. The Plea Rolls of Edward I's army of 1296[42] include a reference to an officer, Richard Tailleur, being fined for failing to ensure that his company performed sentry duty when it was their turn to do so, and so there was clearly an operational function. Whether this was the case on the battlefield is another matter, though it would seem peculiar if Edward had failed to make use of an existing tool of articulation. Even the relatively substantial formations of the millenars were not deployed as discrete units on the battlefield, but were brigaded to form larger units as required. It is not certain that these larger units necessarily consisted of the same formations throughout a campaign, though the advantages of maintaining an order having a consistent chain of command would surely have been obvious to the commanders of armies given that armies were, as a general rule, divided into major divisions for tactical purposes.

The spear-armed element in each army must have functioned in broadly similar ways, since the behaviour of such units in the field was largely dictated by the nature of their equipment. One issue that might be construed as a radical difference in the approach to battle between the English and Scottish infantry is the question of the schiltrom. In the popular imagination, a schiltrom was a circular formation of spearmen, arrayed with their spears pointing outwards, thus providing an all-round defence against cavalry. Modern descriptions and depictions of the battle of Bannockburn are replete with such formations. There are, however, only two examples of the Scots adopting circular schiltroms. The first was at the battle of Falkirk, where Wallace's four large formations stood in circles to receive – and initially repulse – Edward I's cavalry. The second occurred on the first day of Bannockburn, when the Earl of Moray's force adopted a circular, or perhaps oval, formation against Clifford and Beaumont's division of the English cavalry with rather more success. Other than these two examples, the Scots seem to have invariably deployed for battle in linear formations.

The problem of the circular formation – primarily lack of mobility and a reduction in the number of men who could be brought into combat without compromising the integrity of the circle – were not significant when standing against cavalry, but would have been paramount issues when committing to the attack. In particular, it would have been very difficult indeed to dominate the front ranks of the enemy. At the initial contact the leading men of the circular schiltrom would have been very heavily outnumbered by their opponents in a linear formation. By the time the weight of the schiltrom was really brought to bear on the enemy, those leading elements might well have been crushed, thus breaking the continuity of the formation and allowing an aggressive opponent to break into the centre. Additionally, though the evolutions required of a block of spearmen were not very demanding, it is not easy to keep men in regular formation on the move unless that formation has clear and simple ranks. Moving a circular formation can only be achieved with any degree of security if the men in the unit have been trained to exacting standards in the way of foot-drill. In an age when cadenced marching had yet to be invented the advance (or retreat) of a circular schiltrom would have been challenging to say the least.

This is not to imply that it was impossible to manoeuvre a circular or elliptical schiltrom. If we are to accept Barbour's description of Moray's action against English cavalry on the first day of the battle – and there is no reason why we should not – it is clear that Moray was able to manoeuvre his force with some confidence against a mounted enemy. However, there are at least three significant factors to be borne in mind. Barbour's account does not describe an action by a great body of Scots, but an action involving a portion of the men under Moray's command. These are referred to as Moray's 'mengne'.[43] We might debate what exactly Barbour meant by the term, though it is reasonable to assume that its meaning was clear enough to Barbour's audience. The most logical interpretation would be to assume that Moray's 'mengne' comprised the men who owed him military service, whether as his tenants or because they were members of communities over which Moray had rights of military leadership. Clearly this was not the formation that Moray commanded on the following day. Virtually all estimates of the Scottish army put the close-order element in the region of 6–8,000 including the archers and the cavalry, and all the contemporary accounts refer to either three (or in Barbour's case four) formations. We should therefore assume that the divisions committed to the fight on the second day of the battle were anything from 1,500 to more than 2,000 strong, and that Moray's own 'mengne' was a formation within the division that he led on 24 June.

Mr Stuart Reid[44] has suggested that the major formations of Robert's army were, in turn, divided into three or four individual schiltroms. Although there is no evidence to support this, it is a plausible proposition to some extent. It would be extremely difficult to instil basic drill practices in very large formations of 1,000 men or more. It would be rational to assume that the troops were taught their 'basic' skills in relatively small groups, before these groups were combined into larger formations for more advanced training. His suggestion that these sub-unit schiltroms would have been drawn up with a distance between them is less convincing. The gaps between the units would have greatly reduced the ability of the Scots to form an effective barrier across the stretch of land between the Bannock and Pelstream burns, and the collapse of just one sub-unit might seriously imperil those to the left and right. Mr Reid also suggests that Barbour's description of the Scottish deployment on 24 June is 'consistent with the normal Scottish practice of deploying four divisions rather than the three common to most medieval armies', however, the four schiltroms of Wallace's army at Falkirk would seem to be only one example and may be a reflection of the scale of Wallace's army. It would probably have been very difficult to control a single body of more than 2,000 men.

Even so, Barbour's description of the fighting at St Ninians may offer some support for the existence of articulation at a lower level than that of the three (or four) battlefield formations employed by the Scots. The Earl of Moray had been active in the Bruce cause for some years and had attained great rank and status as one of King Robert's most trusted commanders. It would be reasonable to assume that he had brought his troops to a high standard of efficiency. He could therefore depend on the quality of the training and experience of his troops and his subordinate commanders to maintain the cohesion of formation necessary for manoeuvres against a more mobile enemy. Barbour gives Moray's 'mengne' a strength of no more than 500 men. Interestingly, although Barbour tells us that Moray ordered his men:

> ... bak to bak set all your rout
> And all the speris poyntis out

he does not use the term schiltrom, or indeed any other term, to describe Moray's formation, though what significance – if any – can be attached to this is unclear. He was certainly familiar with the term, since he used it to describe the appearance of the English army.[45]

Barbour's description of Moray's force as his own 'mengne' is possibly of interest in an administrative context. There must surely have been some form of articulation in the Scottish army, if only for the sake of organising the distribution of rations and apportioning guard duties and work-parties. Moray's 500 men may be an indication that the major battlefield formations of King Robert's army had a degree of internal sub-division and that those sub-divisions could be allotted to specific operations as discrete units. But the deployment of one body of men from a major formation is not sufficient evidence to indicate that this was normal practice.

Articulation at the smallest scale is occasionally indicated by the wording of charter evidence. A body of men required from the recipient of a charter might comprise so many archers and an 'armed man' to lead them. An example from Formulary 'E'[46] indicates that a burgh might be expected to supply a given number of troops and a man – or men – 'sufficiently' equipped to lead them. These examples do, however, refer to very small groups. We know that rights of military leadership over quite extensive areas might be granted to an individual regardless of whether the men concerned were tenants of that individual. We also know that a lord – Sir James Douglas, for example[47] – might be granted military leadership rights over all of his tenants throughout the kingdom regardless of existing custom. An individual might also be granted leadership rights over men who lived on properties that did not belong to him.[48] This surely implies that as a general rule those men would fall under the authority of a local officer of the crown – whether earl, baron or sheriff – but that that authority might be passed on to another.

We might ask how that would be of benefit either to the person receiving this privilege or to the king, who obviously granted it in the first place. For the beneficiary of such a grant there was an element of enhanced prestige – he evidently enjoyed the confidence and favour of the king, but there must surely have been some practical advantage as well. Such grants may have simplified the business of getting men into the field. There was obviously some potential for conflicts in the chain of command if, for example, a lord's tenant owed military obedience to both his superior and the local sheriff. It may have been a means of assisting lords to raise larger and/or discrete formations. The tenants of Sir Thomas Randolph in his capacity as Earl of Moray were, presumably, under his command when they took to the field, but his tenants in other parts of the country may have been the responsibility of the local sheriff or Earl with specified local military responsibilities. By granting someone the leadership 'of all his men throughout the realm' the king may have been able to obtain 'army units' with a common allegiance to one man, and thus achieve some degree of tactical articulation and cohesion at a more practical level. The administrative challenge of leading an army which consisted of a great many lordly retinues of varying sizes would be enormous, so it would be in the interests of the crown to encourage the development of larger formations for campaigning generally and for the battlefield in particular.

There is no extensive body of evidence to suggest that the Scots adopted a system of administrative articulation of any kind, though it is hard to see how the daily life of an army could be maintained without one. Wallace allegedly imposed a system of junior commanders of units down to the level of five men, though this is probably an example of the literary fancy of the writer rather than a valid description of the Scots at war in 1296–98. On the other hand, Bower describes two Scottish men-at-arms, John Stirling and Alan Boyd, as being commanders of the Scottish archers at the siege of Perth in 1339.[49]

It would therefore seem that the archers at least were considered to be a distinct portion of the army, rather than consisting of men from the rank and file who just happened to be armed with bows. Neither Boyd nor Stirling were men of the first rank in the Scottish nobility, but they were certainly not commoners.

Enlistment

The experiences of the three Edwards in Scotland brought about a number of changes in the English approach to mustering armies. Long before the end of Edward III's reign in 1377 the contracted soldier in receipt of government wages had become more the rule than the exception. His pay was poor – 2*d* to 4*d* a day – and we have little knowledge of the conditions of his employment. He might volunteer in search of adventure or perhaps to avoid problems at home, but most infantrymen were chosen by local authorities such as the sheriff or the borough council. They were not, therefore, always the best specimens, but rather the dregs of the community. Counties and towns were asked for contingents of men, and might be obliged to furnish those men with arms, armour and foodstuffs. In some instances they were also burdened with the provision of the men's wages for the duration of their march from their community to the muster point of the army, where the crown assumed responsibility for pay. The pay scale might be adjusted for service inside and outside England on the premise that the men would be able to supplement their wages through foraging and plunder – a rather short-sighted policy given that plundering would inevitably alienate residents in areas under Plantagenet control. Moreover the areas through which the army passed were likely to have been stripped bare before the army arrived, leaving very little for hungry soldiers to requisition.

Scottish soldiers, in theory, were seldom paid at all, though it is likely that the large sums collected by Robert I from the communities of northern England did in fact find their way into the pockets of his soldiers. As Professor Duncan has pointed out in reference to King Robert's campaigns of 1312–13,[50] 'such protracted campaigning cannot have been carried out with only the free service of the common army'. If Robert did not provide wages, it is difficult to see how he could keep such firm control of his troops as they marched through Northumberland, Westmorland, Cumbria, Durham and Yorkshire. Numerous medieval documents give us scraps of information about Scots in military service, but they are – largely – documents which describe personal liability. There are few that shed light on the wider issues of army enlistment. Broadly speaking, the rank and file of Scottish armies were recruited or con-scripted under the authority of specific local potentates. For most people this probably meant the sheriff or a senior noble – an earl or baron. Naturally, the earls and barons had their own resources to call on, either as landholders with military obligations, or as local officers of the crown whose rights and responsibilities included mustering men for war in time of need. The right to call out men for service was not a simple matter of authority. While still Earl of Carrick, Robert Bruce was obliged to give an undertaking that he would not, in future, use his authority to call out the tenants of Melrose Abbey to fight in support of his personal career ambitions, but only when the whole com-munity was called upon to serve in the national interest.[51] As Earl of Carrick or Lord of Annandale, Robert had a responsibility to conscript men to serve in defence of the realm, and the authority to do so, but men were not obliged to fight for the baronial interests of the Bruce family. Naturally the situation was somewhat different once Robert had made his kingship a reality; the desires of the king and the duties of community being – in the eyes of contemporaries – virtually one and the same.

An extract from 'Formulary E' (see above), possibly detailing the military obligations of the Burgh of Ayr as an example, indicated that the town had to find a given number of properly equipped infantry and a man-at-arms to lead them. The same applies to the 1304 charter of the Earl of Fife relating to Kilsyth (see above), the recipient of the grant being obliged to provide ten archers. Clearly infantry service was considered important enough for it to figure in the charters of great lords, but there is insufficient evidence to allow us to formulate a rationale for the practical integration of such men into a large field army. To some extent this may have been offset by the extension of rights of military leadership. As we have already seen, men like Sir James Douglas and Sir Alexander Seton might be given charters which cut across the customary practices of the day, in that they were given the 'leadership' of all their tenants, regardless of which sheriffdom those tenants came from.

Although the bulk of Robert's army was certainly recruited on the basis of customary military duty, we should not assume that they were all men dis-charging obligations. Barbour tells us that the king turned away volunteers who did not have adequate arms and armour, but there is no reason to assume that properly equipped men were not acceptable wherever they came from. There may have been no prospect of regular wages, but there was the prospect of plunder if the Scots were triumphant or – as had happened in the past – the English had failed to force battle and were obliged to withdraw. Service in the army might also attract men who, for whatever reasons, had fallen into banditry. Pardons granted for army service were a normal part of the recruiting structure of English armies, and there is no reason to presume that a similar practice was not acceptable in Scotland just because we have no record of it.

Military obligations were not necessarily as simple as the supply of soldiers for the crown. Religious houses in Scotland (unlike their counterparts in England and France) were not obliged to provide knight service for the King's army, though their tenants certainly were. This does not mean that the convents, abbeys and monasteries of Scotland were automatically exempt from providing a contribution to the military, either in wartime or peacetime. An undated charter of Robert I relieved the community of Paisley Abbey from the annual burden of providing five chalders of oats to the garrison of Dumbarton Castle.[52] Robert's policy of slighting castles to render them useless to future English invasions may have made the existing obligation redundant. If there was no castle there would be no garrison to support, and the church might undertake other tasks connected with the finances of war. In 1339 Robert the Steward (later Robert II) relieved the Priory of St Andrews from an undertaking to collect funds from the 'community' (that is to say the lords, landholders and burgesses of the county) for the upkeep of the garrison of Loch Leven Castle.[53]

The burdens of Paisley Abbey or St Andrews Priory were probably not dissimilar in principle to those of other religious houses, and individual clerics certainly took up arms in pursuit of political aims. Bishops Lamberton and Wishart were certainly very active in the Bruce cause and, among the Edinburgh garrison of Edward III, we find the Parson of Pencaitland serving, not just as a man-at-arms, but as a knight.[54] Several other clerics appear in record and narrative sources in military roles – perhaps the most famous of these being Antony Bek, Bishop of Durham, who served Edward I on more than one campaign. Bek commanded an expeditionary force from the main body of the army of 1298 in a brief campaign to recover three castles in Lothian which had fallen (or whose garrisons had defected) to Wallace's army in the year or so since the Battle of Stirling Bridge.

The Logistic Effort

The large forces raised in 1314 required huge quantities of foodstuffs for both men and beasts, quantities that could not be achieved through foraging or through reliance on supplies provided by the troops themselves or by merchants following the army. Dr McNamee has examined the scale of provisions collected at Berwick and Newcastle[55] and has concluded that, if collection of material continued on the same scale, it would be sufficient to allow 'English garrisons to remain in Scotland indefinitely'. However, such a concentration of supplies would have been very hard to maintain for any length of time and was achieved only by buying huge shipments of produce from Italian merchants and bankers like Antonio Pessagno.[56] Maintaining garrisons would, naturally enough, depend on recovering towns and castles to house them, a practical proposition if Edward could secure a major victory on the battlefield, but not if the Scots were able to evade battle long enough to force Edward to abandon the campaign – a strong possibility given the campaign of 1310–11. However, maintaining garrisons was not simply a matter of providing food and funds. If the garrison could not impose Edward's lordship effectively they would be no more than an expensive way of keeping the Scots occupied.

Provisions were obviously a major issue for both armies, but there were other logistical requirements. Scottish commerce could supply any form of equipment and armourers and lorimers appear in many medieval Scottish documents long before the wars of independence. As early as the reign of William the Lion, a 'galeator' (a specialist helmet-maker) was operating in Perth, but local tradesmen could not provide arms in the quantities necessary for a long-term, large-scale war. War materials were certainly being imported for the Balliol party in 1302 when a Flemish ship carrying arms, probably bound for Aberdeen, was captured by the English.[57] In addition, in the autumn of 1309, Edward II complained to the count of Flanders that the Scots were receiving aid from German merchants operating through the ports of his province.[58] Edward even found that his own merchants could not be trusted to desist from selling arms to the Scots either directly or through Irish ports.

We can say very little indeed about the Scottish approach to supply. It is evident from charter material (see above) that institutions might carry a responsibility to provide foodstuffs for royal garrisons on a formal, regular basis, but there is no evidence of a government department with responsibility for providing arms, food or wages to Scottish troops. This does not mean that we should assume the Scottish armies were expected to live on supplies that they had brought to the army personally, nor that they lived by foraging, though that was unquestionably a major source of rations when communities in the north of England had failed to come up with ransoms.

The army that King Robert assembled at Stirling could not possibly have survived simply by requisitioning material from the local community. Apart from anything else the army of summer 1314 was probably of at least the same order of magnitude as the largest burghs in the realm. If non-combatants are included, the number of mouths to feed may have amounted to 10–12,000, conceivably more. Mr Nusbacher[66] categorically states that King Robert cannot have recruited more than 5,000 men for service in 1314, but offers no supporting evidence or rationale. Even if the army itself was as small as 5,000 – and that would be a very low estimate indeed – we can be confident that the collection of metalworkers, cooks, servants, prostitutes and general 'hangers on' that were part and parcel of any army would have inflated that number very considerably. Strictly speaking, these people were not part of the army in the sense of being combat soldiers, but they still lived – or at least attempted to live – at the expense of the army.

By the time of the Bannockburn campaign, Robert had gained control of the majority of Scotland. In fact, Robert's army may have been very much greater, even twice the size of Nusbacher's estimate. There are a number of issues to be considered here. Obviously the size of the population as a whole cannot be adequately estimated, and figures extrapolated from estimates of fourteenth-century population figures should not be taken too seriously. We might more usefully consider the estimates of other Scottish armies. The army that David II led to defeat at Neville's Cross is generally believed to have been of the order of 10,000 troops, including 1–2,000 men-at-arms. We might consider the possibility that David was able to raise a larger army than his father. It is quite possible that Robert had not been able to establish his lordship sufficiently in Berwickshire, Lothian and Roxburghshire to be able to fully exploit the manpower of those counties, but on the other hand, King Robert very obviously made more extensive use of men from the West Highlands and the Western Isles in 1314 than King David did in 1346. Estimates of the strength of Robert's army have, in essence, been arrived at by assuming that Barbour's numbers should be divided by four to give a reasonable 'working guide' to Robert's army, however Barbour's figure is a literary one and was therefore not intended to give an accurate account. A figure of 7,000 is not unreasonable, but neither is a figure of 10,000. Robert had, after all, been gathering troops and training them for several weeks before the battle and, since his army was not on the march, the potential for deserters to slip away unnoticed would have been very much reduced. We should not doubt that Robert's army included a detachment tasked with the security of the camp, and therefore, almost inevitably, with the apprehension of would-be deserters.

Whether the army comprised 5,000 or 10,000 – and we are probably safe in assuming that these are the upper and lower limits – it was still a very considerable body of men and would have demanded a sophisticated system of administration. The army would have had to have some form of articulation, if only for the sake of arranging training groups, work details and ration parties, and there would also have to have been a regulated system for the collection of provisions from the rest of the country.

A force of several thousand might be able to live 'off the land' if it was on the march, but King Robert's army was unquestionably static. This had the advantage that his lieutenants could concentrate on training and organisation, but there would be no prospect of gathering the sheer volume of foodstuffs necessary to feed several thousand people and horses from the immediate vicinity. Even if the community of Stirlingshire had been wealthy enough to provide the rations, the ill-will generated by wholesale requisition would have done nothing to enhance Robert's prestige as king – he would be failing to provide the 'good lordship' on which acceptance of medieval kingship rested. We do not know what measures were taken to feed the army, but clearly something was done or the army would either have starved to death or simply disintegrated.

If we do not know how supplies were collected, we do at least have some idea about where they were deposited. During the night of 23–24 June the Earl of Atholl – who had recently defected to the English after Edward Bruce's jilting of his sister – led an attack on the Scottish supply trains at Cambuskenneth Abbey. The attack seems to have had little or no effect on King Robert's plans, nor on his army, but clearly there was an established centre for supplies which could be identified and raided.

The administrative and logistical elements of the English army can be described with more confidence, though a good deal of material has not survived. No doubt some portion was lost on the battlefield. There are no muster rolls or horse valuation rolls for the army of 1314. These records would be of great benefit in estimating the strength of the army overall, but more importantly the proportions of different troops present. They would also provide us with some idea of the ancillary effort that was required to make and keep such an army ready for battle.

Right: 1 The last remaining building of Cambuskenneth Abbey. Scene of the only action of the battle which can be located with complete confidence.

Below: 2 View toward 'The Entry' into the New Park. The first action probably took place in the vicinity of the gentle ridge line slightly to the south of what is now the National Trust Visitor Centre.

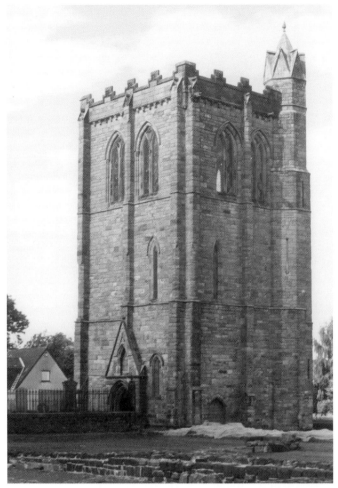

3 View south from the Visitor Centre. The Earls of Gloucester and Hereford led their troops into 'The Entry' and were defeated by Scottish spearmen and archers. King Robert's famous duel with De Bohun probably occurred close to this area.

4 View toward Stirling Castle. The medieval town did not extend far beyond the tail and eskar on which the castle stands.

5 Looking south from the centre of the level area now occupied by Bannockburn High School. All of the most reliable source material indicates that the Scots moved downhill from woods onto the 'carse'. This would have been an ideal 'forming up' area for Robert's army.

6 Looking north from the same location.

7 The slope down to the carse. King Robert's army would have had to negotiate this incline to advance to contact with the English army down on the carse.

8 The Bannock Burn from the Telford Bridge. The Scots, concentrated on the high ground to the west of the carse, would have been quite invisible to the English below, giving King Robert a tremendous reconnaissance advantage.

9 The Bannock Burn runs through the carse and formed the southern boundary of the English camp and deployment area.

10 The carse. Although primarily pasture today, this area was predominantly arable in the fourteenth century due to the high value of grain. Modern tradition would have us believe that the English army camped in a swamp among pools, but medieval writers are clear that the fighting took place on firm, flat terrain.

11 Medieval infantryman. English and Scottish troops were armed and armoured in much the same manner. The cap below this soldier's bacinet provides vital cushioning.

12 Heavy cavalry soldier. This man's flat-topped helmet would have been a little old-fashioned, but still serviceable.

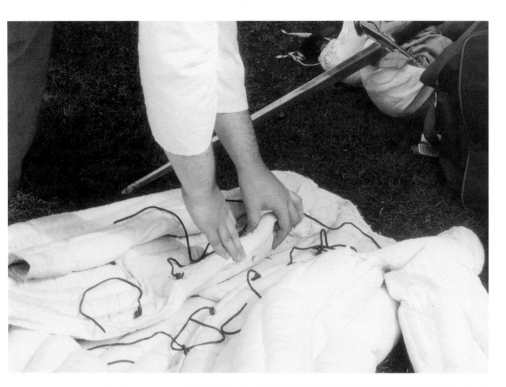

Above: 13 Padded jackets stuffed with raw wool would give good protection against impact weapons, but would become terribly hot on a summer day, leading to heat exhaustion.

Right: 14 This soldier's armour is, arguably, a little late in period for Bannockburn, but articulated plate armour for the arms and legs was becoming very fashionable. The picture was taken on the high ground overlooking the approximate area from which Gloucester and Hereford advanced on the first day of the battle.

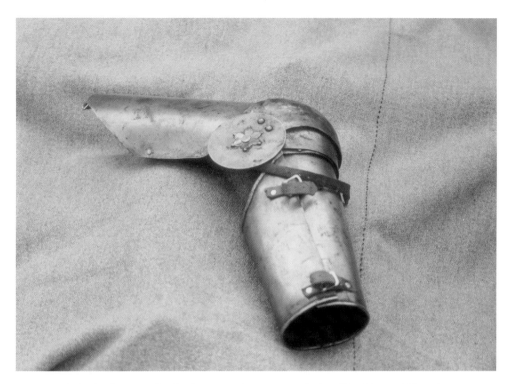

15 Articulated armour for the forearm and upper arm. A piece like this would have been the height of military fashion, worn by men-at-arms of both armies.

16 Medieval spearmen. Troops armed and armoured like these would have formed a large part of the army of Edward II and a very large proportion of that of Robert I, though we should expect the spears to have been rather longer than the 10 foot weapons shown here.

17 Close-up of spearmen. As long as spearmen maintained their formation they were virtually invulnerable to cavalry.

18 An archer. Contrary to a tradition that has developed over the past century, there is no evidence to suggest that Scottish and English archers used different types of bow.

19 Livery – the practice of dressing troops in particular colours – was only just becoming fashionable in the early fourteenth century.

20 An archer in padded coat 'nocking' his arrow.

21 The film *Braveheart* popularised myths about the nature of Scottish military equipment, in particular a belief that Scottish troops wore very distinctive leather tunics like this one.

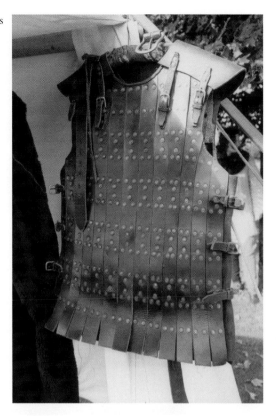

22 Arms of Scottish some of the Scottish Earls, barons and knights who served at at Bannockburn.

Left: 23 A well-equipped infantryman with three layers of protection – a thick padded coat worn over a chainmail hauberk over a thinner padded jacket.

Below: 24 A considerable proportion of the men-at-arms in the Scottish army – including the earls of Carrick and Moray and the King himself – served on foot with spear in hand.

25 Receiving cavalry. The strong modern tradition that Scottish spearmen knelt down to rest the butts of their spears on the ground is supported by medieval evidence.

26 Inchcolm Abbey, where Abbot Bower composed his *Scotichronicon*.

27 Torphichen, headquarters of the Hospitallers in Scotland. Contrary to modern tradition, there is no evidence to suggest that a body of Templars received sanctuary in Scotland and continued to exist as a branch of he Hospitallers or that they served under King Robert at Bannockburn.

28 A re-enactor in the role of Edward II. In reality, the king would have been rather better armoured, with plates for his arms and legs, plate gloves and a helmet, probably a bacinet.

29 Pilkington Jackson's statue of Robert I at the Bannockburn Visitor Centre.

Horse valuation – restauro – was an important process in the enlistment of men-at-arms. In order to qualify for his 12*d*/day wage, each man-at-arms had to have his charger valued by a panel of officers. If the animal was lost on campaign, the owner would be reimbursed accordingly by the crown. Only one horse could be assessed for restauro, but if the animal was lost, or simply unfit for action, the man-at-arms could lose his day's wages. Therefore, the vast majority of the men concerned would actually take at least two mounts to war, and men of greater status might well take several. If we can realistically accept a contingent of roughly 2,000 men-at-arms in the army of Edward II from contemporary accounts, we can be reasonably confident that the army's supply arrangements had to cater for an absolute minimum of 4,000 cavalry chargers and a vast number of grooms and farriers.

To some extent, issues of pay and supply could be the responsibility of the leaders of retinues. Men of great status might choose to serve without pay as a means of demonstrating personal independence, exceptional loyalty to the crown or simply to show off their wealth. For the majority of the army there were four principal sources of supply: foraging; carrying personal supplies; purchase from merchants travelling with the army and purchase from stores of food arranged by the crown. The first of these was, in a sense, the most attractive option. There was no need to pay for the materials collected and the requisition of foodstuffs by an English soldier obviously prevented them being consumed by a Scottish one, however there was little to be gained by foraging the same area twice. Foraging was therefore only really valuable as a supply source when the army was on the move. Moreover in the southern and eastern areas foraging was likely to push Scots who had accepted Plantagenet rule – in some cases more or less continuously since 1296 – into the arms of the Bruce party. Finally there was little chance of acquiring all of the materials necessary for war by foraging alone. A force which involved at least 4,000 horses as remounts would consume a vast number of hay, oats, barley, harness, horseshoes, nails and other items that would be scarce in an area that had already been scoured by the Scots. Carrying a good supply of one's own foodstuffs was an option, but only for men with the wealth to provide themselves with a wagon, a team, a driver and perhaps a guard for the wagon. Obviously the common infantryman would be capable of carrying some quantity of flour, and a cavalryman more, but neither was likely to be able to carry enough to feed himself, let alone a horse, for the duration of the campaign.

Commercial involvement in campaigning could help to ease supply problems so long as merchants could maintain stocks in the vicinity of the army.

So long as the troops were receiving regular issues of pay, there was every incentive for merchants to tend to the military, though presumably the risk of theft from one's own army, let alone the actions of the enemy, must have discouraged some from participating in that market. Merchants might, in any case, have some difficulty in just keeping up with an army on the move, and might well experience problems in trying to maintain adequate stocks of the foodstuffs, weapons, harness and other items that the troops would want to buy.

The provision of foodstuffs through the efforts of the government was a long-established part of English campaigning in Scotland. Each campaign since 1296 had seen calls for shipping and crews from virtually every significant port in England. As a broad rule, ships from the north and west of England were requisitioned for the purposes of transporting troops from Ireland and to the replenishment of castles and formations operating in the west of Scotland. Those from the eastern seaboard were dedicated to the supply of English armies marching through eastern Scotland. Although very sound in principle, the logic of re-supply by sea was a complicated and unreliable business. The ships were dependent on favourable winds to carry them north from their home ports, so their arrival could hardly be guaranteed, let alone accurately predicted. When vessels did arrive at a convenient location and at a convenient time, there was no certainty that they would be carrying the stores most urgently required. A delivery of wine to Edward I's army in 1298 was one of the root causes of a dangerous riot which, had it not been strenuously suppressed, might have led to a major conflict within Edward's army at a point when the army of William Wallace was quite close at hand.

Crown supplies, whether delivered by sea or by land, were not necessarily distributed free to the troops, but could be sold by officers of the crown, thus recouping some portion of the money paid out in soldiers' wages. The range of products available through each of these sources was fairly limited. Supply contracts and inventories of stores in garrisons suggest a rather monotonous diet of wheat bread, beef, bacon, dried fish, ale and wine. The last of these was much prized, but was often in short supply. Each year's vintage was very fugitive compared to the 'shelf life' that we expect today. Little of the wine produced in the late summer and autumn would last beyond the late spring or early summer of the following year. The rations may have been predictable, and there were frequent failures of delivery for a variety of reasons. Shortages of shipping, wagons, draught animals, money and produce were compounded by failures of administration and by widespread dishonesty, but the sheer quantities of grain and meat demanded and delivered are staggering.[67]

Delivering supplies to English garrisons in Scotland was fraught with difficulty. In addition to the risks of sea and weather there was the prospect of piracy and the problem of transporting provisions from the point of delivery to the point of use. This was less of a problem for those fortresses and burghs which lay on the coast, but a landlocked installation – Linlithgow for example – had to depend on the ability of the surrounding garrisons to ensure that convoys could pass from Blackness Castle (where the supplies were landed) to Linlithgow, Livingstone and other garrisons. Providing foodstuffs for a major field army was an altogether more challenging proposition. Overland transport was slow, cumbersome and expensive. The fodder for the draught animals and the provisions for the men who drove and guarded the wagons must have represented a considerable drain on the victuals they were transporting. This could be offset to some extent by carrying the goods in ships. This practice was certainly cheaper in the sense of miles, tonnage and money, but it was not necessarily very effective. Adverse weather could prevent the landing of provisions, or even lead to the loss of ships, whose owners would need to be recompensed. To complicate the issue further, the demand for ships and mariners might not be met, with the result that the foodstuffs desperately needed by the army might be rotting in warehouses in ports up and down the length of England. Even if material was delivered to the right place at the right time, an imbalance of supplies could lead still to difficulties.

A substantial fleet amounting to at least sixty vessels[68] was requisitioned for the Bannockburn campaign, but a considerable part of the major effort depended on land transport – over 200 heavy wagons were ordered from English county authorities for service in Scotland. Even so, this major collection of vehicles cannot possibly have provided for the needs of the army and was probably only intended as the transport element of the royal household. The balance of the army's supplies would have to be transported at the expense of individuals and leaders of retinues, or would have to be acquired en route. Those acquisitions can be divided into two categories: supplies bought from merchants travelling with the army, and supplies bought or requisitioned from the communities through which the army passed. Both of these means of provisioning an army were well-established practices, but the latter presented Edward with a political problem. His adherents in southeast Scotland had already made at least one major representation to Edward concerning the behaviour of his garrisons. If he wanted to establish his rule effectively he had to be seen as a man who could provide 'good lordship' to the men in his allegiance. If his army plundered its way from Berwick to Stirling it would inevitably be damaging to the very people whose loyalty Edward hoped to retain.

Edward seems to have made no effort to requisition transport until 6 June,[61] when thirteen sheriffs of English counties were ordered to send a total of more than 140 wagons of different types to arrive in Berwick for 6 July. Since the intention was that the army would have arrived at Stirling and either have fought an action against the Scots or have forced them to retire, the date seems something of a curiosity. However, it is possible that this considerable train of wagons, and many others ordered for 8, 15 and 22 July, plus a further draft of transport for August, meant that Edward – or his staff – envisaged a campaign that would last well beyond the few weeks that Edward seems to have expected initially. It may even signify an intention to bring substantial forces into Scotland to supplement, or perhaps replace, the troops enlisted for the June campaign.

The lack of records relating to transport requirements before 6 June is not a clear indication that no effort had been made to form a baggage train for the campaign. Much has been made of Edward's general incompetence and of his lack of military skill, but he did have a certain level of war experience. It is unthinkable that he would have embarked on a major campaign without making transport arrangements, if only to provide for the needs of the royal household at war. It is all too easy to dismiss the defeat at Bannockburn as simply the consequence of Edward's incompetence. It is worth bearing in mind, however, that he did only lose *one* battle in a career that may not have seen much in the way of major engagements, but certainly involved a good deal of time in the field.

6

Going to the War:
October 1313–May 1314

The traditional view that the campaign of 1314 was prompted by the threat to Stirling Castle is well established, but not well founded. By late 1313 the occupation government was already in a perilous condition. Many of the great castles of the southern counties were still in English hands. Bothwell, Stirling, Edinburgh, Roxburgh, Berwick and perhaps some of the baronial castles – Dirleton, Yester and Hailes – continued to hold out against the Bruce party, but the ability of the Plantagenet administration to actually impose Edward's rule was very limited. In October or November 1313 Edward II received a petition for aid from 'the people of Scotland' (in practice this meant that part of the political community of the southeast which was still in English allegiance) pleading for help against the Scots. They claimed that the counties of the southeast had lost the sum of £20,000 over the preceding three years and had recently been forced to find 1,000 quarters[1] of wheat for King Robert's armies in exchange for a truce until Martinmas (2 November).

The Bruce party was not the only problem faced by the people of Lothian, Berwickshire and Roxburghshire. The English garrison at Berwick, possibly for want of adequate and regular supplies from England, had taken to raiding the very people that they were there to protect. A foray into the lands of the Earl of Dunbar had resulted in the loss of 4,000 sheep and the kidnapping of thirty people who were held for ransom.[2] Naturally, this soured relations between the administration and the community, but it also undermined the credibility of King Edward's lordship. If he could not protect the community from his own troops, let alone from the activities of the enemy, there was little to recommend support for the Plantagenet cause. Even the senior officials of the administration were vulnerable to the depredations of the Berwick garrison. Sir Adam Gordon, a significant landowner and Edward II's justiciar for Lothian had been taken prisoner and had the humiliation of having to promise to appear before Edward for judgement, though no specific charges seem to have been levelled against him. Gordon had been a consistent supporter of the Plantagenet party for many years,[3] and obviously enjoyed King Edward's trust. If a man of his prominence and proven loyalty could be treated in such a manner, there was little prospect of good government for the rest of the community.

By the time Edward received the 'envoys' of the people of Scotland – Sir Adam Gordon and Patrick Earl of Dunbar – the truce was either close to expiry or had in fact already expired, and the community was clearly desperate for a resolution to their problems. On 28 November Edward issued a response in which he declared his intention to mount a major offensive in the summer of 1314. This may not have given very much encouragement to his remaining supporters in southern Scotland, but realistically it was probably as much as he could do. Raising an army – and finding the funds to keep it paid and fed – was a complicated business and could not be achieved on the spur of the moment. It is not impossible that Edward had already decided to lead an army to Scotland before this. It is also credible to assume that the presentation of the petition was a political device used in order to give Edward opportunity to announce his intentions appropriately. What cannot be seriously doubted is that Edward planned to march into Scotland long before Edward Bruce made his pact with Philip Moubray.

This would not be Edward's first attempt to restore his fortunes. His campaign of 1310–11 was not wholly ineffective and Edward was certainly active in the Roxburghshire/Selkirkshire/Peebleshire area in September 1310.[4] He had taken an army north and had remained in Scotland until July 1311, but had achieved very little. In part, this was because he could not bring the Scots to battle. King Robert retired before him, stripping the countryside of livestock and crops, thus putting a considerable strain on Edward's logistical situation. Edward's withdrawal from Scotland was a great boost to Robert's reputation as well as a blow to the credibility of the occupation government and the prestige of English kingship. The 1310–11 campaign may have helped to bolster the occupation forces for a brief period, but Edward's withdrawal undermined confidence in his ability to push the Scots onto the defensive. A number of prominent lords, including the earls of Atholl and Strathearn, who had previously supported the Balliol or Plantagenet causes, defected to King Robert. For Edward, the return to England was a matter of 'out of the frying pan and into the fire', since his own magnates were now plotting to restrict his authority.

By late 1313 there were a number of factors fuelling Edward's desire to seize the military initiative in Scotland: the growing power of the Bruce party; the increasing vulnerability of the remaining garrisons; the plight of his Scottish supporters and the need to restore his authority at home. There was also a pressing political dimension in Scotland. He had already lost the resources of several significant adherents among the Scottish nobility to military action and through disenchantment, but in October – probably at a Parliament held at Cambuskenneth Abbey or a meeting of the King's council at Dundee[5] – it would seem that King Robert had issued a proclamation to the effect that any Scottish landholders who were still in the peace of Edward II would have one year to join the Bruce party or be forfeited forever. The fact that Robert could safely hold a Parliament at Cambuskenneth at all was an indication both of his own confidence and of the weakness of the occupation forces. Cambuskenneth lies close to Stirling, so clearly the commanders of the garrisons at Stirling and Edinburgh did not believe that their forces were adequate to the task of preventing Robert from making what was both a political statement and a military challenge. Robert may have been emboldened by the fall of Linlithgow pele in the late summer of 1313. The loss of Linlithgow was a serious blow since it had held one of the largest of the occupation garrisons, but it was also a political loss of some magnitude. Before the war, Linlithgow had been one of the three constabularies of the sheriffdom of Edinburgh with little or nothing in the way of a standing garrison – there was no castle, but it was a fairly important centre of local government. In 1301[6] Edward I had chosen the town as the location for a major military base capable of housing a substantial body of men-at-arms. Its loss increased the isolation of Stirling, but could also be seen as a failure to protect the legacy of Edward I.

Robert's threat to forfeit men who remained in Plantagenet allegiance was obviously valueless if he could not secure the territory in question, but by late 1313 his progress against the occupation government had made that a real possibility. Edward had no choice but to take action in the light of Robert's declaration, but it would be unreasonable to assume that he had not planned to do so anyway. The threats to Stirling and to Edward's Scottish adherents may have put pressure on Edward to move more quickly and perhaps to choose Stirling as the primary objective, but he was surely intending to take action of some sort from October 1313 at the latest.

The fall of Roxburgh in February and Edinburgh in March increased the pressure on Edward further. As well as the blow to his prestige and political credibility there was the practical issue of the advantage that the capture of

Lothian and Roxburghshire gave to King Robert. Obviously it was politically advantageous in that it enhanced Robert's standing, but it also extended his power base. Lothian was probably the most populous and wealthy sheriffdom in Scotland, and, though the county had suffered from having to pay large sums to avoid incursions by the Bruce party, the fact that they had been spared pillage and destruction meant that the local economy was largely undamaged. Robert could reasonably expect to acquire considerable amounts of money, provisions and manpower if he could impose his kingship over the Lothian communities.

All of these factors would have brought about an invasion sooner or later regardless of the situation at Stirling. However important Stirling castle might be, it was hardly likely to be worthwhile to mount a major offensive just to save one stronghold. It is, in any case, easy to exaggerate the significance of Stirling castle as a military installation. The castle is generally seen as the means of dominating the lowest crossing of the River Forth – 'the gateway to the Highlands' – and to central and north eastern Scotland generally. It was perfectly possible to cross the Forth lower in its course, but only by ferry – not really a practical route for a major army. However the castle could only control the crossing if the garrison could operate freely. The Bridge was far too far from the castle to allow the garrison to control the crossing with the missile weapons of the day. If the striking force of the garrison was contained within the walls and precincts of the castle they might as well not be there at all. Containment would, of course, require a considerable commitment of men, and Robert would probably have struggled to maintain such a force indefinitely. For military reasons as well as political ones, Robert would have been eager to capture it and release the troops for other operations.

The various turns of events in late 1313 – Gordon and Dunbar's petition, King Robert's proclamation about forfeiture, the general decay of the occupation government and the political situation of Edward II – were all factors that made an English offensive in 1314 a strong possibility. Had it not been for the challenge of Edward Bruce's pact, Edward could have chosen to make the recovery of Edinburgh. He could invade Scotland by the western route, pass over the Clyde and carry the war into Bruce-held territory with the intention of forcing Robert to abandon his position at Stirling and either meet Edward's army at a different location, or continue his policy of avoiding battle. Either of these options might have proved more effective than seeking battle at the earliest opportunity.

It would seem that no historian has considered the possibility that Robert, aware that Edward was preparing to make a move against him, deliberately chose to encourage Edward to make Stirling his target. The advantages in such a plan would have been considerable. If Robert could be confident that Edward would take his forces to Stirling, he would not have to commit extensive forces anywhere else and could therefore concentrate the largest possible force in a location central enough to make the mustering of troops and gathering of supplies relatively straightforward. The terrain offered good options for a defensive battle and possibilities for an offensive one, but it was also a place from which he could retire safely if necessary. It is not safe to assume that Robert always intended to fight a major action at all, but equally it would not be safe to assume that he did not deliberately exploit the political conditions to try to ensure that Edward's army would aim for Stirling. It is even conceivable that Robert's dismay on hearing of Edward Bruce's pact with Moubray was in itself a piece of deception.[7] If Robert was eager to induce Edward to march on Stirling, he can hardly have wanted Edward to know that this was the case.

Regardless of whether or not King Robert intended to offer or accept battle, there were several factors which might have encouraged him to gather an army. His own prestige might suffer considerable damage if he allowed Edward to enter Scotland without fear of serious opposition, and failure to prevent the English from crossing the Forth might well lead to the loss of much of what had been gained since 1307. In 1296, Edward I had been able to march as far north as Elgin without serious opposition. Of course, Edward had been aware that there was no Scottish army worthy of the name to obstruct his progress, whereas Robert had assembled a major army in 1314. Even so, if Edward was able to cross the Forth, Robert might not be able to find a suitable location in which he could offer battle on reasonable terms, and Edward's undoubted superiority in cavalry would give him a tremendous advantage in a mobile campaign. Just as significantly, Edward would not actually need to procure a victory on the battlefield to undermine Robert's kingship, nor did he necessarily need to gain and retain a great deal of territory. If he could march through eastern Scotland, perhaps as far as Aberdeen, destroying crops and towns, Robert's credibility as a source of good lordship would be seriously undermined and his reputation for military effectiveness might sustain a blow from which it would never recover. The political and military situation may not have made a confrontation absolutely unavoidable from Robert's perspective, but failure to make effective resistance certainly carried a high risk. The risk would have been greater if Robert had raised a large army and then not led it into battle. Mustering a major army called for a national effort in both manpower and produce. If men came to believe that they were deserting their homes, families and livelihoods to no apparent purpose it might well prove difficult to motivate them to serve in the future. Even if the army mustered at Stirling was not committed to battle, so long as the English were prevented from achieving their objective of destabilising the Bruce government and so long as the men in the army could see that their sacrifices were not in vain, then Robert's reputation was probably safe.

The risks of raising an army and then disbanding it without coming to blows with the enemy may have been significant, but there were potential gains to be had from doing so and successfully preventing Edward from achieving anything very positive from the campaign.

The act of raising a large army was a matter of some political importance. Demanding military service helped to make people accustomed to his kingship, and there had been a good deal of military activity over the past years. For the infantry who formed the majority of Robert's force, the bulk of that service had been discharged at sieges. The value of that experience was, perhaps, rather limited. Sieges were, by and large, more a matter of containment and isolation than of combat, but the fact that men were accustomed to life with the army – even if it was only for forty days a year at most – would have been of considerable benefit to King Robert. Such men were accustomed to following particular leaders, and they were accustomed to – and understood the importance of – obeying orders. More importantly, given the success of Robert and his lieutenants in capturing towns and castles – whether through failure of supply, surrender pacts, coup-de-main operations or stormings – the men were also accustomed to winning. This is not to say that all of the men in Robert's army of 1314 had seen action in the past, or that they had always been victorious, but that a large proportion of them had taken part in successful operations. Service at a siege may not have been very exciting, but it did provide opportunities for training and building confidence.

Robert started to muster his army around the end of May and thus had several weeks to develop the skills and esprit de corps that any army needs if it is to have confidence and strong morale. He would not have failed to ensure that his men were properly fed and we know, from Barbour's account, that he was careful to restrict recruitment to those who had proper equipment. Additionally, Robert – and no doubt the army as a whole – would have been aware that their opponents were almost bound to arrive at the battlefield in a less than ideal condition.

The Scottish army, on the other hand, would be rested, well trained and well organised. Further, the experience of the Scots over the preceding eight years or so had largely been one of repeated success. The only major operation to have failed utterly was an attempt on Berwick in 1312 which had been foiled by the barking of a dog, alerting the garrison to the approach of the Scots. There can be little doubt that King Robert was prepared to avoid battle in the summer of 1314, but equally we cannot assume that he was unwilling to give battle if the circumstances were propitious. He had evidently raised a substantial army and brought it to a good standard of training. Quite how large that army was is open to question; chronicle estimates cannot be taken at face value. Barbour's assertion that Robert had 30,000 men under arms as well as a great number of ancillaries is obviously a gross exaggeration, but we should not assume that he intended the reader to take the figure literally. Quite how strong that army may have been is open to question. The assumption that the Scots numbered somewhere in the region of 5–10,000 men is probably well founded in the sense that we might reasonably take these figures as the parameters of the army. We might assume that his strength would have been limited by the fact that some of the most populous and prosperous counties of Scotland had only come under his control since the capture of Edinburgh and Roxburgh castles. This would, however, depend on the assumption that the Edinburgh and Roxburgh garrisons were able to maintain Plantagenet administration in those areas right up to the moment when they fell to the Scots. Given the strong commitment of the political communities to the Bruce cause in the 1330s, despite the power of Edward III's occupation government – over 100 men and women were forfeited for resistance in 1335–37[8] – it would be rash to assume that Robert did not enjoy a degree of support in 1314. Indeed, the men of Lothian and Roxburghshire faced a variety of pressures to turn out for the Bruce cause. If Robert stripped the counties to deny produce to the advancing English army, as he did in later campaigns, Lothian men would have had little choice other than to serve. Furthermore, there would be some pressure to join the army to show loyalty to the new regime, particularly if their families and goods had been evacuated north of the Forth.

Even so, what we know of Scottish armies in the later Middle Ages generally would suggest that an absolute outside limit of 10,000 combatants is a realistic estimate, though it is possible that Robert could only field 5000 men. Equally, he may have brought as many as 10,000 men to the fight. There is no particularly good reason to assume otherwise, though it would surely have been very difficult to control three formations, each consisting of the better part of 3,000 men, if we assume that the balance of the army consisted of men-at-arms and archers.

There seems to be a general assumption that the archery element of a Scottish army would not exceed 10 per cent of the whole, though the army that served in France in the early 1400s seems to have consisted of about 4,000 archers and 2,000 men-at-arms and spearmen. The quantity of archer service stipulated in charters is no guide to availability of archers from the community as a whole. The latter would be trained, competent men – men for whom military service over and above universal obligation was a normal part of life. Of course, successful massed archery in large numbers did not depend on individual marksmanship, but in the effectiveness of a large number of arrows delivered in controlled concentrations.

The proportion of different troops within the close-combat element of the army is as hard to judge as the total strength. We might assume that the men-at-arms were concentrated in one body under the Earl Marischal, Sir Robert Keith, as a subtracted reserve to react to threats or to exploit opportunities, however it is evident that several senior magnates served on foot in the main formations of the army, including the king himself. It is unthinkable that he, or Edward Bruce, did not go into action in the company of their immediate military entourages, thus the man-at-arms element of the Scottish army as a whole is likely to have been considerably in excess of the 500 men-at-arms mentioned by Barbour. The army that David II led to defeat at Neville's Cross may have had as many as 2,000 men-at-arms in its ranks, which would certainly represent a really successful mobilisation, but not one beyond credibility. David may of course have been able to recruit more men-at-arms than his father thirty years before, since there was no real competition for authority in the southern counties. But even if we were to assume that Robert could not call on the men-at-arms of Lothian and Roxburghshire, it would be unrealistic to assume that the loss of two counties would deprive him of seventy-five per cent of the available men-at-arms. If pressed to give an estimate of the total number of men-at-arms under Robert's command at Bannockburn, it would not be unreasonable to suggest a total of somewhere in the region of 1,000.

The absence of English records relating to the army of 1314 means that estimating the numbers in Edward's army is fraught with difficulties. It is, for example, very easy to assume that of the 22,140 men called to service from English and Welsh counties and a further 4,000 demanded from Ireland,[9] only a modest proportion turned up at all and that a very large number would have deserted by 23–24 June. To assume that the turnout was only in the region of fifty or sixty per cent – the case in a previous campaign – is not altogether convincing.

We can certainly be confident that fewer served than were called and that desertion would have been a problem, but the rate of desertion in an army raised for service in winter would almost certainly be very much greater than in a force raised for a summer campaign. We should also be wary of assumptions that large numbers should never be taken seriously, simply because they refer to the strength of a medieval army. In February 1298, an army of about 21,000 had been assembled at Newcastle for service in Scotland. This may have been an exceptionally successful muster, however sizeable infantry forces were raised on this, and other occasions. Professor Barrow[10] has drawn attention to material which might suggest that Edward I had arranged for 60,000 to be in pay at Newcastle for March 1296, however there was a great difference between calling men to arms and actually having them turn up. Edward called for 16,000 men for his campaign in 1300,[11] but the force peaked at about 9,000. Similarly, we cannot assume that all of the demands for troops have actually survived. Edward II's writ of 27 May 1314 only sought to enlist 3,000 troops from Wales, which is in sharp contrast to the Falkirk campaign, where the majority of the infantry were Welshmen. Although he could count on the support of some Scottish lords, Edward cannot have gained much in the way of infantrymen from Scottish sources. Most of the Scots in English allegiance were men who had been driven from their estates and were not, therefore, in a position to demand the service due from their erstwhile tenants. Some men may have been forthcoming from the properties of lords in the border areas, assuming that the Bruce party had yet to establish its authority in those localities, but the contribution, if any at all, must surely have been insignificant.

Additionally, the writs issued in 1314 refer only to demands placed on specific communities. They take no account of men volunteering for service in search of plunder, adventure or pardons for criminal behaviour. There is no record material relating to Irish troops at Bannockburn, but considerable numbers had served in earlier Scottish campaigns and it is quite possible that records of their service did not survive defeat. Even so, it is unlikely (but not impossible) that the infantry component of Edward's army exceeded a figure in the region of 15,000 men. The same applies to the cavalry element, however here we can have a little more faith in the estimates of chroniclers. There is no obvious reason to assume that Edward II's army in 1314 was less well furnished with men-at-arms than that of Edward I in 1298, in which case we would probably be quite close to the mark in accepting a figure of something a little in excess of 2,000 heavy cavalry, indeed it would be difficult to make a case for anything less given the chronicle estimates, what we know of English armies of the period generally and the fact that Edward's army was seen by contemporaries as an impressive force by the standards of the day.

It would be easy to dismiss estimates of the strength of both the Scottish and English armies as mere guesswork, which, to a considerable degree, they are. Barbour and the other chroniclers offer quite incredible numbers, but as Dr McKisack has pointed out, modern attempts to reduce Edward's army to 'Between 6,000 and 7,000 infantry with no more than 450–500 cavalry, are hardly less so'.[12]

Even if that estimate of infantry strength is a valid assessment – and there is no particular reason to assume that it is – the cavalry estimate does not bear examination. J.E. Morris[13] suggests that the heavy cavalry element of the 1298 army was in the region of 2,400, and has drawn attention to the fact that 830 protections were issued for the 1314 campaign, however these protections were issued for the members of the retinues of particular lords. The Earl of Gloucester's retinue alone received 132 protections and a large proportion of the balance of 698 were given for the retinues of just eight men: the Despensers (62), the Earl of Pembroke (96), the Earl of Hereford (45), Richard Grey (26), John Moubray (26), Henry Beaumont (29) and Robert Clifford (12). At least another sixty protections can be found in Bain's *Calendar of Documents Relating to Scotland*. Again, we must remember that not all of the men who served would have sought protections and that we have no way of estimating numbers of those who might have served voluntarily or of any Irish contingent. In 1296 Richard De Burgh, Earl of Ulster, supplied a body of 310 men-at-arms including seven bannerets, and in 1301 he provided 264 men-at-arms.[14] De Burgh may not have served at Bannockburn, but he was certainly with Edward at Newminster on 29 May and, as Professor Barrow has pointed out,[15] he is unlikely to have come empty-handed. Further, there is no record material to allow us to make an estimate of foreign volunteers (though they are likely to have been few in number) or of Scots in English service. Again, these men are not likely to have constituted a major contribution, but it is difficult to believe that the various major Scottish lords who had been driven from their estates did not bring parties of men-at-arms. Sir Laurence Abernethy led a party of eighty men-at-arms, and it would be unrealistic to assume that he was the only Scot who was able and willing to provide a retinue for Edward's army.

There is no unequivocal evidence to prove the presence of either light cavalry or hobelars in the English army, though equally there is no evidence to indicate otherwise. J.E.Morris, making the point that light cavalry were a rarity in the armies of Edward I and Edward II, dismisses Walter of Hemingburgh's assertion that the army of the Falkirk campaign included 4,000 light cavalry in addition to 3,000 men-at-arms, but it is difficult to imagine that there was no light cavalry or hobelar element at all. In 1298 and again in 1310, the Earl of Ulster provided modest, but not negligible, numbers of light cavalry in addition to his contribution of men-at-arms, but there is no reason to suppose that there was a substantial body of such troops in the army as a whole, useful though they might have been. They certainly had no role in the battle as far as the chronicle records go, but there again, hobelars and perhaps other cavalry below the status of men-at-arms, would have dismounted for action and would therefore not be distinguished from the infantry.

Finally, there may have been contingents of troops who served, but whose presence was not recorded, or rather that no record of their service has survived. Edward I employed a company of mounted crossbowmen for the 1298 campaign, though there is no record of their presence in battle. We should also expect that there would have been modest units of specialists of one kind or another – pioneers, miners, etc. – whose normal role would not necessarily have excused them from combat.

On balance, though we must obviously reject the wilder claims of chroniclers, we must accept that the English army of 1314 was an imposing force, sufficiently so to give Edward and his lieutenants confidence that they could attack the Scots, even if they were deployed in a very strong defensive position, with every confidence of gaining a major victory.

There can be no doubt that Edward and his lieutenants did expect to defeat the Scots. Not only did they lead a larger force, but their experience indicated that the Scots were likely to avoid battle if they could, and that if they could have battle forced upon them, they would be very likely to lose. The English army was a versatile tool, and if victory could not be secured through the power of a cavalry attack, the deployment of the army could be adjusted to disrupt Scottish formations and allow the cavalry to break their ranks. There was nothing particularly innovative about fielding large bodies of spearmen. The Scots had done that at Falkirk and had been defeated by the application of combined arms tactics.

This had been achieved in the past. Like the Scots, the Welsh had depended on spearmen in their wars with Edward I. At Builth in 1282 the English archers had played a vital part in the fighting, and as Hemingburgh put it:

> ... through our archers, who were fighting by concert in between our cavalry, many of them fell.

Similarly at the battle of Maes Madoc, an attack by the English cavalry was initially unsuccessful, but then the archers and crossbowmen were deployed:

> ... and when many of the spearmen had been brought down by the bolts, the horse charged again and defeated them with greater slaughter, it is thought, than had ever been suffered by them in past times.

Some writers have taken this to mean that the English had developed a habitual posture for battle which placed bodies of archers between bodies of men-at-arms, but this takes no account of other battlefield experiences such as Falkirk. Here, the cavalry formations were very clearly separate bodies, and in smaller actions, such as Dunbar or Roslin, the cavalry fought without any infantry support at all. The practice of deploying archers on the wings of close-combat troops which would bring about the great longbow victories of Dupplin Muir, Halidon Hill, Crécy, Poitiers and Agincourt had yet to be invented.

One of the considerations which may have given the English commanders confidence of victory was the knowledge that the Scots had very little experience of large engagements, however there was very little experience of that kind in the English army either. The last great battle of manoeuvre for both sides was Falkirk. Given that the army of Robert I was little different in structure to that of William Wallace, Edward and his subordinates may well have felt that the tactical principles which had brought victory in 1298 would give them another victory in 1314. This might well have proved correct if the Scots had followed Wallace's example and stood on the defensive. If they withstood an initial attack – whether by foot or horse – the army could be reformed for another attempt. If, on the other hand, the Scots chose to attack, there would be neither space nor time to achieve redeployment and mount a new attack.

Most of the more senior members of the national political and military elites of England and Scotland were present at Bannockburn: the Earls of Moray and Carrick; Lord Douglas and the Stewart for the Scots; the Earls of Pembroke, Hereford, and Gloucester, and several prominent barons such as Beaumont and Clifford for the English. Equally, several major figures were conspicuous by their absence. The Earl of Lancaster's failure to attend his king is hardly surprising; the two men were hardly on good terms. On the other hand, the Earl of Dunbar was a remarkable absentee. He was certainly in the peace of Edward II in the summer of 1314 and was instrumental in helping Edward to make his escape to Berwick after the battle. Earl Patrick – and his father before him – had been steadfast in support of the Plantagenet cause for nearly twenty years. Under normal circumstances, Edward would surely have expected his presence in the English army at the head of the men-at-arms of Roxburghshire and other areas in which the Earl had extensive property and influence, however the circumstances were far from normal. The network of garrisons that had imposed Plantagenet rule in the east of Scotland had fallen to the Scots over the preceding year and more. By the spring of 1313 Patrick's position had become precarious in the extreme. The only English garrison close enough to give him any kind of support was Berwick, and he could not afford to rely on the effectiveness or commitment of the troops there. Both Patrick and Sir Adam Gordon had had cause to petition Edward on behalf of the communities of Lothian, Roxburghshire and Berwickshire in late 1313 about the behaviour of the Berwick garrison. They were inclined to help themselves to the property of the locals, even kidnapping them for ransom, but worse than that, they were prone to mounting operations that infringed the truces that the local people had made with the Bruce party. These truces were expensive undertakings. Since he enjoyed complete operational superiority, Robert could impose a truce on terms that suited him. Generally, they involved very considerable sums of money and very often a right for Robert's troops to pass freely through the area in question. Evidently Edward's administration in Lothian and the south east had more or less collapsed by the summer of 1314. Whether King Robert was in a position to impose his rule effectively is a different matter. Clearly he had not been able to exert the level of lordship necessary to force the Earl of Dunbar to turn out for the Bruce cause.

The Earl was not the only notable Scottish absentee. Sir Alexander Seton, a prominent baron with interests in the south eastern counties, had in fact been one of the first men to commit himself to the Bruce cause in 1306,[16] but had defected to the Plantagenet party by 1308. He had continued in the peace of Edward II for the next six years, presumably fulfilling his duties and obligations as a senior member of the political community of Lothian. He joined Edward's army in 1314, but chose to return to the Bruce party during the night of 23–24 June.[17] The political choices of a man like Seton were not simply a matter of personal commitment. As a prominent baron, he would obviously have a strong influence on his tenants and relatives, but he would also have a more general leadership role in the wider community. Neighbouring landholders might well look to him for a lead in political matters, perhaps assuming that a man of his stature would have better sources of information, but certainly well aware of the power that he could wield in the vicinity. Seton's defection may have been one of the factors that persuaded Robert to carry the fight to the English. Seton was an experienced soldier and his change of heart would not have occurred if he had been confident that Edward II would achieve a victory on the 24 June. He can hardly have been unaware of the progress of the Bruce party and the nature and strength of the Scottish army, so we must assume that he was making an informed choice on the basis of the capabilities of Edward's and Robert's forces, and on their relative merits as commanders.

Seton was a useful addition to Robert's cause, but he was not yet a man of very great substance either politically or militarily. Failure to attract the support of the Earl of Dunbar and other senior figures in the political community was a more pressing problem for Robert I. The prestige of his kingship was undermined by the absence of any major noble, but failure to procure the support of men like Dunbar and, to a lesser extent, Adam Gordon, had a military dimension. Although men-at-arms could be, and were, recruited from all over Scotland, the availability of such service was very much smaller in the north and west than in the south and east. Although the cavalry service due to the crown from Gordon and Dunbar for their lands would not have provided a significant force in itself, the political influence of these men was very extensive, and undoubtedly discouraged support for the Bruce cause from other members of the landholding communities. As long as Bothwell castle was retained in Plantagenet control, there would be considerable pressure for the local landholders to continue in their allegiance to Edward II. This was a matter of some importance militarily, since failure to bring these areas under control would have had an adverse effect on the numbers of men-at-arms that Robert could call to his service.

Equally, the absence of the Earl of Dunbar and the defection of Seton can be seen as indications of the state of the English administration in Scotland. Both could claim – perhaps with some justice – that their resources were already fully committed in resisting the expansion of Bruce administration, but seemingly neither was very confident of Edward's ability to bring Bruce to battle and achieve victory. The former point was probably more of an issue than the latter in the minds of Dunbar, Seton and others. If, as had happened in the past, Edward failed to force battle on the Scots, he would almost certainly be forced to disband his army and return to England without having made any serious progress against the Bruce party. This would inevitably strengthen Robert's hand against those who remained in English allegiance.

Confidence in Edward to protect the interests of landholders had obviously diminished by 1314, but clearly not to the extent of a universal defection to the Bruce cause. By mounting an expedition to Scotland, Edward was declaring his intention to restore his administration through armed strength. He certainly had every intention of bringing the Scots to battle if at all possible, but was probably realistic enough to realise that the Scots would very probably choose to avoid a major engagement, as they had in the past. On the other hand, if he could force a battle – and he would have every confidence that he would win one – he might well be able to finish off the Bruce party once and for all. In the event of Robert and Edward Bruce being killed in action or taken prisoner, the Bruce cause would really have no future at all, in which case, Edward would almost certainly be able to establish his rule with little, if any, political opposition. Clearly a victory for Edward would have the potential to bring the Scottish war to a successful conclusion, an outcome that would greatly enhance his political prestige credibility at home and abroad. Even if the Bruce party survived a major battle in the sense that Robert or Edward escaped to fight another day, the credibility of the patriotic party would have been dealt a major blow. A significant battlefield defeat at Stirling would probably have led to wholesale defections from the Bruce party and the recovery of towns and territory across the country.

7

Locating the Battle

In the late eighteenth century, the battle was believed to have been fought in the area around a feature known as the borestone. The stone itself has long disappeared, but it is believed to have lain in the vicinity of the Bannockburn Visitor Centre maintained by the National Trust for Scotland. Ascribing specific locations for the different actions that occurred on 23 and 24 June is a thankless and ultimately futile undertaking. Of the four separate fights – at 'The Entry', St Ninians, Cambuskenneth Abbey and the main engagement itself – only the raid that David de Strathbogie mounted on King Robert's trains at Cambuskenneth can be identified with any great degree of confidence; the remaining tower of the Abbey still stands.

In a sense, this is not really a problem of any great significance. For the purposes of tactical analysis it matters very little whether an action took place at 'this spot' or at another location in the vicinity, so long as the topography is compatible with what we know from the source material. The narrative sources do not give us sufficient information to allow absolute precision in locating the fighting, but the principles are absolutely clear. Again, whether the fighting was conducted at one given spot or another is not of great importance, though of course it would be very satisfying if the locations could be ascertained with more precision. It is not impossible that this may yet be settled by archaeology.

One of the very few finds which, on balance, can reasonably be attributed to the summer of 1314 is a bodkin arrowhead which was uncovered in the vicinity of the National Trust for Scotland's Visitor Centre. It is of course possible that the arrowhead has no connection with Bannockburn at all, and that it was used – or even just mislaid – at an earlier or later date. It has been suggested that it may not even have any connection with military activity at all; the New Park was, after all, a hunting preserve. However, bodkin arrows were developed for warfare, and hunting arrows were generally much broader and more heavily barbed. Even so, though we can probably safely assume that the arrowhead was at one time in the hands of a Scottish archer, we cannot be sure that it was actually used in the fighting at the Entry. How can we be certain that it was not shot in an incident relating to the Scottish siege of Stirling Castle in 1299 or the English siege of 1304? It could even be argued that, since only one arrowhead has been recovered from the area, it is actually unlikely that the fighting occurred in the vicinity of the find at all, but this is hard to accept.

A medieval battlefield was likely to be picked clean after the event by local salvagers. More importantly, once the action was completed, the archers of the victorious side would surely search the field for arrows to replenish their quivers; arrows were not cheap. There is, however, more material to support the National Trust site as the location for the fight at the Entry. We are aware that the southern boundary of the New Park lay in that general area and that a road ran through it, probably along much the same route as the modern A80. Further, the lie of the land immediately to the south of the Visitor Centre would have provided a good site for the Scots, since the English force would not have been able to see them until they reached the brow of the hill. It would seem, then, that neither the source material nor archaeology allows us to agree on a precise identification, but that the cumulative value of the sources and tactical analysis can give an *approximate* location and a reasonably clear picture of the *nature* of the action. The same problems apply to the other action of 23 June – Moray's engagement with Beaumont and Clifford.

Moray may have met Clifford and Beaumont at a distance of 100 metres or 1,000 metres from St Ninians chapel, indeed we cannot be certain that the location that we associate with the chapel was identical to the location of the chapel 700 years ago, though the only alternative, Dunipace, does not seem to be a realistic possibility.[1] If we cannot be certain of the precise location, we can at least identify the general area by the course of the action as described by Barbour and by Sir Thomas Grey, whose father was captured in the fighting.

An advance party of English cavalry passed across the low-lying ground to the east of the Torwood, keeping to the open ground to avoid ambush. They were then intercepted by a Scottish force which moved out of wooded terrain and on to the lower ground to the east of St Ninians chapel (see 'First Clash – St Ninians'). Beyond that, all we can be sure of is that the two forces met on the plain. Further, battles are not static events. Moray's men were stationary when the English cavalry came into contact, but once they had achieved supremacy they pushed the English away. Other than the fact that the English force seems to have split in two with one party making for Stirling castle and the other retiring on the main body of the army, we cannot even say in which direction the Scots advanced. Again, this is not terribly significant. Moray's force was able to push the English cavalry hard enough to split them into two parties, but they could hardly pursue either body. As Barbour tells us, they halted to catch their breath, having performed a considerable feat of arms. The nature and progress of both of these actions are quite clear from contemporary accounts, but unless more information comes to light, there is very little prospect of furthering our current level of knowledge.

The same is true of the main action on the morning of 24 June. We can be reasonably confident that the Scots made their way from higher ground to lower ground and advanced to contact on a stretch of relatively narrow but firm, flat terrain to the south and east of Stirling on the north side of the Bannock Burn, but no more can be said with any great degree of certainty. We can, however, make some valid observations about the nature of the terrain and of the nature of the fighting. All contemporary accounts agree on the nature of the ground, though a great many historians have chosen to reject that information.

Early references to the battle often do not mention the name Bannockburn at all, but realte to a battle at or near Stirling. This should not come as a surprise; few people outside of Stirlingshire would ever have heard of Bannockburn, but many people in England, let alone Scotland, would have heard of Stirling. As Professor Barrow has pointed out,[2] we should not think of Bannockburn as a village, but as a hamlet. It was certainly an identifiable community, long known as Bannock, and the Burn was named for the hamlet, not vice versa. The hamlet of Bannock was significant enough to have two subdivisions: Ochtirbannok and Skeoch. Skeoch at least was a fairly valuable property. In 1329, the 'ferm', that is the rental due to the crown, amounted to the not inconsiderable sum of £26, 13s, 4d. Superficially, this would seem to be a carefully calculated sum, but in fact the figure is an expression of a round sum of forty marks.[3] According to Trokelowe, the main action occurred on Bannokesmora. This should not be confused with the modern usage of Muir of Bannockburn, which lies to the south of the burn. The term 'muir' can itself lead to confusion; it is not necessarily synonymous with the English 'moor'. The latter may be interpreted as rough heathland of no real value, but 'muir' tends to indicate grazing in common use by a community such as the Burgh Muirs of Edinburgh or Peebles. Medieval battles were generally named for a settlement, not a geographical feature, and Professor Barrow[4] is surely correct to reject MacKenzie's belief that the fighting occurred on the fields of the farms of Upper Taylorton or Muirton. Alternatively, it is not impossible that Bannockburn was adopted as a name for the fight because it was the last settlement that the English army passed through on their way to the battlefield.

The biggest single barrier to understanding the nature of the physical combat of the main battle is the distribution of the bogs, pools, swamps and trenches which prevented the English from delivering effective attacks. Curiously, none of the contemporary writers seem to have been aware of the dramatic effect these various barriers had on the course of the main battle. Grey, admittedly, refers to the ditch of the Bannock Burn, but he also makes it very clear that the English army had already crossed over the Bannock before the fighting commenced, that the battle had already been decided and that the ditch became a problem for the English in retreat, not in attack.

The only source which makes any reference to trenches is Trokelowe, who tells us that the Scots dug extended ditches three feet deep and three feet wide from the right to the left flanks of the army, filling them with a brittle plait of twigs, reeds and sticks, and covering them with grass and weeds. Infantry might be aware of a safe passage through these, but the heavy cavalry would not be able to pass over them.

The design and execution that would be required to make the coverings of the trenches effective should be enough to warn historians not to take their existence too seriously at all, but there are other problems to be considered. In order for these trenches to be effective in the sense of being in the right place, King Robert would have had to be extremely confident that the English army would camp in a very specific location, not simply 'down in the Carse'. Just as importantly, he would have to depend on the English army failing to make even the most rudimentary reconnaissance in the immediate vicinity of their camp, and to trust that no word of these trenches would reach the ears of the Stirling garrison. Despite being contained in a tactical sense, they were clearly capable of making contact with the English army, as Sir Philip Moubray was able to meet with King Edward on the evening of 23 June.

If the trenches were located between the Scottish and English armies it is difficult, if not impossible, to see how they could have failed to be an impediment to the advance of the Scots. Dr De Vries[5] sets much store by these trenches in his account of the battle. He gets around the issue of whether the trenches would have affected the Scottish formations by asserting that Trokelowe missed the essential point, that is, that the Scots were on the defensive and the English attacked. All contemporary material, however, points in exactly the opposite direction. Source material points to a Scottish attack, indeed it is a challenge to see how the Scots could possibly have won the battle unless they attacked. Had they remained static, the English army would have been able to reform and adopt a different form of attack with impunity. Finally, we might expect that the trenches would have left some archaeological trace in the way of parch-marks, but none have been identified.

We can make similar observations about the pools, bogs and swamps which litter modern plans of the battle. The 'pools' originate in a misunderstanding of the word 'pows' – small slow streams which crossed the lower areas of the Carse. There is nothing in the contemporary evidence to indicate that they had any effect whatsoever on the course of the battle. The same applies to marshes and bogs. Edward II believed that his enemies were gathering:

> … in strong and marshy places, where access for horses will be difficult, between us and our castle of Stirling.[6]

but this communication was written well in advance of the campaign and is not in any sense a description of the battlefield. Edward clearly expected the Scots to adopt a defensive posture in a location which would be a challenge to cavalry, but he still expected to fight on horseback; access to the Scots might be difficult, but he did not expect it to be impossible. Furthermore, it is not as if the terrain around Stirling would have been *terra incognita* to his lieutenants, or even perhaps to himself. Several of the senior officers of Edward's army had visited Stirling at some point in their career; Edward himself may have been present at his father's siege of Stirling Castle in 1304. Sir Philip Moubray can hardly have been unaware of the nature of the terrain and was certainly in contact with Edward on the night of 23/24 June. Surely he would have brought any treacherous swampland to Edward's attention.

Not only do bogs and marshes fail to appear in any of the contemporary material, what we know of the terrain as it stood in the later Middle Ages does not fit well with any suggestion of a battle in the mire. There were several mills in the immediate vicinity, including Milton of Bannock, Park Mill, Skeoch, Ochtirbannock and very possibly another mill at the Kirkton of St Ninians. We know from earlier record material that the corn teinds of the area were worth having,[7] that it is extremely difficult to grow wheat, barley or oats in a swamp, and that it is, in any case, difficult to believe that anyone would build mills if there was no grain to grind. Additionally, as Professor Barrow has pointed out, the name Balquiderock − a Gaelic place-name in what was most certainly an English-speaking area long before 1314 − 'would hardly have survived continually as a farm name had this area been out of cultivation for a long time.'

There is also the matter of the choice of a suitable battlefield for large bodies of spearmen and cavalry. If the major action took place in a swamp, it would have been very difficult indeed for Gloucester's force to make their charge on Carrick's formation. Just as importantly, it would have been very difficult indeed for the Scots to make an effective advance. Large bodies of men in close order cannot be expected to drill efficiently on anything other than firm ground, and if they could not keep very good dressing they would almost inevitably be overcome by a cavalry charge. Maintaining control over a body of troops which might easily be 200 metres across and 5 or 10 metres deep would be virtually impossible if the men did not have secure footing.

Despite the absence of marshes from contemporary accounts of the main action, we cannot utterly dismiss soft ground as an issue, only as an issue in the decisive phase of the fighting. Mr Sadler[8] suggests that 'the English were pushed back toward the morass around the Pelstream', which is certainly a possibility, though it is hardly a proven fact that the Pelstream − at least in the immediate vicinity of the action − was surrounded by morasses at all. More significantly, Sir Thomas Grey was of the opinion that the English were forced back on the Bannock Burn, not the Pelstream. Given that the English army had crossed the Bannock during the night of the 23rd and that armies in precipitate retreat are inclined to retire in the direction from which they have advanced, it is difficult to see why they might move northward rather than southward.

Evidently the ground on which the battle was decided was quite firm, but the area of deployment was evidently quite narrow, since the English were unable to mount effective flanking attacks despite a very considerable superiority in cavalry. We can be reasonably sure, therefore, that the main action took place in an area bounded by serious obstacles and that these obstacles were the ditches of burns.

This does not, unfortunately, allow us to locate the battle with any great precision, other than to conclude that it occurred on firm ground and probably between the Bannock and the Pelstream. Even if we assume that the courses of these two burns today are identical to their courses in 1314, the fighting could have taken place at any point over a distance of more than a mile. There is, of course, a remote possibility that Gardiner and Oman were correct in their analysis and that far from facing the Scots across firm terrain between the Bannock and the Pelstream, the English camped on the south side of the Bannock, the Scots deployed on the north bank, and the battle took the form of an opposed river crossing. There are two insurmountable problems with that analysis which cannot be ignored. The primary problem is that none of the contemporary evidence suggests that the English had to advance across a burn on the morning of 24 June in order to attack the Scots. On the contrary, the overwhelming weight of evidence from the narrative records clearly indicates that the Scots advanced on the English and that a portion of the English cavalry under the Earl of Gloucester made a hasty counter-attack on the leading Scottish formation under the Earl of Carrick.

The other problem is one of tactical analysis. Edward II had no experience of command in a large-scale battle, but he was not a complete novice at soldiering. It is hard to see why he might choose to make an attack over terrain that would put his force at a severe disadvantage unless there was a pressing need to mount his attack immediately. The argument that he needed to move rapidly to prevent the Stirling garrison from having to surrender under the terms of the pact does not bear examination. The English army was already close enough to the castle to have effected a technical relief, and it is in any case extremely unlikely that the garrison commander would have chosen to surrender his charge as long as there was a strong and undefeated English army close at hand.

Although he was not thought of as a particularly wise or intelligent man – and with good reason – there is no reason to assume that Edward II was completely witless, but he has certainly come in for a good deal of criticism for his decision to make camp in the vicinity of the River Forth. There is no way of knowing the precise time of Edward's arrival on the scene, but it is clear that the day was well advanced. His army had made a considerable march on a hot day and must have been tired, so Edward's primary requirements were security and water. The first of these could, perhaps, have been achieved simply by making camp at some distance from the Scots somewhere south and east of the Bannock. Concentrating the army for the night two or three miles from the Bannock might well have been enough to discourage the Scots from mounting a night attack, which seems to have been regarded as a real possibility. The drawback to such a plan was that the Scots might take advantage of the distance between the armies to effect a withdrawal through the night. Since the destruction of Robert's army was a primary objective of the whole invasion project, Edward could hardly afford to let his enemy slip away, so establishing his force in the vicinity of the Scots was, if not necessarily crucial, certainly desirable. Regardless of the exact location chosen, it is clear that Edward's army crossed over the Bannock on the evening, or through the night of 23–24 June, and therefore lay in an area bounded by the Bannock Burn to the south, the Pelstream burn to the north, and with the River Forth in his rear. This afforded the English army a degree of protection against a sudden night attack by the Scots on three out of four possible approaches. It also meant that the English were well provided with water points. It is difficult to exaggerate the importance of access to water to any classical, medieval or early modern army. The army did not consist of men alone; there were several thousand animals to consider. A dehydrated horse is a skittish and unpredictable creature and will very quickly run out of stamina, a matter of some importance if there is the prospect of a major battle and possibly a lengthy pursuit. It is possible to explain to a man that there is no prospect of water and that he will have to make do until tomorrow, but there is little value in trying to explain that to a horse. Further, it is important to remember that we are talking about a great many horses.

If we accept that the heavy cavalry element of Edward's army amounted to 2–3,000 men, we must assume that between them they had at least 4–6,000 horses, probably more. In fact, the whole tally of beasts would probably have been rather greater than that. Even a relatively obscure knight or baron with a handful of animals would inevitable need at least one groom who in turn would need a horse of their own if they were to lead two or three beasts for their master. In addition there were draught animals – some horses, some oxen – and probably meat 'on the hoof,' all of which would need to be watered. Finally, if Edward camped his army to the east of Broomridge, as Professor Barrow suggests,[9] he would have a relatively level and firm area to the front (west) of his army between his forces and the Scots on which he could deploy his troops for the attack that he intended to mount the following morning. To the modern observer, the site seems to be rather constricted which, for an army whose main striking arm was mounted, would be something of a risk, as mobility might be impaired in the event of a general attack by the Scots. However, we should also consider the possibility that the two operations conducted on the evening of 23 June – at St Ninians and at the Entry – were part of a plan, as opposed to accidental engagements.

BATTLE of
BANNOCKBURN
June 24TH 1314.

........English.
........Scots.

Above: Plan of the main action at Bannockburn as presented by Gardiner, Oman and many others since. This interpretation has the English perform an opposed river crossing then moving across a swamp to attack the Scots, utterly contradicting all of the contemporary source material.

Below: Illuminated letter depicting the defence of Carlisle.

If Hereford and Gloucester had been able to establish themselves to the south of the Scots and Clifford and Beaumont to the north, any advance by the Scots could easily result in their flanks and rear being left open to English cavalry attacks, in which case the English would have been able to defeat the Scots. Alternatively, if the Scots had been discouraged from making such an attack but had been unable to withdraw through the night, the entirety of the English army could have been brought into the fight much more effectively since Edward would have had plenty of space to form up his troops for an advance into the New Park. In this case, an ensuing victory would be regarded as a stroke of genius by historians. Indeed, Edward may even have had the battle of Falkirk in mind as a model. Wallace's army was not very different from that of King Robert. Robert may have had a rather larger number of men-at-arms under his command, and the average quality of the armour of his rank and file may have been rather higher given that he apparently turned away men whose equipment was not up to the mark, but the vast majority of both armies were spearmen. Like William Wallace, Robert chose to deploy his army initially on high ground, from which he could observe the enemy. It would not have seemed unreasonable to Edward or his lieutenants to assume that Robert intended to fight a defensive battle if, indeed, he chose to fight at all. Professor Duncan finds Barrow's site unacceptable because it includes a steep incline which is not mentioned by any of the contemporary accounts, however this rather misses the point. The Scots advanced on the English and therefore deployed from the higher ground down to the plain, leaving the wooded New Park to array themselves on flat ground in front of the English position. This would rather undermine the proposition that the main action took place in the area now covered by Bannockburn High School. The school is of relatively recent construction and the ground had been levelled for the buildings and also for the extensive playing fields, but seems to have been a relatively flat expanse before that. The site would not, however, fit with the 'flat' terrain which all of the contemporary sources agree was the location of the fighting. It would, however, form a good place for King Robert to marshal his troops before their advance down to the plain, in which case it is surely a strong possibility that the initial clash between Carrick and Gloucester may have taken place in the vicinity of the railway line which cuts across the flat ground to the east of Bannockburn High School. The school grounds would also have provided a suitable location for King Robert to meet the English if he had chosen to fight a defensive action. Edward's cavalry could not have negotiated the slope to the south of the school grounds, nor could it have made a good charge pace up the slopes to the east and north. Further, although he could have marched his archers up the slope to engage the Scots, they would have been very close to the enemy and vulnerable to an advance by their infantry or a charge from their cavalry.

Edward's deployment on 24 June is open to criticism because he lost his battle, but in fairness, he did not get to fight the sort of battle that he would have envisaged. On balance, both commanders chose their concentration and deployment areas for rational reasons; Edward's position gave him water, night protection and a clearly defined bivouac area which his officers could control reasonably easily, and Robert's move to the New Park had similar advantages. Several burns pass through the boundaries of the Park, so there was no shortage of water and the Park itself would have been defined by fences and/or ditches to control the movement of game, thus providing his officers with a clear definition of boundaries which could be monitored to prevent, or at least impede, desertion.

8

Muster and March to Battle:
17–18 June 1314 to 22 June 1314

The March to Stirling

The English army left its muster areas at Wark and Berwick on 17–18 June[1] and marched through Lauderdale and Tweeddale to Edinburgh, arriving on or before the 22nd.[2] Here they may have collected provisions from shipping[3] before marching on to Falkirk, where they spent the night of the 22–23rd. They had made reasonably good time, but had hardly been setting speed records, even by the rather slow rates of march common to medieval armies. There is no reason to assume that the troops arrived at Falkirk in a state of exhaustion. The final leg, from Falkirk to Stirling, may have well been the longest single day's march performed by the army but, again, it was not so great a distance as to cause excessive fatigue. A similar march in mid-winter would have been a far greater achievement given the very short period of day-light. At midsummer, dawn would break before four o'clock and there would still be enough light to march by at ten o'clock. Obviously the army could not march continuously for eighteen hours, save, perhaps in a dire emergency. It would take some time to get the army on the road and there would need to be an allowance for making camp and an opportunity for men and beasts to be fed and watered. Medieval estimates of the time of day cannot be taken too seriously, but it is clear that the day was well advanced by the time the leading elements of Edward's force came within sight of Stirling. Even so, the army appears to have been able to cross the Bannock Burn and make camp by dusk on 23 June. There is nothing in the contemporary material to indicate that the army had suffered a heavy loss from men or horses dropping by the wayside. Any degree of exhaustion would be as much a product of heat as anything else. Scottish summer days can be very warm, but the issue would have been more the effort of carrying arms and armour than the physical temperature. Assuming that the army had commenced its march from Falkirk within two hours of dawn and made an average of about two miles per hour, the forward elements of the infantry would probably have arrived at the Bannock Burn by late afternoon. The wagons and carts of the supply train may have taken a little longer to arrive, but there is no reason to assume that they had not crossed the Bannock before the end of the day. The forward elements under the Earls of Hereford and Gloucester and Lords Clifford and Beaumont may have arrived rather earlier in the day. Sir Philip Moubray met with King Edward a few miles from Stirling 'after dinner', which MacKenzie interpreted as meaning around midday, though perhaps mid to late afternoon would be a more realistic assessment.[4]

The army had made reasonably good time and there is no reason to assume that they arrived at Bannockburn in anything other than good order. Barbour had King Robert spread word that the English were in disarray due to the length of their journey and poor march-discipline, but this was clearly a matter of propaganda. Robert took the precaution of moving his men into the woods of the New Park, thus ensuring that his force could not be observed by the advancing English or by the Stirling garrison, but by doing so he also ensured that his troops could not see the enemy as they made their way across the Bannock and into their bivouac area. This allowed him to control information within his own army, and anything the troops knew about the enemy was only what Robert chose for them to know.

This was not the case in Edward's camp. The defeats at the Entry and St Ninians prevented any adequate reconnaissance of the Scottish position and the acquisition of detailed intelligence relating to the Scottish army. The latter, though it would obviously have been desirable, was not, perhaps, as significant as all that. The English cannot have waged war in Scotland for more than eighteen years without gaining a reasonable working knowledge of Scottish military practice and of the scale of army that a Scottish government could raise. This does not mean that any conclusions the English command might come to would necessarily be valid. It is perfectly possible, even probable, that the force under Robert's command was substantially larger than any that he had gathered in the past. He had certainly mustered an army in 1310–11 in the face of invasion, but the force had not been large enough to challenge the English in open battle. In effect, Edward and his lieutenants would have had a good understanding of the nature of Robert's army, but perhaps little idea of its strength.

Preparing for Battle

The Scots of course were already on-site. They had no need to make camp, their victualling arrangements had been in place for a month or more, and King Robert was able to observe the English army as it arrived. Robert started to muster his army several weeks before the battle, but we should not assume that he achieved his full strength in short order; medieval musters were notoriously slow. He may not, in any case have wanted to bring all of his men together at once. There would be a lot to be said for bringing a relatively modest number of men together initially, so that they could be intensively trained and form a cadre to facilitate the training of others as the army grew, rather than trying to instil all of the necessary drill and weapon training to a very large body of troops.

His army was certainly not idle in the weeks before the battle. Sir Philip Moubray informed Edward II that the Scots were gathering at Stirling and that they were blocking up the paths that passed through the New Park. There were several reasons why he might do this. Robert would have been very rash indeed had he assumed that no one in the English army would have been familiar with the area. Since the army was mustering in or around a hunting reserve and since hunting was such an important and popular entertainment for the noble classes, it would be very unlikely indeed that there were no English gentlemen who had, at one time or another, hunted in the New Park. They would therefore be familiar with the paths, tracks and views that would have traversed the woods and thickets of the Park. By rendering these paths impassable, Robert would obviously have reduced the possibility that a body of English troops might make their way into the rear of his army unnoticed.

He may have undertaken a more ambitious project at the same time. If he could block paths to impede the English, he could also make new paths which would allow him to move troops quickly and unobtrusively to react to developments. We might consider this as a possible factor of some importance to the opening phase of the main action on 24 June. It is clear that the Scots moved down to the plain from the higher wooded terrain of the Park in order to engage the English. This would not have been easy to accomplish either quickly or in good order if the troops had had to make their way down the slope through the trees in line abreast. If, on the other hand, they could march down the hill in column along paths which led directly to the plain, there would be a very good chance that they could move from column to line at the edge of the wooded area out of sight of the enemy before advancing into view and kneeling to pray.

In addition to training his men and ensuring that they were adequately armed, Robert put some effort into preparing the field. If we can reject Trokelowe's trenches we cannot reject the 'pots' which Barbour tells us were dug in a field near the Entry. Barbour tells us that the king stationed his army in the New Park and ordered the construction of these pots to channel the route of the English advance:

Tharfor withoutyn mar delay
He til the New park held his way
With all that in his leding war
And in the New park herberyt thar
And in a plane field by the way,
Quhar he thocht ned behovyd away
The Inglismen gif that thai wald
Thou the park to the castel hald
He gret men mony pottis ma
Off a fute-breid round , and all tha
War dep up til a mannys kne,
Sa thyk that thai may liknyt be
Til a wax cayme that beis mais.

[*Therefore the king immediately made his way to the new park with all the men under his command, and made camp in the Park, then, in a clear field beside the road, which he thought the English would need to take if they were to pass to the castle, he had his men dig many holes a foot wide and as deep as a man's knee, so thickly that they might be likened to a wax comb, such as bees make.*]

The pits have been an important fixture of secondary accounts of the battle, but have yet to be reliably identified by archaeology. Even if they were deliberately filled in after the fighting, one might have expected that they would still show up as parch-marks in aerial photography. Although they appear in many plans of the battle, they have never been reliably identified by observers. J.E. Morris[5] cites a Lieutenant Campbell who, visiting the generally accepted site of the time (prior to 1845), claimed to have observed marshes bordering the Bannock being drained and to have seen:

... many circular holes about eighteen inches deep, very close to one another, with a sharp pointed stake in the centre of each. The stakes were in a state of decomposition ... There were some swords and spearheads, horseshoes ...

Campbell asserted that these pots were at the western end of Halbert Marsh, which Morris takes to mean that they were distributed along the western foot of Coxet Hill. Campbell's description does not appear in later editions of Tytler; and, as Morris says, no one corroborates him. It is surely very unlikely that these pits could have been exposed without more investigation. Further, medieval swords and spearheads were already considered to be desirable arte-facts by antiquarians and collectors and would therefore have a good potential cash value to the men working on the drainage project. If Campbell's claims were true, one would have expected that some of the swords and spearheads would have survived in local collections. More to the point perhaps, one must question why the Scots would choose to arm the pots with expensive items such as swords and spearheads, indeed one must wonder why Lt Campbell did not help himself to a few examples as curiosities or souvenirs.

This does not mean that we can arbitrarily discount the existence of the pots. On the contrary, we should assume that the pots were dug and that they fulfilled their purpose in forcing the English cavalry to advance on a very nar-row front and into an area where they would be vulnerable to Scottish archery attacks to their flanks and spearmen attacks to their front. But we have, as yet, no evidence to show exactly where they were situated. In the absence of fur-ther evidence, we should accept that they lay close to the course of the road that ran through the New Park to the town and castle of Stirling and that they were distributed on either side of the road to deny space to the English and to protect the flanks of the Scots from significant infiltration. It is, of course, quite possible that individual English men-at-arms could have made their way to the rear of the Scots by gingerly picking a path through the pots and wood-land to the left and right of the Scottish position, but we can be confident that there was no viable route for a formed body of any strength. Any intrepid souls who did try to pass around the flanks of the main body of the Scots would also have had to brave the shooting of King Robert's archers, who were stationed among the trees and shrubs of the Park.

Clearly, at least in Barbour's view, the 'pots' were dug in one location: a flat field aside the road near to where it passed into the New Park. Neither he, nor any of the chroniclers, suggests that they played any part in the main action. Interestingly, Barbour was sure that the pots were dug in the course of one night, Saturday 22 June. Robert's army had been gathered at Stirling for some weeks by this point, so one might assume that any preparation of the field would have been made well before this juncture. Digging a vast number of holes would, after all, be a very labour-intensive business, and since Robert was, by this point, very familiar with the terrain, it can hardly have been news to him that the English army would very probably attempt to force a passage to Stirling through the New Park. With a force of several thousand combatants and a considerable number of non-combatants on hand, Robert was not short of labour, but there may also have been a security aspect. The earlier the pots were constructed, the more chance there would be of their location coming to the attention of the Stirling garrison and of that information being passed to the English army, which would rather compromise their value. Setting the army to a lengthy physical task through the Saturday night may have had another advantage, in that it gave the troops something to keep them occupied rather than allowing them to dwell on the prospect of combat. It would also have made the army rather easier to observe, reducing the opportunities for desertion.

Blocking paths in the New Park and digging pots may possibly have been supplemented by the distribution of caltrops. A number of these wicked instruments are alleged to have been recovered from the battlefield. If used at all they must have been limited to the areas around the Entry and St Ninians. If they had been scattered between the armies prior to the main battle they would have been more of a problem for the Scots than the English. Had they been used at St Ninians, we should certainly expect that Grey would have mentioned them since they would have been an instrumental part in the defeat of Clifford and Beaumont's command – this was where Sir Thomas Grey senior was taken prisoner after all. Caltrops are also conspicuous by their absence in *Lanercost* or the other accounts. Mr Shearer, citing Oman's 'History of the Art of War', offers a useful comment, one which we should take seriously since there are several caltrops in private collections which are claimed to have been recovered from various locations in the Bannockburn area:

> It is whispered that caltrops for tourists are occasionally manufactured by modern enterprise.[6]

It is of course impossible to prove definitively that no caltrops were used at Bannockburn, though they do not seem to have been a part of the normal equipment and tactical practice of the Scots of the Middle Ages, but it would seem very unlikely that they played any part in the battle. Even so, Shearer was quite wrong to assert that those caltrops which are alleged to have been recovered from the area would have been ineffective due to their small size, being only 'two or three inches' in height and of rather flimsy construction. It is true that they might be crushed by the hoof of a horse, but the 'frog' enclosed by the hoof is quite delicate and easily damaged by a lodged stone, let alone a sharp spike and anyone who has stood on a drawing pin in their stocking soles will be aware that even a very small object can cause a remarkable degree of discomfort.

There seems little doubt that regardless of when Robert decided that he would offer battle, his troops were well prepared for the business of fighting. Professor Duncan makes the observation that the battle was a huge gamble '… which perhaps a wise general would have refused'.[7] This opinion is echoed by several other historians, including Dr McNamee,[8] however observation and experience led Robert to believe that he could achieve a major victory, and his experience of battle, his knowledge of the capacities of his troops – and those of the English army – cannot be discounted. He was clearly confident, and this is an important consideration. Competent generals do not choose to fight lightly; they do so either because they have no real choice or because they believe that they will win.

The same is true of Edward II. He was very confident that his army had the power and expertise to deliver a decisive victory. One might make the observation that the previous great victory over the Scots – Falkirk – had been a tactical success, but brought the English no closer to victory in war, but that is a different matter. On the morning of 24 June, Edward clearly believed that he was on the cusp of a major military success. Victory might not bring the end of the war, but it would certainly help to restore his political credibility and prestige at the expense of Robert Bruce, and might well allow the recovery of towns and castles in central and southern Scotland at least.

Offering or accepting battle is always something of a gamble regardless of the strength or equipment of the armies involved, but the risks must have seemed rather less serious to Robert than they do to us. There are several reasons why this should have been the case. The disparity of numbers may not have been as apparent to Robert and his lieutenants as we might expect. James Douglas and Sir Robert Keith had made a reconnaissance of the English army and had been impressed by its scale, but it is notoriously difficult to gauge numbers, as we can see from the wildly varying estimates of attendance at demonstration marches. Also, our view of the situation is heavily coloured by questionable perceptions about the nature of Anglo–Scottish battles. It is important to remember that no one at Bannockburn had witnessed more than one really large-scale confrontation between Scottish and English armies for the simple reason that there had only been one such action – Falkirk – since the battle of the Standard in 1138. Wallace's great victory at Stirling Bridge was far from being a conventional general engagement.

There is also the matter of the confidence of the army. If the troops were in good heart, well fed, well armed, well trained and well rested, they were likely to be confident about their own abilities, but they were also likely to have confidence in their leaders. The army was, by Scottish standards, very large, and there would have been a high level of combat experience among the rank and file.

Men would have been aware of the 1310 campaign which had not resulted in a general engagement and would have had confidence in the king's abilities as a commander. If he chose not to fight, it would be for good reasons, and if he chose to give battle, it would be because he believed in his men. The morale of the army was likely to be very high. Not only was the army strong, but all of the heroes of the age were present – Douglas, the Earl of Moray, the Earl of Carrick and, of course, the king himself. The lack of 'big battle' experience may not have been as significant as we might expect. It is not at all clear that there was very much difference between being in the front rank of a formation of 200 and a formation of 2,000; the business of fighting or of being wounded or killed would surely be much the same however many men were engaged. Nor is it certain that past defeat necessarily had very much influence on the morale of the troops. Men who had survived Falkirk and were under arms at Bannockburn may have believed that the quality of the army – and of the commanders – was very much better in 1314 than it had been in 1298.

Evidently Robert was able to persuade his troops that a battle at Bannockburn could be won and that a repeat of the Falkirk debacle was not inevitable. The situations were certainly different in one sense. Unlike Wallace, Bruce had a plan for victory rather than a plan to avoid defeat.

The successful actions at the Entry and St Ninians on 23 June obviously had a positive effect on the army as a whole. The men involved would have been pleased with themselves and the men who had not fought on the Sunday would probably be all the more eager to prove themselves in the greater engagement on the Monday. Familiarity with the ground, confidence in their arms and training and a clear understanding of what was expected of them were all factors that would breed confidence. On top of this there was the inspirational figure of the king. His duel with De Bohun at the Entry cannot have failed to encourage confidence in the king and his cause, but his presence probably had a greater value. The speeches put in the mouths of medieval commanders by chroniclers do have a theatrical unreality about them, but we should not doubt that the king did spend some time on the evening of the 23rd talking to his men, encouraging their self-confidence. This would probably be more effective for those men – and there must have been a good many of them – who had never been in battle before. The veteran soldiers would know the score already, but even the most hardened of them would be likely to draw confidence from the presence of a leader with whom they had shared previous fights and the hardships of life in the field.

The proportion of veterans to novices would have been relatively high for a medieval army since there had been intermittent war with the English for the best part of twenty years; a whole generation of men would have grown up with war as the background of their lives. This would not be an unmixed blessing. Men who have seen a lot of combat are not easily moved to undertake dangerous operations and their experience would tell them whether a particular approach to battle was inherently unsafe. The fact that Robert's army was clearly ready and willing to carry the fight to the enemy, despite the high level of experience among the more experienced troops, is an indication that they saw the movement to the plain from the woods and high ground overlooking the carse as a viable proposition. The implications of this are greater than the matter of abandoning high ground for low ground. An advance against Edward's army would inevitably mean a confrontation with the English horse on terrain that was eminently suitable for mounted combat. Clearly the rank and file of the Scottish army were not intimidated by this prospect. To some extent they would have been encouraged by the successes of Moray and the King's formations on the evening of the 23rd, but those successes could not have happened unless the Scots were already confident of their ability to meet and defeat cavalry with spears. There was nothing terribly revolutionary about this. The initial English cavalry attacks at Falkirk had been repulsed, the Flemings had defeated the French at Courtrai, King Robert's troops had been victorious at Loudon and elsewhere, but the strength of disciplined infantry was well known from theoretical treatises. Many, perhaps most, of the senior commanders would have been familiar with the works of Vegetius, who was very aware of the weaknesses of heavy cavalry:

[who] are safe from being wounded on account of the armour they wear, but because they are hampered by the weight of their arms, are easily taken prisoner.[9]

In the right circumstances and if the opposing infantry failed to keep good order, heavy cavalry could be devastating, but their vulnerability to well-ordered infantry who would keep their formation when attacked, unsupported cavalry had grave weaknesses. To fight at all is always a risk, but for Robert, his commanders and his troops, the risks were outweighed by the advantages. The potential for victory was, in their eyes at least, rather better than the potential for defeat. There were, of course, several political pressures on Robert which made battle an attractive option, but none of these was so great as to make battle a vital step in the process of gaining recognition for his kingship. A great defeat would undo the achievements of the preceding eight years, and it is impossible to believe that he would have led his men into the field if he was not confident that victory would be his.

Robert was not alone in having confidence that he could secure a victory; the English army does not seem to have lacked self-belief. Edward had raised a large and well-found army, probably at least as large as the one that his father had led to victory at Falkirk. The vital man-at-arms component was very much larger than its Scottish counterpart and possibly – though this is not supported by the evidence[10] – equipped and mounted to a higher standard.

Until 23 June, Edward and his lieutenants were at least as confident of victory as King Robert. The army was large and there is no reason to suppose that the troops were not well equipped. The senior commanders included several men with extensive experience of war generally and of campaigning against the Scots in particular. Robert Clifford and Aymer de Valence had been involved in several operations against the Bruce party, and De Valence had even inflicted a defeat on King Robert at Methven in 1306. There were many veterans and at least one internationally acclaimed paladin, Sir Giles d'Argentan. Edward himself had spent a good deal of time campaigning in Scotland during his father's reign and his own; he cannot simply be dismissed as being militarily ignorant. The confidence of the troops may have started to break down because of the two actions on the evening of 23 June, but neither of those engagements was large enough to inflict serious damage on the strength of the English army as a whole. There certainly seems to have been no reluctance to accept or seek battle on 24 June; on the contrary, it would seem that there was a strong belief that the Scots would not be able to withstand a general engagement.

Some of the English chroniclers, such as Baker and the author of the *Vita* in particular, saw over-confidence as a major issue, identifying the impetuous and arrogant behaviour of the commanders as the chief cause of defeat. For others – and this includes the Scottish chronicler, Bower – there was a theological element. In their view, the Scots had put their faith in God and had been suitably rewarded with victory. For these writers, the defeat at Bannockburn was more the product of God's punishment for English arrogance and impetuosity than his endorsement of the Scots.

English confidence was not altogether ill-founded. They had secured a major victory in the only other really grand-scale battle that the war had produced. There had been other victories and defeats. The Scots had won at Stirling Bridge, but that could be dismissed as an anomaly and the cause of defeat was fairly obvious. Roslin had been a fight of some significance politically, and a considerable boost to Scottish morale, but it was not a really major engagement. Similarly, the defeat of De Valence at Loudon had given Robert some domestic military credibility, but the forces engaged were not large and the circumstances unusual. On the other hand, Falkirk was a very large battle of a fairly conventional nature, and the English had unquestionably scored a great victory. Given the nature of their experience to date, the English had every reason to believe that they could and would defeat the Scots in 1314.

Arma Virumque Canto

Whatever planning and preparation took place before the fighting, the action itself came down to the business of men fighting one another with swords, spears and bows. A great deal of effort has been devoted to the study of horseflesh[11] and the construction of armour,[12] but remarkably little attention has been paid to the experience of combat beyond references to spears breaking or men (and horses where appropriate) being mown down by hailstorms of arrows. It is important to remember that one of the reasons – perhaps the chief reason – that the great longbow victories made such an impression on contemporary writers was that they were rare events. On the other hand, the experience of defeat at the hands of longbowmen was not sufficient to prevent the Scots or the French from accepting or even seeking battle. Despite the effect of massed archery, none of the great battles of the Middle Ages was decided by missile combat alone; they all culminated in close combat. No English commander took to the field with an army which consisted of archers alone. Furthermore, all of the longbow battles were essentially defensive actions. Henry V may have advanced on the French at Agincourt, but he did so in order to force the French to attack; his troops did not advance to contact. Archery could not be sustained indefinitely. Even the most practised archer will start to tire after loosing a relatively small number of shafts in quick succession and a man can only carry a relatively slender supply of arrows. Exhaustion of ammunition does not seem to have been a regular problem for medieval archers, but that is, in part at least, because the enemy would come to contact before the archers ran out of arrows, at which point the archer would have to rely on close combat weapons such as swords and axes or on the protection of their spear-armed colleagues.

Our perception of the effect of archery is heavily influenced by the progress of particular battles and, perhaps, a certain amount of 'Robin Hood' romanticism. Our understanding of the experience of close combat at unit level is little better, and numerous questionable perceptions arise from that. It is almost axiomatic that infantry could not withstand cavalry save in very favourable circumstances, though there are few, if any, examples of cavalry defeating disciplined infantry without the support of archers or other missile-armed troops. There is also a risk of conflating the infantry experience of different eras. It is possible, for example, that Oman assumed that the Scots must have adopted a static defensive posture because that was his (correct) observation of successful infantry actions against cavalry in the Napoleonic wars. For example, he would have been well aware that Marshal Ney's cavalry failed to penetrate the Allied squares at Waterloo despite mounting several courageous attacks. The situations were, however, very different. Wellington's infantry were not spearmen, but musketeers with bayonets. Having the front rank of the infantry kneel and place the butts of their weapons on the ground to present a uniform row of bayonet points to the enemy was viable with a five-foot musket. The second and third ranks of the formation were not required to engage the enemy with their bayonets; their contribution was to maintain steady volleys of musket balls. This was obviously not an option for medieval spearmen. If they were to inflict casualties on the enemy at all then they had to make physical contact with the points of their spears.

The assumption that infantry must inevitably take a defensive posture against cavalry is well established. Morris[13] suggests that Robert:

> ... must have trained his men to halt to receive cavalry a few moments before the impact came.

A justification of 'must have' is hardly firm evidence, and we must surely question *why* they 'must have' done anything of the sort. A major element in repulsing cavalry is the fact that a horse, being a reasonably intelligent creature with a well-developed sense of self-preservation, will not throw itself into an apparently solid structure. However well schooled the beast might be, it would be more than difficult to persuade it to crash onto a great immobile hedge of spear points, but it would be even more of a challenge to persuade it to crash into a hedge that was moving steadily toward it in a threatening manner. We must also give some thought to the infantrymen. How would the men know when to halt? If they did not do so in absolute unison, the integrity of the formation would be compromised by some men coming to a halt before others, and the fact that they were allowed to halt in combat under any circumstances would be an encouragement for the less-committed to halt as far away from the enemy as they possibly could. Additionally, any apparent hesitation on the part of one formation might well have an adverse effect on their comrades in formations not yet engaged, which would not help to maintain the confidence required to commit to the fight.

The assumption that sheer impetus would be enough to carry cavalrymen into the heart of an infantry formation cannot be accepted at face value. It is absolutely clear from accounts of early modern warfare that horses would balk and shy rather than plunge into the ranks of the enemy. The 'scrum' effect which many historians have attributed to cavalry formations is simply not credible. The chief effect of one horse cannoning into the hindquarters of another would be to incapacitate both animals. Simplistic mechanics-based assumptions about the weight and speed of a horse against the weight and strength of a man with a spear are similarly unacceptable for a number of reasons. A good charger could probably attain a speed of around twenty miles per hour at a hard gallop, but the strength of a cavalry charge rests primarily in the ability of the leading rank of the formation to make contact with the enemy as a formed body. The speed of the charge is therefore limited by the speed of the slowest animal, not the fastest. Even the most aggressive of animals will slow down as it approaches any sort of threat however competent the rider may be. Additionally, each charging horse was not facing one man with a spear, but several men. Even if we were to accept the mechanistic approach of assuming that a man and horse weighing the better part of a tonne and travelling at twenty miles an hour would simply brush aside or trample a seventy-kilogram soldier, we must take account of the fact that for every cavalryman in the leading rank, there would be six or eight infantrymen –

possibly more – wielding sharp and heavy spears. To some extent, the speed of the horse would actually increase the effectiveness of the spear at the point of contact and, if the spear formation was deep, penetration into that formation might actually allow more spearmen to join the fight.

Two further points about spearmen and our perceptions of spear combat should be considered. There is a medieval sketch[14] which shows a Welsh soldier with only one shoe. The assumption is that removing one shoe would some-how give the man better purchase on the ground. Extensive experiments on differing surfaces, from bare sun-baked soil to grass to wet ground and thick mud, have not given this author any confidence that this would be the case. It is quite possible that there is an aspect to this that has eluded me. Equally, it is possible that the artist happened to observe a soldier who had lost a shoe.

The other issue is the use of shields. Extensive experiments suggest that a shield is more of an encumbrance than it is worth unless the bearer is using a weapon that can be usefully wielded with one hand. Chronicle references to shields are, with one exception, related to the men-at-arms, not the infantry. The one exception is Trokelowe, who describes the Scots as advancing with their shields closely locked together. The assumption that Scottish spearmen went into battle with shields strapped to their fore-arms, though widespread, cannot be taken as a certainty since it would greatly impede the use of the primary weapon, the spear. The lack of shields would help to explain the very real fear of archery among the rank and file of Scottish armies.

9

The First Clash: The Entry, Evening of 23 June 1314

As the main body of Edward's army approached the Scots, two detachments of heavy cavalry made separate advances toward Stirling. A variety of objectives have been attributed to these forces by historians, so it is worth giving some thought to what the English command may have hoped to achieve in mounting these operations. Traditionally, the technical relief of the castle has been offered as the rationale behind the manoeuvres. Affecting that relief would certainly have been an acceptable gambit in itself, but the offensive of 1314 was intended to do more than just secure one castle, however significant. Edward hoped to bring the Scots to a general engagement where his superior numbers, particularly in men-at-arms could be brought into play. Previous invasions of Scotland had failed to force battle on the Scots, with the result that the huge expense of keeping a major force under arms had obliged Edward to disband his troops and return home without having achieved anything very much. These abortive campaigns had done nothing to enhance Edward's popularity or his credibility as king. Additionally, another failed campaign would probably make it more difficult to raise a respectable force in the future. Edward was unquestionably committed to a combat policy, but if he was to pin the Scots down and force battle on Robert, he had to gather all the intelligence he could about the strength and location of the Scottish army. Edward was certainly aware that the Scots had gathered in the area of the New Park, and he and his lieutenants must have had a good working knowledge of the general nature of Scottish armies and of the general military policies of Robert I.

Given that the Scots were lying in wooded ground and uphill from the perspective of the advancing English forces, they were effectively out of sight. Edward decided to carry out two operations that are probably best thought of as reconnaissance in strength – fighting patrols on a grand scale. Alternatively, there may have been a rather more ambitious rationale to these operations. Since failure to bring the Scots to battle would inevitably compromise the general objectives of the campaign – the destruction of the Bruce party and the restoration of Plantagenet rule – discovering the current location of the Scots would only be part of the solution. If Robert was able to extricate his army without loss and continue to evade the English, little or nothing would have been achieved despite an enormous commitment of manpower and money. Robert's prestige might be damaged if he avoided battle, but Edward's prestige would suffer much more if he had nothing to show for his efforts in mounting the invasion. It is possible, therefore, that the intention of committing the force led by the earls of Gloucester and Hereford to the Entry was to 'pin' the Scots in their current position. If the English could establish a strong mobile force at the south end of the Scottish position and possibly another at the north end, it might prove difficult for Robert to lead his troops into the Lennox. It was late in the day by the time the action took place at the Entry, so if the Scots were trapped on the high ground to the south of Stirling they would be accessible to the main body of the English army the following morning. In Barbour's account, it is clear that Robert was not committed to continuing the action, even after the two successful engagements at the Entry and at St Ninians Church. He saw that withdrawal to terrain that would be difficult for a pursuing English force to negotiate safely would be a viable option.

The Entry lay at the point where the road from Falkirk via Denny – roughly the same route as the A80 today – passed into one of the more densely wooded parts of the Park.

The precise location of the Entry, or at least of the scene of the fighting, cannot be ascertained with any great degree of accuracy, though the recent discovery of an armour-piercing arrowhead in the vicinity of the modern Visitor Centre is perhaps an indication that at least some part of the action occurred there. It would seem that the Scots had deployed a considerable force at the top of a rise and across the road at a point where the distribution of trees formed a sort of tunnel with the road at its centre.

As long as the Scots held this point it was effectively impossible for the English to enter the Park, either to make a reconnaissance of the Scottish positions or to pass through to the castle.

This seems, on balance, to be the most likely location for the 'pots' or 'pitfalls' which have figured in virtually every description of Bannockburn ever written. As others have pointed out,[1] the pots can be seen as a form of medieval minefield, but it is worth bearing in mind the practical function of a minefield.

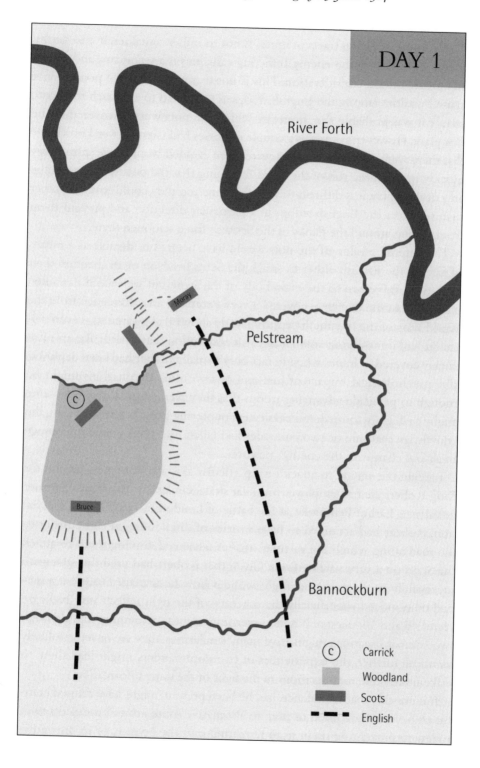

DAY 1

River Forth

Moray

Pelstream

C

Bruce

Bannockburn

C Carrick

Woodland

Scots

English

The purpose of laying tracts of mines is not to inflict casualties, but to deny a stretch of terrain to the enemy. Inflicting casualties is a secondary, and generally rather minor, consideration. This is not to suggest that the pots did not cause casualties among the English troops as they tried to approach the Scots, in fact it was probably the means by which the pots were discovered in the first place. However, as soon as a couple of horses had tripped over, knowledge that there were pots and that they were to be avoided would have spread very quickly through the rest of the force. Assuming that the pots were dug in the area of the Entry, it is difficult to see what function they could have had other than to direct the English troops in a particular direction and prevent them from getting around the flanks of the Scottish force stationed there.

The defensive value of the pots would have been considerable as a means of forcing the English either to attack the Scots head-on or to abandon their operation and return to the main body of the army, but we should not automatically assume that they covered a very extensive area. Evidence from the World Wars of the twentieth century clearly shows that awareness – even suspicion – of mine-laying could lead to an assumption that a particular area was thickly covered in mines when in fact only a small number had been deployed. The psychological impact of just one or two mine detonations might be enough to persuade advancing troops that they were at great risk. The same might well apply to medieval cavalry encountering pots. At the very least, the knowledge that one or two comrades had fallen into traps would discourage an all-out charge on the enemy's position.

Forcing the enemy to attack on a particular axis was not a new gambit for King Robert; he had employed a similar stratagem against the army of Aymer de Valence, Earl of Pembroke, at the battle of Loudon in 1307.[2] On that occasion, Robert had arranged to have a series of ditches dug at right angles to the road along which De Valence's troops advanced, forcing them to attack the Scots on a very narrow front. Given that Robert had used this stratagem successfully in the past, one might wonder how he managed to use it a second time, indeed, superficially, the outcome of the fight reflects very badly on Hereford and Gloucester. It is, however, important to remember that although two combat situations might have many similarities, they are never absolutely identical; further, the experiences of two commanders might lead them to make utterly different decisions in the light of the same information.

It is possible that De Valence, had he been present, might have refused combat or have endeavoured to find an alternative route around the Scots with a view to preventing them from retreating into the Lennox or to disrupting their deployment from the rear. De Valence was not present, however, and even if he had been, he might not assume that the outcome of an action at the Entry would necessarily be the same as that which had occurred at Glentrool six years earlier. He might, for example, have believed that his defeat at Glentrool was not due to the general weakness of unsupported cavalry against formed infantry, but to a lack of 'moral fibre' among the men-at-arms he had led in 1307.

It is, of course, perfectly possible that Hereford and Gloucester did not either expect or intend to come to blows at all, but that they followed the road into the Entry hoping or expecting that the Scots would not attempt to obstruct their passage. There is no good evidence to indicate the strength of their column, though it was undoubtedly a powerful force. It is certainly most unlikely that they intended to engage with the entire Scottish army with only the men under their command, but they may well have felt that their formation was strong enough to deter the Scots from giving battle. Although it is generally assumed that Hereford and Gloucester's party was a force of men-at-arms operating in isolation, there is one piece of evidence to indicate that they led a combined force of horse and foot. Thomas Grey tells us that Henry de Bohun (identified incorrectly by Grey as Piers de Mountforth) who was certainly present – he had the misfortune to be killed by King Robert – was the commander of a body of Welsh infantry. Given that Edward himself had identified the importance of infantry for the campaign of 1314, it would not be surprising if infantry formations were deployed to support cavalry operations. De Bohun seems to have left his command to make a personal reconnaissance when he saw King Robert riding alone some distance from his troops. The famous duel took place after which De Bohun was in no condition to return to his command and bring them into action.

Regardless of the presence or absence of the infantry, the English cavalry formation advanced on the Scots only to find that they could not penetrate the serried ranks of spears. Having been brought to a halt, they were also vulnerable to the Scottish archers in the woods to left and right, and so, after some ferocious fighting in which the Earl of Gloucester was unhorsed, were obliged to retire. The Scots, excited by their own efforts and, no doubt, by the king's duel with De Bohun, pursued for a short distance but were quickly recalled, an indication of the level of control that King Robert had been able to establish over his soldiers. Hereford and Gloucester now retired across the Bannock and made their way toward the main body of the army which was now crossing the Bannock and making camp somewhere in the low-lying area to the west of the River Forth.

The success at the Entry gave Robert a range of choices of action. He could still retire into the Lennox and avoid a major battle. Leaving the field to the English would have some effect on his own prestige and on the morale and confidence of his troops. It would probably give King Edward an opportunity to restore his rule in much of the south of Scotland, but it is unlikely that he would be able to bring about a wave of defections from the Bruce cause among the political community. Without their support, he would struggle to impose, let alone maintain, a stable and secure administration. Even if he could attract support from landholders in the south and east, he could hardly hope to retain their loyalty unless he could dislodge the Bruce party from the rest of the country.

Any political profit from the campaign was likely to be very short-lived if the Bruce party could simply return to their campaigns as soon as Edward's army marched back to England. Alternatively, he could await developments in a position of some strength. Preventing the English from penetrating into the New Park meant that he still had the upper hand in the intelligence and reconnaissance aspects of the battle. Edward was aware of the general location of the Scots, as he had been for some weeks, but was no wiser as to their deployment or strength than he had been before the action. If the Scots were hidden to the English, the reverse was not true. The English were on lower ground and could be kept under observation from the Scottish position. Since Gloucester and Hereford had not managed to establish themselves on the flank or in the rear of the Scottish army, Robert was still able to retire if he chose to do so, but the possibility of offering, or rather forcing, battle must have been in his mind.

The defeat of Gloucester and Hereford would surely have caused some degree of doubt and dismay among the English troops and it certainly had a positive effect on the morale of the Scots. The action at the Entry could hardly have been better for Robert. By the time the fighting was over, it was late in the day, too late for a general advance and attack by the English, many of whom were still filing across the Bannock to their camp area. The English were tired from the march and some of them from the fighting, but only a portion of the Scottish army had been engaged at all. The majority were therefore comparatively well rested, though given the length of the marches executed since the army left Berwick and Wark, none of the English army can really have been considered 'fresh' for the fight.

Additionally, Robert's duel with De Bohun and the action at the Entry would, inevitably, have had a positive effect on the morale of his troops.

No doubt many of them would have been more than happy to follow the king into the Lennox with a view to conducting the sort of evasion campaign that had been so successful in the past but, as events the next day would demonstrate, there was surely some appetite for a fight.

10

The Second Clash: St Ninians and Cambuskenneth Abbey, Evening of 23 June 1314

The action at the Entry was not the only engagement of the day. A second body of men-at-arms marched across the low-lying area to the west and south of the Forth under the command of Sir Robert Clifford and Sir Henry Beaumont. Their most likely approach would have been to take the road past Snabhead, passing to the east of the New Park and St Ninians and on to Stirling. The relief of the castle was surely one of their objectives, possibly the most important one, but it is clear that the commanders were more than happy to fight if an opportunity arose. Dr McKisack[1] has suggested that there was an intention to reinforce the castle garrison, but it is difficult to see what would have been achieved by this. The chief objective of Edward II was to draw the Scots into battle. If the English were victorious the castle would be perfectly secure. In the unlikely event of a defeat Moubray would most certainly have to surrender his charge regardless of whether or not he had been technically relieved. The Scots would simply renew the siege and any reinforcement of the garrison would do nothing more than increase the number of men who would fall prisoner when the castle was eventually forced to surrender. Adding to the complement of men-at-arms under Moubray's command would do little to help his situation and would reduce the cavalry arm of Edward's army.

The size of the party is open to debate. Grey, whose father was a member of the force, gives a strength of 300, but Barbour suggests a strength of 800. If we are to assume that the English army of 1314 was similar in structure and articulation to that of earlier forces, such as the army of 1296 or the army of 1298, it would be a fair guess that the heavy cavalry element was divided into four bodies. Several historians have described these bodies as 'brigades', which is a rather misleading term since the word 'brigade' indicates a group of permanent formations brought together to form a long-term operational formation within the army. The term 'regiment' might therefore be more appropriate. The major formations of cavalry could be considered 'brigades' in the sense that many of the members of the formations did belong to discrete groups, the retinues of more prominent men than themselves. This is not, however, an adequate description of the nature of these 'brigades'. Retinues came in all sorts of shapes and sizes, and the retinue of one earl might be very much larger than that of another. Some minor barons might bring only one or two men-at-arms to the campaign, but they were still leaders of retinues. A good many men were enlisted as individuals, whether through landholding obligations, in exchange for pardons, for pay, or just men who volunteered in search of adventure. No doubt the smaller retinues and individual men-at-arms were apportioned to the formations of the greater magnates at the head of formations based on the core of their own comitiva to achieve a degree of similarity in strength between one formation and another. But there was not, so far as is known, a regular system to define the size of cavalry formations to equal the millenars and centenars of the infantry. There were formation commanders, and the formations consisted of the retinues of bannerets and great lords, but the retinues were not of a uniform size.

Assuming that the total of men-at-arms available to Edward came to something in the region of 2,000–3,000, it would be convenient to assume that each of the cavalry formations was of a similar strength, however this was not the normal practice of the day. The king would almost certainly have personal command of one formation which, unsurprisingly, might well be double the strength of the other cavalry formations of the army. Without a good deal of the material that exists for other English armies of the period, it is quite impossible to make more than a guess at the sizes of the cavalry formations of 1314.

At least one writer has dismissed the possibility that Clifford and Beaumont led a formation as small as 300 men-at-arms. The idea has been dismissed on the grounds that a major formation of cavalry within an English army of such magnitude would surely be a quarter of the total force of men-at-arms and that that total would be at least 2,000 men, thus the formation in question would have some 500 men in its ranks. Another has dismissed Barbour's figure of 800 as being unreasonably large. Neither of these assertions can be supported from the source material relating to the 1314 campaign, nor from material relating to other armies of the period.

Clifford's and Beaumont's command could easily be as small as 300 or as large as 800, though it is probably safe to accept these as the outside parameters, since a force led by two such prominent men would unquestionably be a powerful one. Working from Barbour's description of King Edward's army, Professor Barrow[2] accepts Barbour's assertion that the English cavalry were divided into ten formations, and assumes that each of these formations was of equal size. In this case, the combined total of their command would have been something in the region of 500–600 men-at-arms – a credible figure. One might even suggest that Thomas Grey junior was mistaken in his estimate. If each of the formations consisted of approximately 300 men, it is conceivable that Grey misinterpreted information from his father.

This may have been the case, but if so, it was something of a departure from the usual practice of the period. The heavy cavalry elements of the English armies of 1296 and 1298, both of which had at least 2,000 men-at-arms, were divided into four formations, but they were not of equal strength. The king's own formation being substantially greater than the others.

Regardless of the strength of the Clifford/Beaumont party, the commanders were evidently prepared to fight, but it would be rash to assume that the objective of the operation was to come to blows with the enemy. Naturally, the relief of Stirling Castle was an objective for the whole army, but grasping opportunities to discomfit the Scots would be 'fair game' for a strong armoured column. On the other hand, the nature of Anglo–Scottish war had changed since 1296 when one formation of English men-at-arms had utterly routed the heavy cavalry element of the Scottish army near Dunbar. The lack of infantry support clearly indicated that mobility was an important aspect of the operation, and to some extent that supports the belief that the primary objective was the technical relief of the castle. On the other hand, it is clear that the commanders of the operation did not feel obliged to avoid a fight if the opportunity came their way, and if they felt confident that they could inflict a defeat on the Scots without compromising their orders.

Whether or not their orders really gave them the discretion to engage as they saw fit, Clifford and Beaumont certainly chose to do so. Their march on Stirling was identified and reported to King Robert who promptly sent the Earl of Moray to prevent them entering the town. The only reference to the strength of Moray's force is Barbour, who tells us that this body of troops comprised 500 men. At least one writer has rejected this on the basis of the fact that Moray commanded a very large portion – perhaps a quarter or even a third – of the Scottish army in the main battle, however that is a very misleading contention. It is true that Moray did command a much larger body of troops when the whole army was deployed for battle on the morning of the 24th, however these men were the retainers, tenants and associates of a number of prominent men, whereas the troops that Moray led against Clifford and Beaumont comprised – according to Barbour – his own 'mengne', that is to say, men who lay under Moray's authority for military purposes. Naturally, one would expect that Moray's tenants would fall into that category, but other men would have been encompassed in Moray's military responsibility. As Earl of Moray, he would have authority over men called out from the earldom, many of whom would, of course, be Moray's tenants. Additionally, the Earl of Moray had been at war for several years, during which he would have attracted other men to his banner, members of Moray's comitiva on the basis of their personal relationship. This does not conflict in any sense with Moray's leadership of a larger formation during the fighting on 24 June, indeed it is probably reasonable to assume that Moray's 'mengne' formed part of that larger formation. It was not extraordinary for one individual to have concurrent command responsibilities at more than one level. Clifford and Beaumont were the appointed leaders of a major body of troops, but they were also leaders of personal retinues.[3]

Apparently Clifford and Beaumont's progress took the Scots by surprise to some extent since – according to Barbour – the king had to draw Moray's attention to the threat they posed. That threat may have been considerable. If Clifford's and Beaumont's force was only 300 strong, it is unlikely that they were expected to establish themselves at the northern end of the Scottish position with the intention of forcing a general engagement. They might, however, be considered strong enough to inflict a lot of damage on the Scots if they tried to effect a withdrawal, enough, at least, to cause some disruption in the ranks of Robert's army. This would seem to corroborate the *Lanercost* account, which asserts that Clifford and Beaumont chose to march around the northern end of the New Park to 'prevent the Scots escaping by flight'. It seems to be generally assumed that Clifford's actions were not in any way co-ordinated with those of Gloucester and Hereford. This is certainly true to an extent, since there was no means of effective communication between the two forces. It is crucial to bear in mind that the English command had no reason to believe that the Scots would accept battle unless forced to do so. Alternatively, Clifford may have been tasked with the relief of the castle and with establishing the exact location of the Scots with view to an attack on the following day. Equally, it is quite conceivable that neither of the engagements were really part of a plan at all, and that the commanders of the two columns were acting on their own initiative, eager to build themselves martial reputations. This does not mean that either Gloucester and Hereford or Clifford and Beaumont were exceeding their orders, or that they were incompetent leaders. Senior field commanders are expected to use their initiative and to seek opportunities to damage the enemy.

Had both of these reconnaissance-in-strength operations – Clifford and Beaumont to the north of the Scots, and Gloucester and Hereford to the south – been successful, the Scots would have been in great difficulty. Even if there had been no combat, the inability of the Scots to prevent English troops from reconnoitring their lines would surely have destabilised Scottish morale while simultaneously encouraging the English. More importantly, Robert would have lost the initiative which allowed him to mount his attack on the morning of 24 June.

As it turned out, the Scots intervened successfully and prevented Clifford and Beaumont from attaining their objectives whatever they might have been. The story of the action is quite straightforward and the only sources to describe it – Grey and Barbour – accord well with one another. Each has Moray lead his men out of the woods on the high ground and down to the open plain. The English commanders, sure of the offensive capabilities of their troops, actually retired a space to allow the Scots room to deploy, and then executed a charge which failed to penetrate Moray's schiltrom. Eventually the Scots turned to the offensive and split the English force into two parts, one of which made its way to the castle while the other retired to the main body of the army.

This engagement is one of only two in which the popular understanding of a Scottish schiltrom – a circular formation of men with spears turned outward – can be clearly demonstrated. Barbour tells us that Moray had his men stand back to back and that as the action progressed the English became increasingly frustrated, so much so that they eventually stopped trying to charge into the formation and started to throw weapons at the Scots instead.

The fight continued for some time, and the outcome may have been in doubt. In Barbour's account Douglas, concerned that Moray might be overcome, sought permission from the King to intervene. This was only given reluctantly,[4] since Robert was eager to preserve his deployment. Although Douglas moved to support Moray, he did not actually engage the enemy, but halted his command some distance from the action. This was presumably to avoid encroaching on Moray's moment of glory, since the English were, by this time, losing the fight. His arrival may in fact have been the factor that decided the result. Clifford and Beaumont were heavily engaged, and the threat of another Scottish force joining the fight may have been enough to persuade them to abandon their objective. If, as Professor Duncan suggests,[5] Douglas's force consisted of cavalry, there would be a real risk that the English, tired and disorganised, could be pursued and destroyed. Alternatively, the English commanders may have already come to the conclusion that nothing more could be achieved by continuing the action. The arrival of Douglas encouraged them to accept that they could do no more, and suggested that they should therefore retire to avoid pointless loss of life. Grey does not mention Douglas's presence at St Ninians at all. He may not have considered it significant if, in the opinion of his father, the matter had already been decided by the time Douglas arrived. Alternatively, Grey senior may have been completely unaware of this development; he was, after all, a prisoner in the midst of the Scottish formation and may not have been able to see anything beyond their ranks.

Douglas's decision not to engage may, of course, have been no more than a matter of following his orders. It is quite possible that he was under strict instructions not to intervene unless Moray was in danger of being overrun by the English cavalry, but the decision to hold back from the fight may well have been intentional. On a more practical level, leaving Moray to conclude the business unaided may well have been seen as a valuable boost to the morale and confidence of the army as a whole. If Moray could inflict a defeat on the English with just 500 men, what could be achieved if and when the whole army was committed to battle?

The nature of this action tells us a number of things about medieval infantry operations against cavalry. Since Moray seems to have had no difficulty in bringing his men to the fight, it is clear that they were confident in holding their own against mounted opposition. There were examples of successful actions by foot against horse that may have been known to the Scots, such as the victory of the Flemings over the French at Courtrai in 1302, but there is a good deal of difference between occupying a position of strength against a mounted enemy and marching onto flat terrain to confront him. Evidently Moray's men were sure that they could hold their own, but that confidence may have been encouraged by the nature of the English force. Without the close support of infantry, particularly archers, the English force was actually very vulnerable. If they could not break into the schiltrom, they could achieve nothing beyond providing targets for the Scots. If they chose to retire, the Scots could not pursue them very effectively since a man on a horse is a good deal more mobile than a man on foot. On the other hand, any withdrawal would be an admission of defeat.

Equally, the willingness of Clifford and Beaumont to give the Scots space to 'come on' before launching their attack is also an indication of the confidence of English men-at-arms and their leaders. They too will have been aware of Courtrai and of Stirling Bridge and, perhaps most significantly, of Falkirk. Students of history who are steeped in the narratives and records of the time will be aware that the defeat of the Scottish schiltroms at Falkirk was a product of 'combined arms' tactics, though these were not employed until the cavalry had already failed to achieve a breakthrough. The men who served under Clifford and Beaumont were probably rather more conscious of the eventual victorious charges of the men-at-arms at Falkirk than of the archery that disrupted the Scottish formations and made those charges possible.

Assuming that Barbour is correct in his assertion that Moray's force consisted of only 500 men, it is quite possible that Clifford and Beaumont believed that their own force was more than capable of scattering their opponents. Assuming that they were aware of the nature of the action at Falkirk – and they surely must have been, seeing as they had both taken part in the battle – they were obviously also aware that Wallace's schiltroms had been able to hold off the English cavalry. But the situations were not the same. Wallace's schiltroms were probably something of the order of 2,000 men strong, not 500, and they had been deployed at the top of a fairly steep rise. On top of that, the English men-at-arms had had to negotiate soft ground and muddy burns in order to engage and had had to endure shooting from Scottish archers positioned around and between the schiltroms. At St Ninians, the schiltrom was only 500 strong and, most significantly, the engagement took place on flat, hard ground where the advantages of speed and impetus should have lain with the English.

The inability of Clifford and Beaumont's troops to force their way into the Scottish ranks should not be regarded as a mystery. As a general rule throughout history, cavalry have struggled to impose themselves against formed and confident infantry, particularly in circumstances where the infantry carried spears or other pole arms. This was not merely a medieval phenomenon; there are several examples from the Napoleonic wars of infantry squares maintaining their formations against cavalry charges even when they themselves had run out of ammunition. The explanation for this must surely lie in the psychology of the horse. An inspiring leader might be able to persuade a body of men to throw themselves onto a thicket of spears, but it is very difficult to persuade a horse to do anything so rash. It is true that training and the herd instinct might be sufficient to bring a mounted formation close to a body of infantry, but as long as the infantry stood fast, the majority of horses would pull up, rather like show-jumpers 'refusing' a fence. The horses in the rear ranks of the cavalry formation would obviously have rather less of a view of the enemy and might well press on, but only into the backs of the foremost ranks. Some historians seem to believe that this would bring about a scrummaging effect which would push the leading ranks of the cavalry in to the front ranks of the infantry. It is perfectly credible that this might occur in a few isolated instances within a formation, but it is difficult to imagine that anything of that nature could be adopted as a tactical practice. In general, if a horse really does not want to proceed, it can always stop. Far from pushing into the midst of a schiltrom, a cavalry formation forcing a close attack on infantry would be much more likely to dissolve into a great mass of collisions and fallen chargers.

This was not, of course, the intention of cavalry commanders. What they hoped to achieve was the collapse of order among the opposing infantry as terrified soldiers cast away their weapons and fled. When this occurred, the cavalry would be in their element, pursuing the hapless infantry to their hearts content. Given the nature of the terrain at St Ninians, the absence of Scottish archers and boggy streams, and the strength of their formation, it would be unreasonable to accuse Clifford and Beaumont of rash behaviour. They were both experienced and competent soldiers with, presumably, a good understanding of what cavalry could or could not achieve on the battlefield. Like any commanders worthy of the name, they chose to engage the enemy because they were confident that they could defeat them, not because they were an available target.

The two actions of 23 June are well known, but it would seem that there was a third engagement. Barbour is the only source for a raid on King Robert's stores at Cambuskenneth. The Earl of Atholl, David de Strathbogie, had been active on behalf of Edward II since his defection from the Bruce party before May 1307. He had been entrusted with truce negotiations in 1311–12, but had entered the peace of King Robert before the end of the year. In 1314 he left the Bruce party again, this time because his sister Isabella had been jilted by Edward Bruce. To what extent this action was a matter of defecting to the English or of defying the Bruces is unclear, but he did not return to Robert's peace. Professor Duncan[6] has suggested that the stores at Cambuskenneth may have been the fodder for the royal horses, and that Strathbogie, who was the King's constable, would have been aware of this. It is possible, however, that the Abbey was the chief supply head for the Scottish army. It would have been a well-known institution, well served for roads and situated beside the Forth at a

11

The Night of 23 June 1314

Defeat in the actions at the Entry and at St Ninians prevented Edward's forces from making an adequate reconnaissance of the Scottish positions. It was probably far too late in the day to concentrate the army and array it for an immediate full-scale attack. His forces had covered a considerable distance on 23 June and would surely benefit from a night's rest. Virtually all of the chronicle accounts agree that the English army crossed the Bannock on the Sunday night and must therefore have made camp on low ground to the east of the New Park. There is no reason to suppose that the great train of wagons and carts carrying provisions, tentage, tools and other supplies were not brought into the camp before the end of the day and that rations were distributed to the troops.

On the morning of the 24th the English army was drawn up in front of their camp, which would indicate that the supply trains and the pavilions of the wealthy were concentrated toward the eastern end of the camp site, as far from the Scots as was practical. In Barbour's account, D'Umfraville[1] suggests that Edward should withdraw his army through the camp so that the Scottish attack might be disrupted by the attraction of looting the English baggage, in which case there would need to have been a considerable space of firm, flat terrain behind the camp on which the English could deploy. It is, of course, quite possible that Barbour was misinformed or that he misinterpreted the available data, or even that he invented the episode for the sake of his story.

The camp certainly seems to have been reasonably well established and the supplies brought up in good time, since there are indications that some of the English troops spent the evening drinking and socialising. We should not assume that they all did so. Grey tells us that at least some of the English cavalry spent the night beside their chargers ready for battle. The practical business of campaigning – more a matter of marches and supplies than of combat – was not virgin territory to the English; they had mounted many campaigns in Wales, France, Flanders and Scotland over the preceding thirty years and must have accumulated a wealth of experience in arranging and administering temporary camps. We should not assume that the troops were especially comfortable, but they were probably as well found as they could reasonably hope to be, given that they were in a field in Scotland and in fairly close proximity to the enemy.

The Scots had been on site for some weeks and we can safely assume that they had made themselves reasonably comfortable with tents for the wealthy and shelters for the many. It is possible that there were effectively two Scottish camps; one for the fighting troops and another, which would be quite substantial in itself, for the various craftsmen, merchants, servants and the rest of the hangers-on that were part and parcel of the medieval army. The infantry of either army could at least expect to sleep in relative warmth by wrapping themselves in padded jackets. These garments were *de rigueur* for the close-combat men, but there is no reason to assume that archers could not acquire them if they wanted to. The drawback to sleeping in a jack is the weather. If the jack is soaked, it can become too heavy to wear. It is not difficult, however, to make a crude personal shelter out of a piece of cloth and a couple of sticks. Such a 'bivvy' would not keep the jack dry exactly, but it would keep off the worst of the wet. No doubt the medieval armies were aware of such a technique.

The troops could bed down for the night, but the commanders had to make plans for the battle or withdrawal and pursuit that they expected to take place the following day.

With hindsight, it is far too easy to criticise Edward's approach to a battle which he had actively sought. His own experience, and that of the men around him, had led him to believe that there was no prospect of the Scots making a conventional attack, and he would therefore have to carry the fight to the enemy. This was not an unreasonable analysis, but it was a mistaken one, and Edward's army paid a heavy price for it.

On the night of the 23rd, the Scots were stationed on higher ground than Edward's troops, and were out of sight. He had no means of gauging their strength beyond the estimates that his own experience and that of his subordinates might generate, plus any information that he may have received from Sir Philip Moubray. If the Scots were to be engaged, then Edward's army was going to have to advance from the plain, find the enemy and then engage. The manner and order in which he was to commit his men to the fight would have to depend on the nature of the Scottish deployment. If they intended to fight a purely defensive action, they might well have constructed trenches and barriers which would present too much of a challenge for a simple cavalry attack. In this case, the English would need to use archers in the initial phases of the action in order to disrupt the Scots and possibly drive them from their positions. The cavalry could then make effective attacks on the Scots once they were in motion.

The events of the evening of the 23rd may have caused him some concern. The outcome of the action at the Entry was easily understood. The cavalry had attacked a force of disciplined infantry who had taken up a strong position in an area where the cavalry could not deploy freely. Their repulse was not, in all probability, too much of a surprise. The vulnerability of armoured cavalry against heavy infantry would have been well known to any student of Vegetius. The fact that Gloucester had attacked at all would have been open to criticism, but not incomprehensible. The English had a poor opinion of the capacity of the Scots to fight large engagements, and Gloucester may have thought there was a real possibility that the Scots at the Entry would break and run if threatened by a powerful mounted force. They did not do so, and Gloucester's men were defeated, but there is no evidence to indicate that they had suffered heavy casualties and been driven from the field. It is more likely that Gloucester, realising that there was nothing to be gained from pressing the attack, withdrew his force to rejoin the main body of the army with a view to renewing the action in the morning with infantry support.

The action at St Ninians may have been harder to take. The Scots had met Clifford and Beaumont's force on the open field with no trenches, woods, streams or pots to disrupt the cavalry and, so far as we are aware, no archers either, but had still won the day. There were no mitigating factors to explain or excuse the failure of the cavalry to penetrate the Scottish ranks. This was not the case at the Entry. The Scots had prepared the ground with pots and had archer support on hand. Edward may have been dismayed by the defeat at St Ninians, but equally he may have identified factors – unknown to us – which put a very different complexion on the fight. Neither Edward nor his subordinates seem to have taken the view that the success of the Scots at St Ninians could be repeated on a larger scale.

The English command did not, apparently, make any contingency plans to meet a Scottish attack, but that does not mean that they had not given careful thought to the manner in which they were going to mount their own offensive. They had every reason to believe that the Scots, if they accepted battle at all, would retain their position on the high ground and wait for the English to attack them. Ordering and re-ordering great bodies of men and horses was not an easy thing to achieve. Given that the English commanders were eager to bring the Scots to battle before they could escape, it is reasonable to assume that Edward and his officers made a conscious and deliberate effort to ensure that the deployment adopted by the army for the morning of the 24th would be consistent with their intention to move toward the high ground to attack. It would also have to be flexible enough to be adjusted once a clearer picture of the Scottish position and strength had been acquired, but this does not mean that they had necessarily chosen to array the army in the optimum deployment for an immediate attack. The Scots were some distance away and the army would have to march, possibly for as much as an hour, before they could come into contact if the Scots maintained their position on the New Park.

The English position was strong in the sense that the Scots could not hope to approach on the flanks of the English without being noticed, and so Edward's staff could be confident that there would be ample opportunity to put the army into the posture that they felt most appropriate without interference from the Scots. The maxim that 'plans do not survive contact with the enemy' was demonstrated by the Scottish attack; it was a contingency that had not been seriously considered. We should not assume that the English deployment was unwise for the purpose for which it was designed, just that it was not suitable for a defensive battle on a plain. On the other hand, if the Scots did not move to the attack until four or five hours after first light (see below) it is perfectly feasible that Robert did not make a final decision about his own movements until the English had completed their deployment, or at least until their intentions were obvious. Nor should we assume that he saw attack or withdrawal as his only options. His position in the New Park was a strong one. He had made some preparation of the field at the Entry and may well have made similar arrangements at other locations.

Robert had probably blocked up paths in the Park to channel the English advance as much as to deny them access to the Park, so it would be no surprise if he had constructed pots and trenches at the points where he expected to confront them. He could not be sure that the English would not mount their attack at the first opportunity, nor that they would take a careful and measured approach. If they could position elements of their army in such a way as to prevent the Scots from making a safe withdrawal, Robert might well find himself obliged to fight a defensive battle in the New Park rather than mounting an attack on the plain. It is simply inconceivable that he did not have a plan for a defensive battle as well as one for attack; indeed, the attack option may not even have been his first choice, but the one that made most sense in the light of the English choices of bivouac and deployment areas. Had Edward become aware of the risks facing his army, he might well have chosen to deploy his army in such a way as to make a Scottish attack impractical, in which case we should expect that Robert would have adopted a different policy – either retreat to the hills or stand his ground and fight on the defensive.

Attack was clearly Edward's preference, but it is by no means certain that he would have committed his troops to a simple frontal assault on Robert's positions. He could have attempted to move his entire force across the Pelstream burn and endeavoured to force battle on the Scots from the north rather than the east. Alternatively, he could have divided his army, committing a substantial force to pin the right flank formations of the Scottish army while the rest of the troops advanced westwards from the camp area. He may even have considered avoiding battle in the short term and moving across the plain to seize the bridge at Stirling to pursue a campaign north of the Forth.

If so, the action at St Ninians may have persuaded him that the risks were too great. The Scots were clearly capable of putting a force between the bridge and the main body of the army which would be capable of preventing a body of men-at-arms from capturing the bridge. The bridge itself might be very difficult to take 'at a run'. It was quite narrow – wide enough for a wagon to cross, but not for two wagons to pass one another and might therefore be held for some time by the modest force of archers and spearmen, even in the face of a very much larger force.

Edward may even have planned on keeping the bulk of his army in camp rather than making an attack on the 24th. According to the *Vita*, Gloucester suggested he should wait another day in order to rest the troops. Edward's rejection of his advice may be no more than the assumption of the writer. The Scots had obviously developed a reliable supply system, but Edward had a much larger cavalry arm than Robert. There was every chance that he could destroy the Scottish logistical chain with columns of heavy cavalry that would be more than equal to the task of countering their Scottish counterparts. Edward could not await developments indefinitely. His wagon train could not sustain his army for long and the livestock – horses, draught oxen, meat on the hoof – would need fresh grazing, but there is no suggestion from contemporary evidence that the army was facing serious shortages. The advance of the Scots on the morning of the 24th meant that Edward had no choice but to accept battle on Robert's terms. This does not imply, though, that Edward had not considered a number of options, any of which might have brought him victory or at least saved him from total defeat.

12

The Great Battle at Stirling: 24 June 1314

Given the need for security and water and a 'forming up' area, it is difficult to see a better location for the English army on the night of the 23rd than the one that was chosen. We should also bear in mind that Edward was not alone. He was surrounded by men with considerable professional experience of war in general and of war against the Scots in particular, including Aymer de Valence, Robert Clifford, Henry de Beaumont, John Comyn and Ingram D'Umfraville. As far as one can judge from the contemporary material, none of Edward's officers took issue with the choice of camp site. Indeed, it is by no means certain that Edward chose the site at all. We might assume that Edward was at the head of the main body of his army as it followed the forward formations under Gloucester, Hereford, Clifford and Beaumont.

It cannot be too heavily stressed that the English expected to have to force battle on the Scots. The experience of Edward, and of his lieutenants, was that the Scots would do their utmost to avoid a major confrontation with a large field army. Previous expeditions had foundered for that very reason. A great force could only be maintained for a matter of weeks before desertion, illness and financial stress reduced the ration strength dramatically, so if the opportunity arose to commit that force to battle on reasonable terms, it was best to get on with it before the army dwindled away to nothing. Furthermore, Edward had raised his army with every intention of bringing the Scots to battle if he possibly could; his credibility would be undermined if the armies passed a night in close proximity but did not come to blows.

The onus, then, was on Edward to force battle, and both his troops and his lieutenants seem, in the main, to have been confident of victory, but the condition of the army was not good. The marches from Edinburgh to Falkirk and then to Stirling had been made at some speed, and though they were

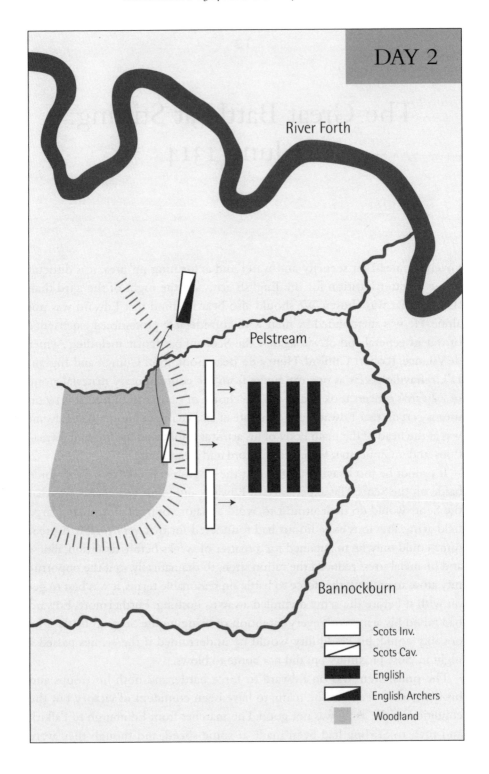

River Forth

DAY 2

Pelstream

Bannockburn

Scots Inv.

Scots Cav.

English

English Archers

Woodland

hardly remarkable feats, both men and horses were less than completely fresh. Two substantial formations had already been in action and been defeated. In all probability, neither had suffered very heavy casualties, but they can hardly have been encouraged by their repulse. Even if the chroniclers did not tell us that the troops were tired and hungry, common sense would tell us that, since the supply wagons were at the tail of the column and had not crossed the Bannock Burn until late in the day, there may have been very little time for the preparation and distribution of food. It is, of course, quite possible that the army completed its concentration early enough on the evening of the 23rd to allow a reasonable period for feeding the troops, watering the horses and pitching tents. If, however, this was not the case, any rations ready for consumption that were carried by individuals – bread, cooked meat, cheese, wine and ale – would almost certainly have been consumed during the march from Edinburgh. Additionally, waiting for rations to be distributed would have meant less time for sleep, so it would not be surprising if men chose to forgo food in favour of rest.

The poor condition of the horses can be exaggerated. The majority of the cavalry would not have ridden their primary charger on the march, but would have saved the stamina of their mount for battle. According to Grey, the English cavalry spent the night beside their mounts with the beasts bitted and, perhaps, saddled ready for battle in the morning. This in itself would have involved a good deal of activity in the camp. Men-at-arms who had travelled to the field on 'riding' horses rather than their chargers would have had to retrieve their mounts from the grooms as well as ensuring that their animals were watered and, if possible, fed. It would be unrealistic to assume that the English camp was inefficiently organised; there were plenty of men in the army with extensive campaign experience, but forming the camp would still have taken some time and midsummer nights are short.

Edward's army had suffered two significant rebuffs during the later afternoon or early evening of the 23rd, but they were far from defeated. Only a relatively small portion of one element of the army, the cavalry, had been engaged at all and it is probable that casualties had not been particularly heavy. It is easy to assume that the army did not achieve concentration for the night until very late in the day, but it is impossible to give a definitive timing for the actions at the Entry and St Ninians. It is perfectly possible that both of these fights had been concluded by late afternoon and that the army as a whole had established its bivouac long before dusk. We cannot even be certain that the day was too far advanced to force a major action. Edward and his lieutenants may have decided that it would be better to let the army have time to eat and rest rather than to press for an immediate battle. This would be the wiser course, since it would allow time to consider their options and would allow for a more careful deployment.

There can be no doubt that the army crossed the Bannock Burn before making camp and that the leading formations which had already fought the Scots re-joined the army. The Bannock did not present a great obstacle to the troops, but it would appear that it was something of a challenge for the wagons. In Barbour's account, the roofs and doors of neighbouring houses were stripped to provide materials for making ramps and bridges to ease their transit. The sources are not unanimous in their description of the condition of the army. According to Trokelowe the English were:

> ... bitter because of their repulse and vowed to be revenged on the morrow or die ... they were hungry and had had no sleep.

On the other hand, Baker tells of drinking and revelry, as does Friar Baston, who was of course in the camp on the Sunday night:

> ... while they thus boast with wine in the night revelling, they kill thee Scotland, with vain words upbraidng. They sleep, they snore.

Grey, whose father was not present since being taken prisoner at St Ninians, tells us that the English cavalry spent the night beside their bitted horses, ready to repulse a surprise attack by the Scots. We should not assume that these views are mutually exclusive. It is perfectly possible that the more experienced commanders of formations or of individual retinues ensured that their men and horses rested, while the less competent allowed their men to indulge in premature celebration. Regardless of their behaviour through the night, it is clear that the army was 'arrayed' early on the morning of the 24th, but we cannot assume that they were deployed for immediate action. The bivouac area must surely have lain some distance from the Scottish position. If the commanders felt there was any chance at all that the Scots would mount a night assault they would hardly have chosen to site their camp within easy striking distance of the New Park, since they were well aware that King Robert's army lay on the high ground overlooking the plain.

Beyond the possibility of a night attack, there was no reason for Edward or his subordinates to believe that the Scots would offer battle; their experience of war against King Robert and against William Wallace before him, would have led them to expect that the Scots would keep to high ground and fight on the defensive. This being the case, it is much more likely than not that the English army was deployed for an advance and might have to march for more than a mile before coming within striking range.

The sources disagree about the nature of the English deployment, but the bulk of the material indicates that at least one body of English cavalry – Gloucester's command – lay to the front of the army, possibly behind a light screen of archers. Mr Nusbacher[1] takes the view that:

> When Edward II deployed his troops for battle on Stirling Carse, he set up a line of units abreast. On his left and right flanks were his archers, in the centre was his horse.

This takes no account of the English close-combat infantry who would undoubtedly have been present in large numbers and is not, in any case, supported by any of the contemporary accounts. *Lanercost* gives Gloucester a command of cavalry and infantry which advanced to counter the Scots, Trokelowe has the English deployed with the cavalry in the rear of the infantry. Grey does not discuss the deployment of the army as a whole, but certainly indicates that the initial counter-attack was delivered by cavalry, as does the author of the *Vita*, while the *Lanercost* account tells us that the battle proper commenced with a vigorous attack on Gloucester's command by the leading Scottish formation. There can be little doubt, then, that the forward element of the English army, with the possible exception of *Lanercost's* body of archers, was a cavalry formation under Gloucester, which, with or without attached infantry, made a counter-attack against the Earl of Carrick's formation.

This would make good tactical sense if Edward expected to move in on the Scots. A screen of archers would provide a degree of night protection against an approach from the west, and the Pelstream and Bannock Burns would form a barrier to approaches from the south and the north. Edward may have positioned Gloucester to the front of the main body of the army to prevent the Scots escaping or to pin them in one position should they choose to fight. If the Scots chose to attack – and this was clearly thought highly improbable – Edward would have a strong force that he could commit immediately with a view to disrupting their plans. Edward, of course, expected that he would be moving against the Scots and not vice versa. His father had adopted a similar plan at Falkirk, where the Earl of Surrey had been tasked with attacking

Wallace's right flank while the other cavalry formations under the Bishop of Durham, the Earl of Lincoln and the King's own formation assaulted the centre and the left flank of the Scottish army. Those attacks had failed, but they did prevent Wallace from adjusting his deployment while the English infantry moved up to support the cavalry.

Edward II may have adopted a more sophisticated plan than his father. Trokelowe describes the English army as having the infantry to the fore with three bodies of cavalry – the 'centre and wings' – in their rear.[2] This does not necessarily contradict other sources which have Gloucester in front of the main body of the army. It seems to have been common practice for English cavalry to be divided into four formations. If this was the case at Bannockburn, then it is quite possible that there were indeed three formations to the rear of the infantry, with Gloucester deployed in front of the army as a whole. This would give him a mounted striking force which would prevent the Scots from redeploying if they were arrayed in static schiltroms. The infantry could then advance to the bulk of the cavalry in reserve ready to break into the Scottish formations or to mount a really effective pursuit if they were to break and run.

Whatever Edward's intentions may have been, his plans were thrown into confusion by the advance of the Scots. Once again, we cannot be sure of the time of day. Dawn would have broken at about half past three and it would have been full light shortly after four o'clock at the latest, but it is not at all certain that the Scots attacked in the early dawn. None of the source material suggests that the English were still abed when the Scots moved out of the woods and into the open field. Whatever arrangements Robert made for moving his troops from the New Park to the lower ground, he can hardly have chosen to march his men down a relatively steep incline and through woodland while it was still dark. He may of course have brought his men to field late on the evening of 23 June, trusting to darkness to keep his movements and intentions secret from the enemy, but this would be a grave risk. Manoeuvring several thousand men in complete silence would have been a considerable challenge, and there was always the risk that an English patrol would alert the English army to his presence. Assuming that the Scots did not start their move down to the plain until first light, it is difficult to see how they could have been in position until at least an hour after dawn.

In Trokelowe's account, the battle commenced at 'about the third hour' which we might expect to mean about nine o'clock. Quite who was monitoring the time – and how – is not clear, and the timing may be no more than a guess, but it is by no means impossible. King Robert was in a good position to observe the behaviour of the English army and may well have been waiting to see what sort of approach they would adopt before making his own move. Robert had very extensive experience of war and had spent the preceding month or more training large infantry formations. He very obviously had a good understanding of what infantry could and could not do. It is therefore a possibility that he decided to keep his troops concealed until the English army had completed deployment for a march on the New Park. He would then advance, confident that Edward would not be able to rearrange his army into formations suitable for receiving an attack while they were in the process of changing their positions.

The move to battle certainly began with the emergence of the Scottish army from the woods. The *Lanercost* account – based on the experience of a 'reliable' eye witness – states that both armies were 'arrayed' and that each had a screen of archers in front of the main concentration of troops. It is reasonable to assume that the body of English archers was not particularly large; they were able to drive off their immediate adversaries – the Scottish archers – with little difficulty, but were not prepared to attempt to force the spear formations to halt through shooting.

Famously, the main bodies of Scots knelt, either to hear mass or to say the Lord's Prayer. It is quite possible that this remarkable act was not performed by the whole army, but only by the forward elements to divert attention while the balance of the army entered the field. It is also possible that the real purpose of this exercise was to give the junior officers an opportunity to ensure that the ranks and files of the units were correctly aligned (see above). It certainly made an impression on the English. Edward is alleged to have assumed that the Scots were kneeling to beg for mercy, which is surely not a credible claim, but this religious act may have had a significant effect on the morale of both sides since it was an indication of confidence that God would reward the pious.

The English commanders seem to have failed to grasp, even at this late stage, that they were about to be attacked, and watched the proceedings with interest, perhaps incredulity, instead of concentrating on the business of preparing for the fight. Prayers over, the Scots resumed their advance. The weight of evidence suggests that the Scots came on in three bodies, with the commands of the Earls of Carrick and Moray to the fore and that of the King stationed centrally and to the rear. Neither the numerical strength nor the breadth of these units can be ascertained, but it is clear that the extreme flanks of the first two formations were protected by the ditches of burns, presumably the Pelstream and the Bannock. They were arrayed in line abreast and were presumably separated by enough of a distance to allow the third formation to come into action between the first two.

As the Scots advanced, Gloucester – whether on his own initiative or under orders from King Edward – took the only rational course of action and led his men in a charge. No doubt he expected this action to stop the Scots in their tracks.

The time between the first appearance of the Scots and clear identification of their intentions would have been quite short, and so there would have been very little time for analysis or reaction. The analysis aspect was straightforward; the Scots were advancing and would soon be in contact unless they decided to halt and wait for the English to come to them. This would not have been a credible proposition. Every moment lost would give the English more time to adjust their deployment. Some English archers had been driven away from the schwerpunkt[3] of the battle, but there were many more available. If they could be brought into action against stationary Scottish spearmen, Robert would have lost the tactical initiative and his men would have lost impetus, and with it the morale advantage of advancing to combat. Gloucester's counter-attack might provide a little time for adjustment, but what would be the best policy? If the English troops were in marching columns, would it be better for Edward to accept battle in the current deployment or to attempt to change formation in the hope that the troops would have re-formed before the Scots made contact?

If the entirety of the English front line consisted of *cavalry*, it would be very difficult to bring the archers into action. If the first line of battle behind Gloucester's men consisted of *infantry*, it would be very difficult to bring the cavalry into battle against the flanks of the Scots because of the burns to the left and right. Gloucester's counter-attack could not achieve much more than a brief delay unless the Scottish formation collapsed at the first onset. If repulsed – which he clearly was – his troops could outrun the Scots and reform, but that would not present a very encouraging example to the formations in the rear, whether mounted or on foot. Additionally, if Gloucester's men retired, the Scots would naturally follow up, thus rapidly reducing the amount of space available for regrouping, reforming or manoeuvring.

Contemporary accounts are very clear about the constricted nature of the battlefield from north to south – that is, the distance between the Pelstream and the Bannock – but the east–west axis was not terribly extensive either. The English had drawn up in front of their camp, which presumably stretched most of the way back to the River Forth. Sir Ingram D'Umfraville is alleged to have advised Edward to draw his troops back through the camp when the Scots first came into view, but there would have been great problems in doing so. The area would have been littered with hundreds of wagons, tents, remounts and draught animals which would have been a severe impediment to an orderly withdrawal. Even if such a retreat could have been performed safely, there may not have been sufficient room between the camp and the Forth to deploy the army at all, and even if there *was*, there would probably not have been time to array the troops in an effective manner before the Scots were upon them.

Time was not the only problem; Edward's army was short of space. Gloucester's attack on the leading Scottish formation under Carrick (the *Vita* author ascribes this formation to Douglas, but is alone in this) had not achieved anything. Gloucester himself was dead, either because he had neglected to put on his surcoat or because he was deserted by his comrades. Having failed to break through Carrick's spearmen, Gloucester's troops were pushed back in disarray and, having had little opportunity to regroup, were probably driven into the main body of the English army. On the other side of the field, Moray's formation advanced to contact and a stiff fight ensued in which the Scots quickly gained the upper hand.

Even so, all was not yet lost. The English army still outnumbered the Scots by a respectable margin and it would seem that there was still an appetite for the fight. There was now a development which only Barbour relates. A body of English archers started to concentrate on one particular flank of the engagement. Their shooting was effective and the battle might have turned in favour of the English, however this was an eventuality that King Robert had foreseen. He had retained a body of mounted men-at-arms as a subtracted reserve, and this formation, 500 strong and under the command of the Earl Marischal, Sir Robert Keith, made a charge and scattered them. It has been suggested that Keith's charge is no more than a figment of Barbour's imagination. This is possible, though it is unlikely that he would have been able to persuade his audience to suspend their disbelief to such an extent.

It is certainly in conflict with other sources which tell us that the entire Scottish army fought on foot, but this may be no more than a conflict of physical perspective. Just because none of the English witnesses saw this part of the action taking place does not mean that it did not happen. At least one English commentator – Baker – tells us that the English archers were unable to come into the fight since they were in the second tier of units and were therefore screened by their own men. This does not compromise Barbour's interpretation. Accepting that there were archers in the rearmost portions of the English army does not mean that there were no archers in other areas. There is no reason to assume that the men who had faced the Scots archers in the *Lanercost* account of the initial phase of the battle had been destroyed; they had, apparently, seen off their opposition, but there is no compelling reason to assume that they had left the battlefield. It is perfectly plausible that they might move out of the way of Carrick and Moray's formations and await an opportunity to rejoin the fight. Further, we cannot simply assume that no one in the English army attempted to gain the initiative by leading a body of archers away from the main body of the army and commit them elsewhere. Edward was not bereft of competent experienced officers with courage and determination.

We might question Barbour's narrative in terms of the relative effectiveness of cavalry and archers, however the various defeats inflicted on men-at-arms by archers were not simply dependent on the effectiveness of the longbow against men and horses. If archers were to defeat horses they needed to be carefully deployed, preferably behind a barrier of some description. They also required an ample supply of ammunition. None of these conditions could be met at Bannockburn. The attention of the archers was focused on the Scottish infantry, relatively few in number and short of ammunition. Whether these factors were relevant or not, the archers can hardly have been expected to withstand a charge unless they had the support of close combat troops, which they clearly did not. Worse still, as they fled from the Scottish cavalry, many of them collided with other English formations who in turn were pushed back onto their neighbours, increasing the crush and confusion.

In Barbour's view this was a crucial moment in the battle. Freed from the attentions of the English archers, the Scottish spearmen could devote their attentions to the enemy in front of them, who were now disorganised and under great pressure. Since the Scottish formations stretched across the field from the Pelstream to the Bannock, there was nowhere to go but backwards.

A controlled withdrawal is a very challenging manoeuvre for any army, but all the more so when it has to be performed in close combat. Moreover the issue for the Scottish formations was really quite straightforward; they just had to press on in the direction in which they had started the battle. For the English formations, the situation was much more complex. When King Robert's troops joined the fight, all of the Scottish units were roughly in a single straight line and they could be sure that anyone to their front was the enemy. If an English commander attempted to extricate his formation from the great heaving mass of cavalry and infantry around him, he could not be sure that he was not exposing his flank to a Scottish force that he had not previously identified, and would in any case have to find a route around other English units. To complicate matters further, his men would have to contend with broken cavalry and panicking rid-erless horses while trying to retire through the tents, wagons and livestock of the camp, as well as keeping a tight formation against the Scots.

Things now went from bad to worse. In Barbour's account, though not in any other, the camp followers, servants, carriage men and grooms of the Scottish army had been watching the spectacle of battle and now decided to make a con-tribution. Grabbing whatever weapons they could find, they chose a leader and, improvising banners from sheets, they advanced to join the fight. The absence of this episode from English accounts does not invalidate it. To Barbour, it was an event of some significance, but it may have passed unnoticed by the witnesses who provided information to English writers. Assuming that the attack of these 'small folk' actually happened – and there is no good reason to discount it – it was probably not an important part of the action in the sense that the battle was already won. Whether the involvement of these grooms, carriage men and camp followers was a matter of planning by King Robert or was a 'group initiative' is open to question. Mr Sadler,[4] citing General Christison, takes the view that the King had stationed them on the rim of high ground overlooking the battlefield to exploit any opportunity that might arise. Barbour, however, indicates that they had been tasked with guarding the provisions and that they were led by a 'captain' of their own choosing. Whether the intervention of the 'small folk' was part of Robert's plan or not, they were obviously close enough to the action to be able to see the progress of the battle and move down to the plain in time to make their own contribution to the fight. Whether they could be seen from the English lines is another matter, but the absence of the small folk from English accounts does not prove their absence from the battle.

No doubt English commanders did their level best to rally their troops and turn the tide, but it was too much to ask of men who had, just a short while before, been looking forward to victory and plunder. The army lost any semblance of good order as the Scots pressed forward and, as it became clear that the day was lost, the men charged with King Edward's personal security decided that it was time to take him away from the battlefield. He does not seem to have been eager to leave, and there should be no question that he lacked personal valour. He had been active in the fighting and though his death might have reflected well upon his character, his capture would be a political disaster of huge proportions. His reins were seized by De Valence and Giles d'Argentan and, accompanied by the knights and men-at-arms of the royal household, they led him toward Stirling Castle.

This was a great blow to the morale of those who were still in the thick of the fighting, and a complete collapse was now inevitable. There was no possibility of an orderly withdrawal and no one to take control of the large numbers of men still milling about on the battlefield. Additionally, Edward's exit would have provided a justification for others to leave the field. If the King was in danger – and he very clearly was – men might decide that their primary duty was to do whatever they could to help protect him. Furthermore, men fleeing the field might be accused of dereliction of duty if they simply made their way home. Finally, when Edward quitted the field there would have been no clear chain of command. Many of the surviving senior officers left with him, and why should those still engaged continue the struggle in his absence? If they could do no more in his cause and were not able to join his company, then their primary duty was to survive, not to add to the horrendous toll of casualties.

Escape was now the only priority, but it was not easy to accomplish. With the Forth in their rear, the only course open to the majority of the army was to head south across the Bannock:

That sua cumbyrsum was
For slyk and depnes for to pas

[*That was difficult to pass over, being deep and slippery.*]

Barbour's claim that men could walk across the burn dry-shod because it was filled to the banks with dead men and horses is undoubtedly an exaggeration, but it was unquestionably a major obstacle in itself and the clamour to escape the advancing did nothing to ease matters.

It would seem that there was an alternative path which some men took; they followed King Edward's party and made for Stirling. To do this, they would have had to pass around the left flank of the Scottish army. This perhaps suggests that the front lines of the army, the men in contact, had swung around to the right so that the Scots no longer occupied the whole of the stretch of land between the Pelstream and the Bannock. A gap would have opened up to their left, through which King Edward had already passed with a portion of his army following behind. Such an account would tally well with Grey's description of the remainder of the English army, who were pressed back into the Bannock rather than forced into the River Forth.

Edward's company reached the castle safely, and although the governor, Moubray, was willing to admit him, he also pointed out that he could not offer a secure haven. Recommending him to make his way through the King's Park, pass around the rear of the Scots and then on to Linlithgow. In the strictest sense, Moubray had been relieved within the terms of his pact with the Earl of Carrick, but realistically there was no point in trying to retain the castle. King Edward would not be able to raise another force for some time, and the castle would certainly fall within a short period. In any case, as a senior Scottish nobleman with little or no property elsewhere, Moubray had his own future to consider. Even if he had been tempted to refuse to surrender his charge, Moubray could hardly have admitted the great crowd of men who, according to Barbour, now ensconced themselves on the castle rock.

For the men still stuck in the Carse it was a different matter. Hemmed in by the Scots and the Bannock, those who could not force their way across the burn could only surrender or fight on to their death.

Of the men who did manage to escape the battle itself, few returned home safely. The Earl of Hereford led a large party of men away from the field and sought shelter at Bothwell – a baronial castle still held for the Plantagenet cause – only to be taken prisoner by its commander, Sir Walter Gilbertson.[5] The Earl of Pembroke, ever the true military professional, having discharged his duty to King Edward by guiding him from the battlefield, collected a considerable number of Welsh troops who had escaped the fight, and led them back to safety in Carlisle.[6] It would not be far-fetched to suppose that these were the men who had made their way to the castle rock, having formed a large enough party to discourage interference from the Scots. Pembroke appears to have left the battlefield with King Edward, but was not in the party that Douglas pursued to Winchburgh and then on to Dunbar. Barbour may have confused Pembroke with Sir Maurice Berkely, who he credits with leading a party of Welsh soldiers away from the battle. However, he also tells us that a great many of them were killed before reaching England.

They were not alone. Other than the party who accompanied Edward and Pembroke, the disintegration of the English army seems to have been more or less complete, and the prospects for individuals or small groups making their way home on their own initiative were very bleak. For many, surrender was the only option. In the words of the *Lanercost Chronicle*:

> Many were taken wandering around outside the castle and in the countryside and many were killed; it was said also that certain knights were taken by women. None of them got back to England unless in a miserable state.

For the chronicler, surrender to women was particularly shameful, but for a shocked and lost knight or man-at-arms, possibly wounded and horseless, it was a sensible course of action. If one was a prisoner, there was at least someone who had an interest in keeping you alive for the sake of a ransom.

Of the great swathe of English soldiers who were captured, the vast majority were either ransomed or exchanged for Scottish prisoners including the Queen, Princess Marjorie, and the Bishop of Glasgow. One notable exception was Sir Marmaduke Twenge, who managed to hide himself in the aftermath of the fighting until he saw an opportunity to surrender to King Robert in person. Quite why he should have done so is not clear, but he may well have been known to the King personally, having been a prisoner of the Scots in 1299 when Robert was acting as one of the Guardians of the Realm on behalf of King John.

English casualties were simply horrendous. If we were to assume that Edward's army amounted to 15,000 combatants – and it is unlikely to have been much less – we cannot take that as the grand total of the number of men he led into Scotland. There would also have been a considerable number of grooms, servants, craftsmen and camp-followers of every description. There may well have been at least as many as 17,000 or 18,000 of Edward's subjects present at Bannockburn, possibly as many as 20,000. There is nothing to indicate that any great number of them survived to tell the tale. This does not mean that they all died or fell prisoner; it is more likely than not that herd instinct brought men together in bodies large enough to dissuade attacks as they passed through the southern counties en route to the border.

Further, pursuit is unlikely to have been very effective; the majority of the Scots were preoccupied with plundering the English camp and the dead and wounded who lay scattered across the battlefield. Even so, it is quite possible that at least a third of Edward's army died on or around the field of Bannockburn or of wounds suffered there. The losses were on a par, perhaps greater than any medieval battle fought between England and a foreign power.[7] In relation to size of population, it was at least as heavy a blow to English society as the first day of the battle of the Somme in 1916. The majority of the infantry were recruited from northern and central England, and very few from south of the River Trent.

Scottish losses were probably considerable, but – as is usually the case for the victor – they were very much lighter than those of the English. Barbour records just two Scottish knights killed in action, William Vipond and Walter Ross, and had nothing whatsoever to say about the men of the rank and file of the army. The fighting had been intense and many Scots must have fallen in battle or died of wounds. Post-combat surgery was rather better than we might expect; men could and did endure the most dreadful injuries and still survive, but there was no effective remedy for infection, gangrene and septicaemia, and peritonitis must have carried off a considerable portion of the non-fatal casualties.

The battle may have been fierce and bloody, but it may have been a fairly brief affair. It was not unknown for a battle to continue for some hours, but there is nothing to suggest that this was the case at Bannockburn. If the Scots took to the field at 'the third hour' and we take that to mean somewhere around nine o'clock, the outcome of the battle may have been decided within little more than an hour. King Edward left the action, rode to the castle, met with the commander and then made a journey from Stirling to Winchburgh. Here he halted his party to rest their horses, before travelling on to reach Dunbar before the end of the day. Dunbar and Stirling are separated by a distance of almost fifty miles as the crow flies, and rather more as the road lies. When his ride to the castle and his journey around the western edge of the New Park are taken into account, it is clear that Edward covered rather more than sixty miles and, to avoid having his men's chargers collapse of exhaustion, he can hardly have averaged more than about six miles per hour. Even if the halt at Winchburgh lasted only an hour or so, Edward must surely have left the battlefield at least eleven or twelve hours before reaching Dunbar. Assuming that he did not arrive there until nightfall, he must have left the battlefield before midday at the very latest.

Understanding defeat or victory is seldom a simple matter of identifying one specific area of superiority or weakness, but there are several factors that we might consider crucial to the outcome of Bannockburn. There is no reason to assume that the English commanders were wilfully negligent or painfully ignorant, but they were over-confident. To some extent, this was the confidence of a larger army faced by a weaker one, but the assumption that the Scots would fight a defensive battle along the lines of Falkirk and the success that Edward I had achieved there led the English commanders to believe that they were invincible. The Scots, on the other hand, were confident because of their faith in King Robert and his subordinates, and they had been intensively trained. The English army fought because they owed service to their King, as did the Scots; but, crucially, they did not feel that their national sovereignty was at stake.

13

After the Fight

Outcomes of the Battle of Bannockburn

For those men who died in the battle or who had escaped unscathed, the business was finished; but for the principals – Robert and Edward – the struggle was far from over. Well over a hundred of the English nobles who fell can be identified by name,[1] a vast number for a battle of this period and an indication of the price paid by the political community. In 1318, Robert de Blakebourne petitioned Edward II for aid in recongnition of his twenty-two years' service in Berwick Castle garrison and against the Scots in other locations. As it was generally known in English record, he had lost his brother and no fewer than ten of his friends at the battle of Stirling.[2] Many more became prisoners of war. They did not expect to remain prisoners until a permanent peace could be negotiated, but they might have to wait many years. Instead, they had to set about agreeing ransoms with their captors. The sums involved could be huge. The younger son of Sir Walter de Fauconberg was freed for 500 marks (a little over £330), Robert Neville of Raby had to find 200 marks for his liberty and William D'Umfraville had to seek permission from Edward II to travel to France to raise the finance for the ransom of Sir Ingram.

Many of those who had escaped had still incurred serious financial damage. The loss of wagons, stores and weapons had to be borne by the individuals, but they could expect at least some degree of compensation for lost chargers, though they might have to wait some time for the money. Roger Heiron[3] claimed £148 for chargers lost at Bannockburn and Sir Richard Lovell was granted the issues of the manor of Eylesham until he had recovered the sum of £96 16s 8d for his eleven mounts lost in the fighting. It is all too easy to assume that the reputation of English armies was ruined by Bannockburn, but it is not clear that they had very much of a reputation in the first place. There had been war with the Scots since 1296, but there had only been one great battle. Edward I had campaigned in Wales, but he had not had to fight against Wales as a united country, as a great deal of the principality had already been under English control for some time. Furthermore, neither Wales nor Scotland was seen as a great military power. Failure to overcome a smaller and – broadly speaking – poorer country in a war of nearly twenty years intermittent duration can hardly have established England as one of the great military powers of the day. On the other hand, while the political damage to Edward II – and to the cause of bringing Scotland under Plantagenet rule – was considerable, neither he, nor his lieutenants, considered the war lost. There would be more campaigns – and defeats – before that became evident.

If the war was not yet lost from the English point of view, it was not yet won for the Scots, however great the victory at Stirling. The assumption that King Robert's kingship was now unchallenged is very misleading. John Balliol was dead, but his son Edward was alive and therefore still the legitimate King of Scotland. Some Scots who would have preferred the Balliol dynasty chose to accept Bruce kingship through *force-majeur* and through fear of forfeiture. Other Scots accepted his rule for lack of another credible Scottish candidate for the throne. No doubt there were those who could not have cared less for any party, but were obliged to accept the government of the day. They may have felt that the Bruces offered the best prospect of peace, security and stability.

Bannockburn empowered Robert as King; it also empowered the Scots militarily. For the rest of Robert's reign, the Scots enjoyed a remarkable level of military superiority which even the failure of the Bruce campaigns in Ireland could not erase. Bannockburn did not, however, end the war with England. In 1316 or 1317[5] an English force which made a landing in Fife was destroyed by a force under the Bishop of Dunkeld, William Sinclair. In 1322 Edward led an army into Lothian, but could not bring King Robert to battle and had to withdraw because of desertion and for want of supplies.[6] The Scots were not idle either. If he was to have peace and establish his family on the throne, Robert needed to force recongnition of his kingship from Edward I. This was not going to be achieved easily. Edward was hardly likely to accept the restoration of Scottish independence and kingship at all, let alone at the behest of a man whose political authority was derived from military force and who was not even the legitimate claimant to the Scottish throne. Of course, pots and kettles are both black; Edward II, like his father before him, had no right whatsoever to try to impose his government on Scotland.

Although Robert was more than willing to have a negotiated settlement, he was not willing to compromise on sovereignty, and the only tool he could wield to force Edward to accept defeat was military action. The policy of raiding into northern England was stepped up; the forces were greater and more daring. English counter-measures were ineffective and led to further defeats at Myton, Byland and Scawton. Edward himself was lucky not to be captured at Rievaulx,[7] and communities as far south as Beverly in Yorkshire found themselves obliged to fork out large sums to avoid being sacked by Scottish forces. Despairing of the capacity of their own king to provide adequate lordship, men in Northumberland, Cumbria and Westmorland started to approach Robert for justice, protection and even for confirmation of their charters.

The war would continue until the disastrous Weardale campaign of 1327, which very nearly resulted in the capture of the young Edward III.[8] The terms of the Treaty of Edinburgh–Northampton of 1328[9] at last gave Robert what he sought – recognition and peace. But he did not have long to enjoy it. On 7 June he died at his country home of Cardross on the River Clyde.[10]

Superficially, his dynasty was secure. He had frustrated an attempted coup in 1320[11] which had been mounted to put Edward Balliol on the throne. He had also restored order and encouraged economic recovery, and had secured a formal peace with England which recognised his kingship and the rights of his heirs. He hoped to ensure his son's safety from English aggression by marrying him to Joan of the Tower, sister of the new English King, Edward III. None of these things prevented Edward III from renewing the war, in the first instance by proxy. In 1332, despite his treaty obligations, he allowed Henry de Beaumont to raise a force of English, French and Low Country adventurers and Scots who had lost their estates through opposition to the Bruce party.[12] Beaumont was the real leader of this army, which mustered on the Humber before taking ship to land in Fife. The titular commander, however, was Edward Balliol, son of the late King John. The army won a great victory over the Scots at Dupplin Muir in August, but by the end of the year, Balliol had already been ejected. The following year, Edward III gave Balliol his overt support; they won another great victory – Halidon Hill – and Edward III was able to impose an occupation government in the south and east of Scotland. There is something of an assumption that only the outbreak of the Hundred Years War prevented Edward III from succeeding where his father and grandfather had failed, but in fact, the occupation government was already failing by the beginning of 1335 when the Earl of Dunbar – who had defected to the English after the disastrous battle of Halidon Hill in 1333 – returned to

Scottish allegiance.[13] Given that virtually all of his property lay within a day's hard ride of the border, he can hardly have chosen to change sides unless he believed that the Scots were going to win this war as they had the last. Success at Stirling was not the only action to have given them confidence in their ability to defeat the English in war. Battles at Myton, Byland, Scawton, Culblean, Crichtondene and many others contributed to a sense of self-belief, but none were as dramatic, or indeed as significant, as that at Bannockburn.

Notes

Preface

1. Myton, 20 September, 1319.
2. Culblean, 30 November, 1335.
3. Burghmuir, 30 July, 1335, Crichtondene, November/December, 1337.
4. Stirling castle fell to Edward I in 1296, to the Scots in 1299, to Edward again in 1304 and to the Scots in 1314.
5. See Dr Fiona Watson's essay, 'The Expression of Power in a Medieval Kingdom; Thirteenth Century Castles.' S. Foster, A. McInnes, R. McInnes (Eds), *Scottish Power Centres* (Edinburgh, 1998).
6. The feature known as the 'Ripple' near Gettysburg, Pennsylvania only appears on maps because it was a feature which had some effect on the course of the fighting. It is too low to be recorded on a conventional map.
7. Two stirrups (not a pair), one bodkin arrowhead and one hammerhead fragment are the sum total of Bannockburn 'finds' to date.

1 The Story So Far

1. S.R. Gardiner, *Outline of English History* (1896). C.W.C. Oman, *History of England* (1910).
2. C.W.C. Oman, *History of the Peninsular War* (5 volumes) (1902–30).
3. W.M. MacKenzie, *The Battle of Bannockburn* (Glasgow, 1913).
4. *Scalacronica, Fordoun, Lanercost, Scotichronicon, Vita Edwardus Secundus,* see 'abbreviations'.
5. E.M. Barron, *The Scottish War of Independence* (Inverness, 1912).
6. G.W.S Barrow, 'Lothian in the War of Independence' (SHR 55, 1976).
7. J. Shearer, *Fact and Fiction in the Story of Bannockburn* (Stirling, 1909).
8. M. Penman, *The Scottish Civil War* (Stroud, 2002).
9. The garrisons of Coull castle, (possibly Aboyne) were relatively large at only 53. A.A.M. Duncan, 'The War of the Scots', p.144 (TRHS, 1991).

10. J. Harvey, *The Plantagenets* (London, 1967), p.121.
11. A.D.M. Barrell, *Medieval Scotland*, p.96 (Cambridge, 2000), hereafter Barrell, *Scotland*.
12. See F. Watson, *Under the Hammer* for a detailed examination of the Balliol resistance to the administration of Edward.
13. See A. Young, The *Comyns. Robert the Bruce's Rivals*, hereafter 'The Comyns', for a detailed examination of the rise and fall of the Comyn family.
14. R. Nicholson, *Scotland. The Later Middle Ages*, p.64 (Edinburgh, 1974), hereafter SLMA.
15. G.W.S. Barrow, *Robert the Bruce and the Community of the Realm of Scotland* (London, 1965 and subsequent editions) for a detailed examination of the career of Robert I, hereafter Barrow, *Bruce*.
16. *The Comyns*, p.208.
17. C. McNamee, *The Wars of the Bruces*, p.59 (East Lothian, 1997), hereafter McNamee, *Wars*.
18. R. Mason, 'Scotching the Brut', in *Scotland Revisited* (Ed.) J. Wormald (London, 1991).
19. G. Donaldson, *Scottish Historical Documents*, p.29 (Edinburgh, 1975), hereafter SHD.
20. W. Fergusson, *Scotland's Relations with England. A Survey to 1707*, p.27 (Edinburgh, 1977).
21. M. McKisack, *England in the Fourteenth Century*, p.35 (Oxford, 1959).
22. J. Harvey, *The Plantagenets*, p.122.
23. *The Comyns*, p.197.
24. J. Harvey, *The Plantagenets*, p.122.
25. *War of the Scots*, p.127.
26. A. Nusbacher, *Bannockburn, 1314*, p.110 (Stroud, 2000).
27. Barrow, *Bruce*, p.62.
28. *Fordoun*, I, p.342.
29. SLMA, p.65.
30. Stevenson, *Documents*, DCXXIV.
31. C. Von Clausewitz, *On War* (Ed.) A. Rapoport (London, 1971).
32. *War of the Scots*, p.127.
33. Barrow, *Bruce*, pp.447–52 lists many southern Scots who supported Robert I in 1306. The list shows only those Scots whose properties were sought by supporters of Edward I, not all of those who accepted Robert's kingship.
34. Only a very modest proportion of town dwellers enjoyed the status of 'burgess', see E. Ewan, *Town Life in Fourteenth Century Scotland* (Edinburgh, 1990).
35. See Barrow's 'Lothian in the War of Independence' for a detailed examination of Scots in Plantagenet garrisons.

2   What Did the Combatants Fight For?

1. Edward took his responsibilities as 'locum' ruler of Scotland pending the outcome of the Great Cause of 1291–92 quite seriously, as indicated by the many surviving documents relating to Scottish affairs calendared by Bain and Stevenson.
2. Barrell, *Scotland*, pp.95–103.
3. The first volume of Stevenson, *Documents*, lists many examples of the fees of sheriffs and household knights who had served Alexander III which were paid under the authority of Edward I for the duration of the Great Cause.
4. 'Itinerary of King Edward I Throughout his Reign', H. Gough, *English Historical Review*, vol. 16 (July 1901).
5. CDS, ii, pp.194–208.
6. Stevenson, *Documents*, ii, p.455.
7. Hugh de Penicuik was forfeited of his chief property at Penicuik, Midlothian and various properties in England for 'rebellion' and had his estates restored under the terms of the Strathord agreement of February 1304. He seems to have been active for the Balliol party throughout the years after 1287/8. CDS, ii, Nos. 1481, 1594.
8. SLMA, p.47.
9. SLMA, p.27.
10. A.A.M. Duncan, *Scotland. The Making of the Kingdom*, pp.590–601 (Edinburgh, 1975).
11. Barrow, *Bruce*, pp.21–2.
12. Ibid, pp.25–7.
13. See *The Comyns*, Chapters 2 and 3 for a detailed examination of the rise of the Comyn family through their service to the crown.
14. M. Prestwich, *The Three Edwards*, pp.44–7 (London, 1980), hereafter *Three Edwards*.
15. SLMA, pp.38–41.
16. Barrell, *Scotland*, pp.95–103 for a brief and lucid discussion of the issues of the Great Cause.
17. Barrow, *Bruce*, p.87.
18. The toll of casualties may well have been confused with an estimate of the number of people killed during the sack of Berwick four weeks earlier.
19. 11 September 1297.
20. Sir Alexander Seton was involved in arranging a truce with the Bruce party in 1308.
21. *Three Edwards*, pp.100–106.
22. Nusbacher, *Bannockburn, 1314*, p.115.
23. SLMA, p.85.
24. Penman, *The Scottish Civil War*, pp.85–6.
25. Barrow, *Bruce*, p.62.

3 Lions and Leopards

1. CDS, ii, 1244.
2. CDS, v, 448.
3. *Three Edwards*, p.80.
4. Ibid.
5. J. Willard, 'The Scottish Raids and the Taxation of Northern England' (Colorado, 1908), cited in McKisack, *England in the Fourteenth Century*.
6. *War of the Scots*, p.144.
7. RRS, v, 41.
8. TNA, C47/22/10/11. Sir Adam had served as Chancellor for Scotland under Edward I.
9. Pierre de Lubaud served as a man-at-arms in Edward I's Lothian garrisons, rising to the post of constable of Linlithgow by September 1305 (CDS, ii, No. 1691). He became a major Lothian landholder under Edward I and Edward II. He defected to the Scots to preserve his position as the Plantagenet administration crumbled, gaining, among other properties, the Barony of Dalkeith, of which he was forfeited in 1316 (RMS, I, 62).
10. Robert de Hastang received temporary grants of the properties of a number of Lothian Scots who were in Bruce allegiance in 1312 (CDS, iii, Nos. 230, 244). Some of these men had been with King Robert for several years before forfeiture, suggesting that Edward II, unlike his heir who forfeited over 100 Lothian men and women in 1335–37, felt that forfeiture was a weapon of last resort.
11. See McNamee, *Wars*, chapter 3 for a detailed examination of Robert I's operations in northern England.
12. Marjorie Comyn, *The Comyns*, p.179.
13. Barrow, *Bruce*, p.118.
14. SLMA, pp.53–4.
15. Ibid, pp.556–6.
16. Barrell, *Scotland*, pp.108–9.
17. Barrow, *Bruce*, pp.151, 188.
18. SLMA, p.59.
19. *The Comyns*, p.174.
20. TNA, C47/22/8.
21. SLMA, p.60.
22. SLMA, p.61.
23. Barrow, *Bruce*, pp.172–5.
24. SLMA, p.67.
25. Barrow, *Bruce*, p.184.
26. Bruce was to be disappointed by his eventual exclusion from senior office. Barrell, *Scotland*, pp.112–3.
27. Barrow, *Bruce*, p.196.
28. C. Brown, *Robert the Bruce. A Life Chronicled*, p.116 (Stroud, 2004).

29. *War of the Scots*, p.135.
30. Barrow, pp.210–13. Robert's coronation or inauguration was witnessed by a surprisingly large section of the senior political community of Scotland including at least three earls – Atholl, Lennox and Menteith – and probably by the young Earl of Mar. According to Guisborough there were five earls, four bishops and 'the people of the land'. The absence of the Comyn family is hardly surprising.
31. Bishop Lamberton, though a strong supporter of Scottish independence, could see the way the wind blew and entered into negotiations to return to the peace of Edward I, claiming that he had been forced to support Bruce, SLMA, 72.
32. McNamee, *Wars*, pp.31–2.
33. Ibid, p.31.
34. SLMA, pp.74–5.
35. McNamee, *Wars*, p.40.
36. Ibid, pp.40–1.
37. Barrow, *Bruce*, p.244.

4   Sources and Interpretation

1. Nusbacher, *Bannockburn, 1314*, p.11.
2. See abbreviations for full title.
3. See abbreviations for full title.
4. See abbreviations for full title.
5. Protections were, as the name applies, documents issued by the crown to give 'protection' from court actions to men who were on active service.
6. *Rot. Scot.* I, p.106.

5   Brave Companies

1. The terms Vallet (or vadlet), Socius, esquire (or escuyer), homines ad arma and occasionally companion are all used interchangeably in many documents calendared by Bain and indicate men-at-arms.
2. CDS 3, pp.376–91, accounts of Sir John de Strivelin, sheriff of Edinburgh for Edward III.
3. SHD, p.54.
4. A.A.M. Duncan, *Scotland. The Making of the Kingdom*, pp.582–3 (Edinburgh, 1975).
5. CDS, ii, Nos 952, 1011
6. CDS, ii, 1011.
7. In a description of one of his early operations, Wallace's force was said to be 'all well mounted'; a term used exclusively of men-at-arms to indicate that they had mounts suitable for war.
8. See Watson's *Under the Hammer* for a detailed and accessible account of the efforts of John Balliol's supporters against Edward I's administration.

9. *Scalacronica*, p.25.
10. CDS, v, No.472.
11. R. Nicholson, *Edward III and the Scots. The Formative Years of a Military Career*, pp.232–6 (Oxford, 1965).
12. TNA, E101/13/15.
13. *War of the Scots*, p.138.
14. A.A.M. Duncan, *The Bruce*, pp.670, 674, 676 (Edinburgh, 1997), hereafter *Barbour*.
15. Barrow, *Bruce*, p.300.
16. 'War and the Later Medieval Scottish Nobility' in (Eds) T. Brotherstone & D. Ditchburn, *Freedom and Authority*, p.120 (East Lothian, 2000).
17. Ibid, p.121.
18. M. Brown, 'The Development of Border Lordship 1332–58', in *Historical Review*, LXXV, February 1997.
19. CDS, v, No. 434.
20. CDS, iii, pp.408–11.
21. CDS, v, No. 514.
22. Ibid, No. 515.
23. CDS, iii, No. 336.
24. CDS, iii, No. 682.
25. J.E. Morris, *Bannockburn*, p.51.
26. *Barbour*, p.420.
27. Ibid, p.423.
28. Nusbacher, *Bannockburn, 1314*, p.116.
29. F. Watson, 'Expressions of Power', p.71.
30. F. Watson, 'The Enigmatic Lion', in (Eds) D. Broun, R. Finlay and M. Lynch, *Image and Identity* (East Lothian, 1998).
31. CDS, v, No. 353.
32. RRS, v, p.414.
33. J. Sadler, *Scottish Battles*, pp.45–53 (Edinburgh, 1996).
34. 'Plea Rolls of the Army of Edward I, 1296', in *Scottish History Society Miscellany* ix, 1990.
35. C. Brown, 'We are Cummand of Gentilmen', p. 51 (PhD thesis, St. Andrews, 2006). *Knights of the Scottish Wars of Independence* (Stroud, 2008).
36. *War of the Scots*, p.145.
37. Barrow, *Bruce*, p.403.
38. Ibid, p.405.
39. RRS, v, pp.48–9.
40. TNA, C47/22/2/57.
41. J. Sadler, *Scottish Battles*, pp.45–53.
42. 'Plea Rolls of the Army of Edward I, 1296', in *Scottish History Society Miscellany* ix, 1990.
43. *Barbour*, p.437.
44. S. Reid, 'Bloody Bannockburn', *Military Illustrated*, No. 224.
45. *Barbour*, p.471.

46. RRS, v, p.261.
47. Ibid, p.453.
48. Ibid, p.459.
49. *Scotichronicon*, viii, p.140.
50. *War of the Scots*, p.148.
51. *Liber Melrose*, I, pp.313–4.
52. RRS, v, p.679.
53. RRS, vi, p.63.
54. CDS, iii, No. 653.
55. McNamee, *Wars*, p.66.
56. Ibid, p.126.
57. CDS, ii, No. 1479.
58. *Rot. Scot*, i, p.78.
59. McNamee, *Wars*, p.126.
60. Barrow, *Bruce*, p.291.
61. *Rot. Scot*, i, p.127

6   Going to the War

1. TNA, C47/22/10/11.
2. CDS, iii, No.337.
3. TNA, SC8/70/3470.
4. *War of the Scots*, p.141.
5. M. Penman, *The Scottish Civil War*, p. 76 (Stroud, 2002), however Professor Duncan suggests that the declaration was issued at the same time as a series of documents issued at a council in Dundee, RRS, v, pp.35–7.
6. C47/3/51/5, PRO 30/26/37.
7. S. Reid, 'Bloody Bannockburn', in *Military Illustrated*, No. 224.
8. CDS, iii, pp.376–91.
9. McNamee, *Wars*, p.62.
10. Barrow, *Bruce*, p.94, n.1, citing TNA E159/69 m.11d.
11. Morris, *Bannockburn*, p.39.
12. McKisack, *England in the Fourteenth Century*, p.35.
13. Morris, *Bannockburn*, p.32.
14. Ibid, p.31.
15. Barrow, *Bruce*, p.293.
16. *Barbour*, p.102. Alexander Seton became a prisoner of war. He was probably taken at the battle of Methven and was sent to York.
17. Barrow, *Bruce*, p.319.

7 Locating the Battle

1. *Barbour*, p.444.
2. Barrow, *Bruce*, p.306.
3. A Merk or Mark was a unit of account; the only coin of this period being the sterling, a silver coin of a given weight and purity, common to what we would now call Germany, The Netherlands and Belgium as well as to Scotland and England. Pennies of all nationalities circulated freely throughout western Europe. A merk was eight score (160) sterlings. Pennies were also accounted in shillings (12) and pounds (240). The fact that a merk was 2/3 of one pound was pure coincidence.
4. Barrow, *Bruce*, p.309.
5. K. De Vries, *Infantry Warfare in the Fourteenth Century. Discipline, Tactics and Technology* (Woodbridge, 1996).
6. CDS, iii, pp.126–7.
7. Barrow, *Bruce*, p.304.
8. J. Sadler, *Scottish Battles*, pp.45–53.
9. Barrow, *Bruce*, p.305.

8 Muster and March to Battle

1. SLMA, p.87.
2. Ibid.
3. MacKenzie, *The Battle of Bannockburn*, p.41 (Glasgow, 1913).
4. Ibid, p.53.
5. Morris, *Bannockburn*, p.62.
6. Shearer, *Fact and Fiction in the Story of Bannockburn*, p.75.
7. *War of the Scots*, p.170.
8. McNamee, *Wars*, p.63.
9. N.P. Milner, *Vegetius; Epitome of Military Science*, p.111 (Liverpool, 1993).
10. See Dr Andrew Ayton, *Knights and Warhorses* (Woodbridge, 1994) and Andy King's paper 'Military Service of Northumbrian Knights' (Durham University medieval Conference, 2001) for a detailed analysis of northern English cavalry service in the later Middle Ages.
11. See R. Davies, *The Medieval Warhorse* (London, 1989) and R. Oakeshott, *A Knight and his Horse* (London, 1995) for a detailed examination of chargers in the later Middle Ages.
12. G. Cameron Stone, *A Glossary of the Construction, Decoration and Use of Arms and Armour* (New York, 1961).
13. Morris, *Bannockburn*, p.87.
14. See C. Brown, *The Second Scottish War of Independence*, p.13 (Stroud, 2002).

9 The First Clash

1. Barrow, *Bruce*, p.311.
2. *Barbour*, pp.296–8, 304–8.

10 The Second Clash

1. McKisack, *England in the Fourteenth Century*, p.36.
2. Barrow, *Bruce*, p.314.
3. The retinue of Sir Robert Clifford included a minimum of twelve men-at-arms, see p.152 above.
4. *Barbour*, p.438.
5. *Barbour*, p.445.
6. *Barbour*, p.505.

11 The Night of 23 June, 1314

1. *Barbour*, p.471.

12 The Great Battle at Stirling

1. Nusbacher, *Bannockburn, 1314*, p.108.
2. Dr De Vries interprets this as meaning that the English cavalry were in two formations behind the infantry, however the words 'wings and centre' surely indicate three separate formations, presumably with King Edward's division in the centre.
3. The focus of the action.
4. J. Sadler, *Scottish Battles*, p.51.
5. *Barbour*, p.500.
6. Barrow, *Bruce*, p.331.
7. Towton, for example, though probably a large battle in terms of numbers, was a purely domestic conflict.

13 After the Fight

1. Walsingham gives a figure of 154 Earls, barons, knights and gentry killed at Bannockburn. Barbour's implied figure of 700 cannot be taken as a careful estimate, but if losses among the men-at-arms were of the order of twenty-five per cent, he might not be so very far from the mark. A song of the time ran 'Maidens of England sore may you mourn/For you have lost your men at Bannockburn.'
2. CDS, iii, No. 627.

3. CDS, iii, No. 624.
4. G. Donaldson, *Scottish Kings*, p.25 (New York, 1967).
5. McNamee, p.214. The expedition was mounted by the Earl of Arundel from the Humber estuary.
6. SLMA, p.104.
7. McNamee, *Wars*, pp.100–101.
8. R. Nicholson, *Edward III and the Scots*, p.35.
9. SHD, pp.61–3.
10. Barrow, *Bruce*, pp.444–5.
11. M. Penman, 'A Fell Coniuracioun Agayn King Robert the Doughty King: the Soules Conspiracy of 1318–20', in *Innes Review*, 50, 1999 is the best examination and analysis of this remarkable event.
12. R. Nicholson, *Edward III and the Scots*, pp.76–84.
13. Ibid, pp.190–1.

Bibliography

Printed Primary Source Material

Acts of the Parliaments of Scotland, C. Innes & T. Thomson (London, 1844).

Anglo-Scottish Relations, 1174–1328, Some Selected Documents, E.L.G. Stones (London, 1965).

Calendar of Chancery Rolls Miscellaneous (London, 1916).

Calendar of Close Rolls, HMSO (London, 1892–1907).

Calendar of Documents Relating to Scotland, vols i-iv, J. Bain (Edinburgh, 1881–88).

Calendar of Documents Relating to Scotland, vol.v, G. Simpson & J. Galbraith (Edinburgh, 1988).

Calendar of Inquisitions (Miscellaneous) (London, 1916).

Calendar of Inquisitions Post Mortem (London, 1908–10).

Carte Monialium de Northberwic, Bannatyne Club (Edinburgh, 1847).

Chronicle of Holyrood (Ed.) O. Anderson, SHS (Edinburgh, 1938).

Chronicle of Melrose (Trans.) J. Stevenson (Llanerch reprint, 1991).

Chronicles (of Jean Froissart) (Tr. & Ed.) G. Brereton (London, 1968).

Chronicles of the Reigns of Edward I and Edward II (Ed.) W. Stubbs (London, 1882).

Chronicon de Lanercost, Bannatyne Club (Edinburgh, 1839).

Chronique de Jean Le Bel (Eds) J. Viard & E. Deprez, *Societe de l'Histoire de France* (Paris, 1904).

Documents and Records Illustrating the History of Scotland, Sir F. Palgrave, Treasury and Exchequer (London, 1837).

Documents Illustrative of the History of Scotland, J. Stevenson (Edinburgh, 1870).

Early Sources of Scottish History, A.O. Anderson (Stamford, 1990).

Edward I and the Throne of Scotland, 1290–96, E.L.G. Stones & G. Simpson (Oxford, 1978).

Exchequer Rolls of Scotland, vol. i (Eds) J. Stuart & G. Burnett (Edinburgh, 1876).

Foedera, Conventiones, Litterae et Cuiuscunque Generis Acta Publica (Ed.) T. Rymer (London, 1816–69).

Gascon Rolls, 1307–17 (Ed.) Y. Renouard (London, 1962).

Liber Cartarum Prioratus Sancti Andree in Scotia, Bannatyne Club (Edinburgh, 1841).

Liber de Sancte Marie de Calchou, Bannatyne Club (Edinburgh, 1846).

Liber Sancte Marie de Melros, Bannatyne Club (Edinburgh, 1887).

Memoranda Rolls 1326–1327 (London, 1968)

Orygenale Cronykil of Scotland, Andrew Wyntoun (Ed.) D. Laing (Edinburgh, 1872–79).

Parliamentary Writs and Writs of Military Summons (Ed.) F. Palgrave (London, 1827–33).

Records of the Wardrobe and Household (Eds) F. & C. Byerley (London, 1985).

Regesta Regum Scottorum, vol. vi. (Ed.) B. Webster, Edinburgh University Press (Edinburgh, 1982).

Regesta Regum Scottorum, vol. v (Ed.) A.A.M. Duncan, Edinburgh University Press (Edinburgh, 1988).

Registrum de Sancte Marie de Neubotle (Ed.) C. Innes (Edinburgh, 1849).

Registrum Honoris de Morton, Bannatyne Club (Edinburgh, 1853).

Registrum Monasterii de Cambuskenneth (Ed.) W. Fraser, Grampian Club (1872).

Rotuli Scotiae, J. MacPherson, Record Commission (London, 1814–19).

Scalacronica of Sir Thomas Grey (Ed. & Trans.) Sir H. Maxwell, Maclehose (Edinburgh, 1907).

Scotichronicon of Walter Bower (Ed.) D. Watt (Aberdeen, 1991).

Scotland in 1298: Documents relating to the campaign of Edward I in that year and especially to the battle of Falkirk, H. Gough (Paisley, 1888).

Scottish Historical Documents, G. Donaldson (Edinburgh, 1974).

Source book of Scottish History (Eds) W. Croft Dickinson, G. Donaldson & I. Milne, Nelson (Edinburgh, 1952).

The Bannatyne Miscellany (Edinburgh, 1836).

The Book of Fayttes of Armes and of Chivalry (Ed.) A. Byles, OUP (Oxford, 1932).

The Bruce, J. Barbour (Ed.) A.A.M. Duncan, Canongate (Edinburgh, 1997).

The Charters of Holyrood, Bannatyne Club (Edinburgh, 1840).

The Chartulary of Newbattle, Bannatyne Club (Edinburgh, 1849).

The Chartulary of Coldstream (Ed.) C. Rogers (London, 1879).

The Chronicle of Lanercost (Trans.) H. Maxwell (Glasgow, 1913).

The Chronicle of Walter of Guisborough (Ed.) J. Rothwell (Camden, 1957).

The Laing Charters (Ed.) J. Anderson, James Thin (Edinburgh, 1899).

The Original Chronicle of Andrew of Wyntoun, STS (Ed.) J. Amours (Edinburgh, 1903–14).

The Register of the Great Seal of Scotland (Ed.) J. Thomson (Edinburgh, 1984).

The Roll of Caerlaverock (Ed.) T. Wright (London, 1864).

Treaty Rolls (Ed.) P. Chaplais (London, 1955).

The Scottish King's Household (Ed.) M. Bateson, SHS Miscellany (Edinburgh, 1904).

Vita Edwardus Secundus (Ed.) N. Denholm-Young (London, 1957).

The National Archives, Kew

The majority of these documents refer to stores, casualties, ransoms and horse valuations. They do not refer specifically to the Battle of Bannockburn, but collectively they make an important contribution to our understanding of the general approach to military service and conditions in the Scottish administrations of Edward I and Edward II.

E101/13/15	SC13/S746
E39/2/21	SC13/S476
E101/7/5	C47/22/3/24
E101/7/1	C47/22/4/2
E101/531/7	C47/22/5/57
E101/531/8	C47/22/9/59
E39/99/19	E101/11/9
E39/99/18	E101/12/38
E101/7/24	E101/17/25
E/39/15/3	E101/68/20
E101/7/9	E101/482/20
E101/7/17	E135/10/1
E101/7/28	E101/16/11
E39/15/1	E39/3/47
E101/10/5	C47/22/2/12
E101/11/14	C47/22/2/32
E101/12/11	E39/100/138
E101/531/13	C47/3/32/25
E101/13/37	C47/22/9/109
E101/17/29	C47/22/6/18
E101/14/21	SC13/S150
E101/68/1/2	SC13/A88
E101/68/1/3	SC1/39/19
E101/428/25	SC32/67
E101/331/5	SC33/3
C47/22/2/33	SC33/31
C143/27/10	SC34/179
SC8/88/4369	SC8/51/2504
SC8/88/4375	SC8/9/432
SC13/A57	C47/22/9/65
SC8/46/2255	E101/12/12
SC8/43/7141	E101/11/14
SC13/A102	C47/22/2/57
SC13/E6	C47/3/51/5
SC13/E9	C47/22/8

National Archives of Scotland

The RH5 series consists of documents transferred to the Scottish Record Office from the Public Records Office in London, most of which also have TNA code references which have been included here. Virtually none of these documents refer specifically to Bannockburn, but they are relevant to our general understanding of military obligation and the political process of late medieval Scotland.

RH5, 39 C47/22/6(43)	RH5, 227
RH5, 20 C47/22/5(1)	RH5, 230
RH5, 22 C47/22/5(3)	RH6, 67
RH5, 31 C47/22/5(16)	RH6, 68
RH5, 32 C47/22/5(15)	RH6, 70
RH5, 41 C47/22/9(2)	RH6, 80
RH5, 53 C47/22/12(5)	RH6, 83
RH5, 56 E93/94/5(1)	RH6, 98
RH5, 66 E39/94/5(11)	RH6, 99
RH5, 86 E39/94/8(1)	RH6, 100
RH5, 90 E39/84/8(5)	RH6, 104
RH5, 98 E39/94/8(14)	RH6, 105
RH5, 114 E99/100/146(2)	RH6, 106
RH5, 115 E39/100/147(1)	RH6, 112
RH5, 120 E39/100/150(1)	RH6, 118
RH5, 205 E39/100/188(8)	RH6, 119
RH5, 220 E39/100/189/5	RH6, 120

Secondary Material

Alger, J., *The Quest for Victory: The History of the Principles of War* (Connecticut, 1982).

Allmand, C., *Society at War. The Experience of England and France during the Hundred Years War* (Edinburgh, 1973).

Allmand, C., *Power, Culture and Religion in France* (Woodbridge, 1989).

Allmand, C., *The Hundred Years War* (Cambridge, 1998).

Anderson, M., *A History of Scottish Forestry* (Ed.) Taylor, C. (London, 1967).

Ayton, A., *Knights and Warhorses* (Woodbridge, 1994).

Bain, J., *The Edwards in Scotland 1296–1377* (Edinburgh, 1901).

Balfour Paul, Sir John., *The Scots Peerage* (Edinburgh, 1904–14).

Barrell, A., *Medieval Scotland* (Cambridge, 2000).

Barrne, J., *War in Medieval Society* (London, 1974).

Barron, E.M., *The Scottish War of Independence* (Inverness, 1934).

Barrow, G.W.S., *Feudal Britain* (London, 1956).

Barrow G.W.S., *The Kingdom of the Scots* (London, 1973).

Barrow G.W.S., *Robert the Bruce and the Community of the Realm of Scotland* (London, 1965).

Barrow, G.W.S., *Kingship and Unity* (London, 1981).

Barrow, G.W.S., *Scotland and its Neighbours in the Middle Ages* (London, 1992).

Barrow, G.W.S., *Scotland and her Neighbours in the Later Middle Ages* (London, 1992).

Barrow, G.W.S., *The Anglo-Norman Era in Scottish History* (Oxford, 1980).

Bingham, C., *The Life and Times of Edward II* (London, 1973).

Blair, C., *European Armour 1066–1700* (New York, 1972).

Boardman, S. & Ross, A. (Eds) *The Exercise of Power in Medieval Scotland* (Chippenham, 2003).

Bothwell, J., *The Age of Edward III* (Woodbridge, 2001).

Bradbury, J., *The Medieval Siege* (Woodbridge, 1992).

Brotherstone, T., & Ditchburn, D. (Eds) *Freedom and Authority* (East Lothian, 2000).

Broun, Finlay & Lynch (Eds) *Image and Identity* (Edinburgh, 1998).

Brown, C., *Encyclopaedia of Scottish Battles* (Stroud, 2008).

Brown, C., *Robert the Bruce. A Life Chronicled* (Stroud, 2003).

Brown, C., *William Wallace* (Stroud, 2005).

Brown, C., *Knights of the Scottish Wars of Independence* (Stroud, 2008).

Brown, M., *The Black Douglases* (East Linton, 1998).

Brown, M., *The Wars of Scotland 1214–1371* (East Linton, 2005).

Brown, R.A., Colvin, H.M. & Taylor, A.J., *The History of the King's Works* vol.i (London, 1963).

Burns, W., *The Scottish War of Independence* (Glasgow, 1874).

Bush, M., *Rich Noble, Poor Noble* (Manchester, 1988).

Clark, J. (Ed.), *The Medieval Horse and its Equipment c.1150–1450* (Woodbridge, 2004).

Clausewitz, C., *On War* (Harmondsworth, 1968).

Contamine, P., (Trans.) Jones, M., *War in the Middle Ages* (Oxford, 1987).

Coss, P., *Lordship, Knighthood and Locality: A Study in English Society* (Cambridge, 1991).

Coss, P., *The Knight in Medieval England* (Stroud, 1993).

Costain, T., *The Three Edwards* (New York, 1958).

Croft Dickinson, W. *Scotland from the Earliest Times to 1603* (Oxford, 1977).

Curry, A. & Hughes, M. (Eds), *Arms, Armies and Fortifications in the Hundred Years War* (Woodbridge, 1994).

Davies, R., *The Medieval Warhorse* (London, 1989).

Davies, R., *Conquest, Co-existence and Change; Wales 1063–1415* (Oxford, 1987).

De Vries, K., *Infantry Warfare in the Early Fourteenth Century: Discipline, Tactics and Technology* (Woodbridge, 1996).

Dickinson, J., *The Battle of Neville's Cross* (Durham, 1991).

Dickinson, W., Croft, *Scotland from the Earliest Times to 1603* (Edinburgh, 1965).

Ditchburn, D., *Scotland and Europe* (East Linton, 2001).

Dixon, P., *Puir Labourers and Busy Husbandmen* (Edinburgh, 2003).

Dodghson, R.A., *Land and Society in Early Scotland* (Oxford, 1981).

Donaldson, G., *Scottish Kings* (New York, 1992).

Dowden, J., *The Medieval Church in Scotland* (Glasgow, 1910).

Duncan, A.A.M., *Scotland. The Making of the Kingdom* (Edinburgh, 1975).

Du Picq, Col. A., *Battle Studies. Ancient and Modern Battle.* (Trans. J. Greeley & R. Cotton) (New York, 1921).

Dunne, D. (Ed.), *War and Society in Early Medieval Britain* (Liverpool, 2000).

Dupuy, R. & T., *Numbers, Prediction and War* (Indianapolis, 1979).

Dupuy, T., *Understanding Defeat* (New York, 1990).

Easson, E., *Medieval Religious Houses in Scotland* (London, 1957).

Ewan, E., *Townlife in Fourteenth Century Scotland* (Edinburgh, 1990).

Fergusson, W., *Scotland's Relations with England. A Survey to 1701* (Edinburgh, 1977).

Fergusson, W., *The Identity of the Scottish Nation: An Historic Quest* (Edinburgh, 1998).

Fowler, K. (Ed.), *The Hundred Years War* (London, 1971).

Frame, R., *The Political Development of the British Isles, 1100–1500* (Oxford 1995).

Fryde, E., *Peasants and Landlords in Later Medieval England* (Stroud, 1986).

Fryde, N., *The Tyranny and Fall of Edward II, 1321–26* (Cambridge, 1979).

Funcken, L. & F., *Le Costume, L'armure et les Armes au Temps de Chevalerie* (France, 1977).

Gilbert, J.M., *Hunting and Hunting Reserves in Medieval Scotland* (Edinburgh, 1979).

Gillingham, J. & Holt, J. (Eds), *War and Government in the Middle Ages* (Woodbridge, 1984).

Grant, A. & Stringer, K. (Eds), *Medieval Scotland, Crown, Lordship and Community* (Edinburgh, 1993).

Grant, A., *Independence and Nationhood* (London, 1984).

Grant, I.F., *The Social and Economic Development of Scotland before 1603* (Edinburgh, 1930).

Gravett, C., *Medieval Siege Warfare* (Oxford, 1991).

Griffiths, R., *The Fourteenth and Fifteenth Centuries* (Oxford, 2003).

Haines, R., *King Edward II. Edward of Caernarfon. His Life, His Reign and its Aftermath* (Dublin, 2006).

Hale, J. (Ed.), *Europe in the Late Middle Ages* (London, 1965).

Hall, D., *Burgess, Merchant and Priest. Burgh life in the Scottish Medieval Town* (Edinburgh, 2002).

Hamilton, G., *Piers Gaveston, Earl of Cornwall, 1307–1312* (London, 1988).

Handel, M., *Masters of War. Classical Strategic Thought* (London, 2004).

Hanawalt, B., *The Ties that Bound; Peasant Families in Medieval England* (Oxford, 1986).

Harding, A., *England in the Thirteenth Century* (Cambridge, 1993).

Hardy, R., *The Longbow, a Social and Military History* (London, 1992).

Harvey, J., *The Plantagenets* (London, 1959).

Herbert, T. and Jones, G.E., *Edward I and Wales* (Cardiff, 1988).

Hewitt, H., *The Black Prince's Expedition 1355–5* (Manchester 1958).

Hilton, R., *The English Peasantry in the Later Middle Ages* (Oxford, 1975).

Howard, M., *War in European History* (Oxford, 1976).

Jones, A., *The Art of War in Western Civilization* (Chicago, 1987).

Jones, M. (Ed.), *Gentry and Lesser Nobility in Later Medieval England* (Gloucester, 1986).
Kaeuper, R., *Chivalry and Violence in Medieval Europe* (Oxford, 2001).
Kagay, D. & Villalon, L., *The Circle of War in the Middle Ages* (Woodbridge, 1999).
Keen. M., *Chivalry* (New Haven, 1984).
Keen, M., *England in the Later Middle Ages* (London, 1973).
Latimer, J., *Deception in War* (London, 2004).
Leyser, H., *Medieval Women. A Social History of England 450–1500* (London, 1995).
Lomas, R., *North-East England in the Middle Ages* (Edinburgh, 1992)
Lord, E., *The Knights Templar in Britain* (London, 2002).
Lucas, H., *The Low Countries and the Hundred Years War* (Michigan, 1929).
Lynch, M., *Scotland: A New History* (London, 1991).
Lynch, M., Spearman, M., & Stell, G. (Eds) *The Scottish Medieval Town* (Edinburgh, 1988).
MacDonald, A., *Border Bloodshed* (East Linton, 2000).
MacDougall, N., (Ed.), *Scotland and War* (Edinburgh, 1991).
MacDougall, N., *An Antidote to the English* (East Lothian, 2001).
MacFarlane, K.B., *The Nobility of Later Medieval England* (Oxford, 1973).
McKenzie, W.M., *The Battle of Bannockburn* (Glasgow, 1913).
McKisack, M., *The Fourteenth Century* (Oxford, 1959).
McLeod, W., *Divided Gaels* (Oxford, 2004).
MacNamee, C., *The Wars of the Bruces* (East Linton, 1997).
McNeill, P. and Nicholson, R., *An Atlas of Scottish History to 1707* (Edinburgh, 1996).
MacQuarrie, A., *Scotland and the Crusades* (Edinburgh, 1997).
McQueen, H.L., *Common Law and Feudal Society in Medieval Scotland* (Edinburgh, 1993).
Mapstone S. & Wood. J. (Eds), *The Rose and the Thistle* (East Lothian 1998).
Mason, R. (Ed.), *Scotland and England, 1286–1817* (Edinburgh, 1987).
Mason, R. & MacDougall, N. (Eds), *People and Power in Scotland* (Edinburgh, 1992).
Mayhew, N. and Gemmill, E., *The Changing Value of Money in Medieval Scotland* (Cambridge, 1996).
Mertes, K., *The English Noble Household 1250–1600* (Oxford, 1988).
Miller, E., *War in the North. The Anglo-Scottish Wars of the Middle Ages* (Hull, 1960).
Miller, E. & Hatcher, J., *Medieval England – Rural Society and Economic Change, 1086–1348* (London, 1978).
Morgan, P., *War and Society in Medieval Cheshire 1277–1403* (Manchester, 1977).
Morris, J., *Bannockburn* (Cambridge, 1914).
Milner, N., *Vegetius: Epitome of Military Science* (Liverpool, 1993).
Nicholson R., *Scotland. The Later Middle Ages* (Edinburgh, 1974).
Nicholson, R., *Edward III and the Scots. The Formative Years of a Military Career* (Oxford, 1965).
Nusbacher, A., *The Battle of Bannockburn* (Stroud, 2000).
Oakeshott, R., *A Knight and His Horse* (London, 1995).

Oman, Sir Charles, *A History of England* (London, 1910).

Oman, Sir Charles, *A History of the Art of War* (London, 1898).

Parry, M.L. & Slater, T., *The Making of the Scottish Countryside* (London, 1980).

Penman, M., *David II* (East Linton, 2002).

Penman, M., *The Scottish Civil War* (Stroud, 2003).

Pillar, P., *Negotiating Peace: War Termination as a Bargaining Process* (New Jersey, 1983).

Phillips, J.R.S., *Aymer de Valence* (Oxford, 1972).

Postan, M., *The Medieval Economy and Society* (Harmondsworth, 1972).

Powicke, F. M., *The Thirteenth Century* (Oxford, 1953).

Powicke, F.M., *Military Obligation in England* (Connecticut, 1975).

Prestwich, M., *Armies and Warfare in the Middle Ages* (New Haven, 1996).

Prestwich, M., *Edward I* (London, 1988).

Prestwich, M., *The Place of War in English History* (Woodbridge, 2004).

Prestwich, M., *The Three Edwards; War and State in England, 1272–1377* (London, 1980).

Prestwich, M., *War, Politics and Finance Under Edward I* (London, 1972).

Rait, R., *The Parliaments of Scotland* (Glasgow, 1924).

Rayner, M., *English Battlefields* (Stroud, 2004).

Reid. N. (Ed.), *Scotland in the Reign of Alexander III* (Edinburgh, 1990).

Ridpath, P., *Border History of England and Scotland* (Berwick, 1848).

Ritchie, R., *The Normans in Scotland* (Edinburgh, 1954).

Rogers, C., *War Cruel and Sharp* (Woodbridge, 2000).

Rollason, D. & Prestwich, M. (Eds), *The Battle of Neville's Cross* (Stamford, 1998).

Ross, A., *In the Footsteps of Robert Bruce Sutton* (Gloucester, 1999).

Saul, N., (Ed.), *Fourteenth Century England* (Woodbridge, 2000).

Sadler, J., *Scottish Battles* (Edinburgh, 1996).

Scott, J., *History of Berwick-upon-Tweed* (London, 1888).

Seynour, W., *Battles in Britain 1066–1745* (Chatham, 1997).

Simpson G., (Ed.) *Scotland and the Low Countries* (East Linton, 1996).

Simpson, G., *Scottish Handwriting 1150–1650* (Aberdeen, 1977).

Simpson, G., (Ed.) *The Scottish Soldier Abroad* (Edinburgh, 1992).

Snell, F., *The Fourteenth Century* (Edinburgh, 1999).

Smurthwaite, D., *Battlefields of Britain* (London, 1984).

Stevenson, J. and Wood, M., *Scottish Heraldic Seals* (Glasgow, 1940).

Stenton, D., *English Society in the Early Middle Ages (1066–1307)* (Harmondsworth, 1965).

Stone, G., *Cameron Glossary of the Construction of Arms and Armour* (London, 1978).

Strickland, M., *Armies, Chivalry and Warfare in Medieval Britain and France* (Stamford, 1998).

Stringer, K., (Ed.) *Essays on the Scottish Nobility* (Edinburgh, 1985).

Sumption, J., *The Hundred Years War* (London, 1990).

Taylor, J. & Childs, W., (Eds) *Politics and Crisis in Fourteenth Century England* (Gloucester, 1990).

Tuck, A., *Crown and Nobility, 1272–1461; Political Conflict in Late Medieval England* (London, 1985).

Tytler, P.F., *A History of Scotland* (Edinburgh 1828, 1845).
Vale, M., *Edward III and Chivalry* (Woodbridge, 1983).
Vale, M., *War and Chivalry* (London, 1981).
Watson, F., *Under the Hammer* (East Linton, 1998).
Whittington, G. and Whyte, I. (Eds) *A Historical Geography of Scotland* (London, 1983).
Young, A., *Robert the Bruce's Rivals; The Comyns* (East Linton, 1997).

Unpublished Theses and Papers

Military Service of Northumbrian Knights. A. King. Durham University Medieval Conference (2001)
Technology and Military Technology in Medieval England. Randall Storey, University of Reading (2003)

Articles

'A Medieval Scots Merchant's Handbook', A. Hanham, SHR l, (1971).
'An Unpublished Early Account of Bruce's Murder of Comyn', T.M. Smallwood, SHR, liv. (1975).
'The Battle of Bannockburn. A Report for Stirling Council', F. Watson and M. Anderson, (2004).
'Battle of Bannockburn Report.' The Battlefield Trust.
'Chronicle Propaganda in Fourteenth Century Scotland', S. Boardman, SHR 76 (1977).
'Clausewitz, Nonlinearity and the Unpredictability of War', A. Beyerchen, *International Security* 17.3 (1992).
'Edinburgh Castle, Iron Age fort to Garrison Fortress.' P. Yeoman, *Fortress Magazine*, 4 (1990).
'Lothian in the First War of Independence.' G.W.S. Barrow, SHR 55 (1976).
'The Aftermath of War.' G.W.S. Barrow, *TRHS*, 28 (1978).
'The Community of the Realm of Scotland and Robert Bruce.' A.A.M. Duncan, SHR xlv.
'The Development of Scottish Border Lordship, 1332–58.' M. Brown, *Historical Research* lxxv, No.171 (February 1997).
'The Guardians of Scotland and a Parliament at Rutherglen in 1300', G. Sayles, SHR xxiv (1945).
'The Use of Money in Scotland, 1124–1230.' W. Scott, *SHR* lviii (1979).
'The War of the Scots, 1306–23' A.A.M. Duncan, Prothero Lecture, *TRHS* (1992).
'War, Allegiance and Community in the Anglo-Scottish Marches; Teviotdale in the Fourteenth Century.' Dr M. Brown, *Northern History*, xli (2004).

Abbreviations

APS: *Acts of the Parliaments of Scotland* (Eds) T. Thomson and C. Innes (Edinburgh, 1814–75).

Barbour, *The Bruce*: *The Bruce*, J. Barbour (Ed.) A.A.M. Duncan, Canongate (Edinburgh, 1997).

Barrow, *Bruce*: G.W.S. Barrow, *Robert the Bruce and the Community of the Realm of Scotland* (London, 1965).

CDS: *Calendar of Documents Relating to Scotland.* Volumes i–iv, (Ed.) J. Bain (Edinburgh, 1881–88), volume v, G. Simpson & J. Galbraith (Edinburgh, 1988).

Chron.Fordun: *Johannes de Fordun, Chronica Gentis Scottorum.* (Ed.) W.F. Skene (Edinburgh, 1871–72).

Chron.Lanercost (Maxwell): *The Chronicle of Lanercost, 1272–1346.* (Ed & Trans.) H. Maxwell, (Glasgow, 1913).

ER: *Exchequer Rolls of Scotland* (Ed.) J. Stuart. (Edinburgh, 1878–1908).

PSAS: *Proceedings of the Society of Antiquarians of Scotland.*

St. Andrews Liber: *Liber Cartorum Prioratus Sancti Andree in Scotia*, Bannatyne Club (Edinburgh, 1841).

Melrose Liber: *Liber Sancte Marie de Melros* Bannatyne Club (Edinburgh, 1837).

RMS vol. i: *Regesta Magni Sigilii Regum Scottorum* (Ed.) M. Livingstone (Edinburgh, 1882–1914).

Rot.Scot i: *Rotuli Scotiae in Turri Londiniensi et in Domo Capitulari Westmonasteriensi Asservati.* (Ed.) D. MacPherson. (London, 1837).

RRS vol. vi.: *Regesta Regum Scottorum* vol. vi, (Ed.) B. Webster (Edinburgh, 1982).

RRS.vol. v: *Regesta Regum Scottorum.* vol. v, (Ed.) A.A.M. Duncan (Edinburgh, 1988).

Scalacronica (Maxwell): *Scalacronica, the Reigns of Edward I, Edward II and Edward III.* H. Maxwell. (Glasgow, 1907).

Scotichronicon: *Scotichronicon of Walter Bower* (Ed.) D.E.R. Watt (Aberdeen, 1996).

SHR: *Scottish Historical Review.*

Stevenson, Documents: *Documents Illustrative of the History of Scotland, 1286–1306.* (Ed.) J. Stevenson. (Edinburgh, 1870).

TRHS: *Transactions of the Royal Historical Society.*

Acknowledgements

As ever, there are several individuals whose interest, information and encouragement demand recognition. In the academic sphere, these include Professor Mason and Dr Reid of the Scottish History Department at St Andrews University, who brought a much needed degree of 'raddure' to my PhD studies, repairing the damage and demoralisation caused by a long period of desultory and incompetent supervision. I cannot thank them enough for reawakening a passion for medieval Scottish history that had come very close to being utterly extinguished. I am also indebted to the unfailingly helpful – and cheerful – archival staff at East Register House and Kew. I also owe a great debt to the many scholars who have written about Scotland, England and France during the fourteenth century, and in particular to the small group of scholars who, since the 1960s, have brought the study of medieval Scotland out of the murk of romance and myth and into the mainstream of medieval historiography – Professors Barrow, Duncan and Nicholson.

I am also grateful for the patience and understanding of my wife, Pat, and my children and their partners – Robert, Colin, Christopher, Charis, Alex and Juliet. They have all had to put up with endless ramblings about the nature of medieval society and war. I have no idea how they have coped, but they have.

I would like to point out that my understanding of the battle is a product of how I see the source material, the terrain and the practice of war at the time of writing. It is perfectly possible that developments in archaeological techniques, a spate of new 'finds', or even a previously unknown piece of source material may yet emerge which might compromise or confirm the evidence on which all of the existing studies of this battle have depended.

Chris Brown, Kennoway, 2008

Index

Robert I, Edward I and Edward II have not been included in this index; their index entries would have a reference to virtually every page For the same reason I have not included 'Bannockburn'

If you enjoyed this book, you may also be interested in…

Battle Story: Bannockburn 1314
CHRIS BROWN

Bannockburn 1314 is the most celebrated battle between Scotland and England. A decisive victory for Robert Bruce, it secured for Scotland independence from England. It was the greatest defeat the English would suffer throughout the Middle Ages, and a huge personal humiliation for Edward II. Chris Brown's account recreates the campaign from the perspectives of both the Scots and English. If you want to know what happened and why read – Battle Story.

978 0 7524 9759 4

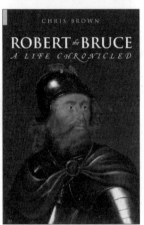

Robert the Bruce
CHRIS BROWN

Much is known about Robert the Bruce's military campaigns for Scottish Independence in Scotland and England but what about his expeditions to Ireland? In the early summer of 1315 a fleet-load of Scots veterans led by Edward Bruce put ashore on the coast of what is now County Antrim in what amounted to a full-scale invasion. What the Bruce brothers hoped to achieve from this is hotly debated. Did the Bruces envisage turning the invasion into a permanent conquest? Was the aim to exploit Irish dissidence to push Edward II into acknowledging Robert's claim to Scotland? This lavishly illustrated study answers these questions and tells the story of the invasion and battles that followed.

978 0 7524 2575 7

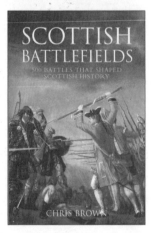

Scottish Battlefields
CHRIS BROWN

This is a painstaking survey of every Scottish battle from Mons Graupius AD 84 to Culloden 1746. Scotland has been formed by war to a greater extent than almost any other nation – against the Romans, the Vikings, between one another and with England. Many of Scotland's battlefields have already been covered by modern developments, many more are at risk, often because their existence and significance is known to so few. If battles are 'no more than the punctuation marks of history' it is not enough to know where these punctuation marks occurred, it is important to understand why.

978 0 7524 3685 2

Visit our website and discover thousands of other History Press books.

www.thehistorypress.co.uk